MW01260187

PREP SCHOOL COWBOYS

PREP SCHOOL COWBOYS

Ranch Schools in the American West

MELISSA BINGMANN

UNIVERSITY OF NEW MEXICO PRESS ☾ ALBUQUERQUE

Library of Congress Cataloging-in-Publication Data

Bingmann, Melissa.
Prep school cowboys : ranch schools in the American West / Melissa Bingmann. —
First edition.
pages cm
Includes bibliographical references and index.
ISBN 978-0-8263-5543-0 (cloth : alk. paper) — ISBN 978-0-8263-5544-7 (electronic)
1. Preparatory schools—West (U.S.)—History. 2. Private schools—West (U.S.)—History.
3. Education—Social aspects—West (U.S.)—History. 4. Ranch life—West (U.S.)
5. Ranchers—West (U.S.) 6. Cowboys—West (U.S.)—Social life and customs.
7. West (U.S.)—Social life and customs. I. Title.
LC58.5.W47B56 2015
373.22'20978—dc23
2014012637

COVER PHOTOGRAPH: Los Alamos School, c. 1917–1920. Goldsberry collection of
open-air school photographs, Library of Congress Prints and Photographs Division,
Washington, D.C.
DESIGNED BY Felicia Cedillos
COMPOSED IN Minion 10/14
DISPLAY FONTS are Rosewood and Century Old Style

CONTENTS

ACKNOWLEDGMENTS

AS WITH MANY RESEARCH ENDEAVORS, THIS PROJECT IS THE RESULT of planned and serendipitous intersections with people and places that occurred over a long span of time. My first encounter with ranch schools was actually in the 1980s, when my youth group rented space at the Judson School in Arizona for a retreat. It was rustic and there were horses, and I remembered thinking, if the school was an expensive private school, why did it resemble a ranch rather than an Ivy League college? I had spent my earliest years in the Northeast and had an idea fixed in my mind of what a private school should look like. A decade and a half later, I worked at the Mesa Southwest Museum in Arizona, and on one rare occasion I happened to be in the collections area when a pamphlet for the Palo Verde Ranch School had just arrived and was waiting for processing. Only after realizing that there were other ranch schools like it did I make the connection between this brochure and the Judson School I had visited as a child.

In exploring these unique institutions, I benefited from several state repositories that work tirelessly to protect the historical records essential to the study of the past. I especially want to thank the Arizona Historical Society and the Archives and Special Collections, Arizona State University Library for the generous assistance I received from the energetic and professional staff and the richness of their collections. Christine Marin, former archivist in the Department of Archives and Special Collections at Hayden Library, went so far as to accompany me to the Judson School in 2000 to see if the school would be interested in donating its records, as it prepared to close, to the Arizona State Library. I was also fortunate to have access to the archives of the National Association of Independent Schools and the Fenster School in Tucson, which holds records from the Southern Arizona School for Boys.

I have been privileged to have support from several institutions and individuals to whom I owe a large debt of gratitude. As a doctoral student at Arizona State University, I received an award from the Arizona Historical Foundation for a seminar paper I wrote on ranch schools in Robert Trennert's research course. Dr. Trennert encouraged me to develop an article for the *Journal of Arizona History*, and I am indebted to Bruce Dinges, who helped me transform my seminar paper into an article. As I continued my research, I received generous funding for travel from the History Department at Indiana University–Purdue University at Indianapolis and the History Department at West Virginia University. Jeff Pappas invited me to participate as a speaker at the American West Program at Colorado State University, providing me a valuable opportunity to present my research to a public audience. I am thankful to Marcia Synnott for encouraging me to present at the History of Education Society, and to Susan Ferentinos for suggesting that I would benefit from participating in the Society for the History of Childhood and Youth. Both have been invaluable to me as I delved into these areas of study.

This project is the result of several years of research and writing. I am especially fortunate to have had the guidance of Gayle Gullett, Noel Stowe, and Robert Trennert at Arizona State University. All provided invaluable encouragement and support as I grew as a professional historian. I will always be indebted to Noel Stowe, who was the ideal role model for working as a public historian in academia. His untimely passing has been a devastating loss to the field and to me personally. I am honored to be able to thank several colleagues and scholars who took the time to read chapters and various versions of the manuscript and provide productive feedback. Carl Ashley, Annie Gilbert Coleman, Lynn Dumenil, Kalyani Fernando, Nancy Jackson, Katherine Morrissey, and Nancy Robertson have made this a much more analytical, accessible, and meaningful book. I am also thankful for the informal conversations I have had at various conferences with Horatio Joyce, Leslie Paris, and Abigail Van Slyk, who shared sources and their knowledge.

I am supremely indebted to Patricia Billingsley, who contacted me several years ago to share her project of editing the journal of Phillip Cummings. She very generously mailed to me the section of the journal from when he was a master at the Valley Ranch School. In conducting her own research, she shared with me sources that I would not have had access to otherwise, including a thesis written by a headmaster at the Arizona Desert School. Because of her generosity, I have been able to include the perspective of some of the men who worked at ranch schools.

Several individuals who have provided support are friends and family who graciously provided housing so I could expand my research to San Francisco, Pittsburgh, Chicago, New Mexico, Rhode Island, and Washington, D.C., and return on several occasions to Arizona. Barb and Steve Hamman, Jennifer Hightower, Jane Lancaster, Rachel and Barry Menard, Jenny Lee and Brad Ryan, Jacqui Schesnol, Leslie and Stephen Ticktin, and Sara Zurier and Jonathan Bell were extremely generous hosts and very kindly inquired about my research after a long day at the archives. Jane Lancaster shared an early version of Emily Post's travel journal as she edited it for publication. This was a wonderful source that I may never have investigated, and I greatly appreciate Jane's interest in my project, which led her to make this important connection. My parents, Marilyn and Richard Bingmann, provided constant support by traveling with me to various ranch school sites, picking up photographs, and providing a nice quiet space to work in the summer of 2011. My mother is probably the only person who has read multiple versions of the manuscript, and her keen editorial skills have been invaluable.

It has been my great fortune to work with Clark Whitehorn at the University of New Mexico Press. He is as patient as he is talented and has provided guidance in everything from selecting photographs to helping me manage the scope of the project. I will be forever thankful for his interest in the history of education in the Southwest and for thinking my work on preparatory schools would make a positive contribution to the University of New Mexico Press.

I am especially indebted to the individuals who invited me into their homes and provided other generous acts of hospitality as they shared their knowledge and experience of western ranch schools. My first contact with an actual ranch school alumnus was at a reunion event that the Judson School very kindly invited me to attend. David C. Lincoln met with me on several occasions, gave me access to several brochures that he had kept over the years, and put me in touch with several more alumni as well as Gloria Judson, who shared a treasure trove of letters and brochures from her late husband's family archives and spent hours talking to me about the school and her family. Fred Dalzell, Barbara Ferris, Robert Kilmarx, Anita McAndrews, Ormonde Parke, and David Wick treated me like an honored guest in their homes when it was really I who had the great fortune of knowing amazing individuals who have lived such interesting lives.

When I called John Donaldson to inquire if he would be willing to participate in an oral history interview about his experience at the Arizona Desert School, he responded positively and asked, "Can I bring all of my friends?" As it turned out, he and his friends from the Arizona Desert School continued to get together annually in Tucson. I had the pleasure of meeting Howard Bremond, David C. Wilhelm, and Alexander (Sandy) Woods at the interview. Since then, I have been assisted by David C. Wilhelm, the only one of the group who survives, who has written a memoir that includes a chapter on his experience at the Arizona Desert School. His generosity in filling in the gaps from the group interview, sharing his personal memories, and graciously allowing me to use his personal photographs in this book have greatly broadened the scope and analysis of this work. After my interview with Charlie Orme Jr. at the Orme School, I was treated to an in-depth tour of the campus. I am thankful to Jeb Rosebrook for initiating my visit and for sharing his experience as a student and board member of the Orme School. At Hacienda Del Sol, I met with the owners, who have transformed the former girls' school into a resort while meticulously maintaining the historic structures, before sitting down to interview Jean Porter Dunn about her memories as a student at the school. Jean then introduced me to her brother, Bob Porter, whom I was able to interview at Sabino Canyon, where he volunteered. The opportunity to visit and meet with alumni at these historic sites was my greatest inspiration and has shaped this narrative more than any other source. It is to these men and women that I dedicate this book. My greatest hope is that I have accurately portrayed their memories as a partial return for the generosity they have shown me.

Men-in-the-Making in the American West

JACK WAS THE GRANDSON OF A SELF-MADE CAPTAIN OF INDUSTRY. He and his brother, Rust, grew up in a wealthy neighborhood in Pittsburgh, Pennsylvania, and attended Shady Side Academy before heading off to Choate to prepare for admittance to Princeton and eventually assume the family business. It was expected that Jack would graduate from an Ivy League college, and his parents spared no expense in his education, sending him to Choate, one of the Select Sixteen boarding schools located on the Atlantic Seaboard. From Choate, Jack dutifully wrote home to his parents about his experience at the elite eastern preparatory school. He described attending football games, but did not participate in this or any other sport. At one point, he was very ill and spent months in a New England hospital. He subsequently transferred to the Evans School in Tucson, Arizona, in 1923 for his senior year.

Jack's letters home reflected his enthusiasm for the Evans School, as he quickly adapted to his new surroundings, even picking up some western slang, concluding one letter with the salutation "Y'Urn Truly." "This A.M. I had the best time I have had for an awfully long time," he wrote, "for I went horseback riding for 2 hours (more money) with two other fellows. We went away out into the country and had a wondrous time and some excitement." Jack thrived at the Evans School and conveyed appreciation for his new freedom and chance to strike out on his own. At Choate, he was lost in the institutional atmosphere, where "everybody has to do things at certain times and the whole is more united." In contrast, at the Evans School, there were "single fellows or little groups of fellows doing almost exactly what they please within a certain limit. . . . I think that the fellows out here on the whole are better than those you find at Choate," he wrote home to his parents. The change for the teenager was "interesting and to say the least quite delightful." His one qualm with the school seemed to be that only the headmaster, H. David Evans himself, could teach the advanced course in Latin he needed to pass the College Entrance Board test.[1]

Jack's grandfather, Henry, was born into an immigrant family who subsisted on agriculture. At age eight, Henry started peddling the family's surplus to other households. By the time he was ten, Henry had his own wheelbarrow for peddling and his family gave him three-quarters of an acre to farm on his own. Two years later he purchased a horse and cart and included some of the local merchants as his customers. In his early twenties, he and other family members invested in a company to produce canned food items. Over a fifteen-year period, the family business experienced economic ups and downs, success followed by bankruptcy, until finally it stabilized and was able to grow. Jack's grandfather became a living example of the American dream and attributed his great business fortune to hard work.

Henry groomed his youngest son, Howard, to take over the family business. Henry believed Howard had great potential and called on phrenological analyst A. S. Fowler to affirm his son had inherited the qualities needed to preserve the company that Henry had worked so hard to create. Fowler found the six-year-old boy "quite a young whirlwind. . . . A natural boss and dominating over everybody. Will be a conspicuous man among men if he doesn't blight young. . . . Will lead a blameless life. . . . Is a handsome, fluent speaker but his controlling feature is originality and power of intellect along with the highest sense of duty. His business talents are well developed." Henry looked forward to the day when his son would work alongside him, and at the age of eight, Howard went to work, six hours a day, in the factory. The family did not need additional income, but Henry wanted to ensure that his son understood the value of hard work and give him a taste of what it was like to work one's way up from the bottom. By the time he was eighteen Howard had toured Europe, mostly on bike, and developed a passion for gas automobiles. His father may have been concerned with his son's conspicuous display of wealth, but he was proud that Howard had labored in the family factories and demonstrated an interest in the development of boys of lesser fortune. When he was a student at Yale, Howard focused his attention on a newspaper boy, concluding that this boy like many others was denied the opportunity to become a self-made man or self-reliant. He and some of his student friends created "a club for newsboys, bootblacks and other lads, who were compelled to earn their own living and, in many instances, had dependents." He continued his philanthropic work in Pittsburgh by establishing a club for the boys who lived in the vicinity of his family's plant. In 1906 Howard married Elizabeth Granger Rust of Saginaw, Michigan, and the couple had two boys of their own, Jack and Rust.[2]

Jack was similarly prepared to succeed his father and grandfather as head of the family business, and he embraced the tests of courage, masculinity, and self-reliance that were inherent in desert living and promoted by the Evans School as part of its focus to prepare boys and young men from wealthy families for life and citizenship. After graduation, while attending Princeton, Jack began learning the business of his father and grandfather from the ground up by working in one of the company's salt plants. By 1941 Henry John (Jack) Heinz II succeeded his father as president of the H. J. Heinz Company, known for its "57 Varieties" of preserved food products. His only son, H. John Heinz III, became a popular state senator.[3]

The Evans School, where Jack Heinz attended for at least one year, was one of several western ranch schools located in Arizona, California, New Mexico, and Wyoming. These unique private schools for boys promised the elite that through "simplicity of living," ranch life would develop "self-reliance" and courage in boys—character traits that many Americans feared had been lost in modern urban society. Ranch school owners made this affirmation based upon an American concept of a mythic West of the past—the West that Frederick Jackson Turner declared had disappeared in the 1890s. By re-creating ranch life in the formation of preparatory schools, ranch schools offered children an opportunity to relive the experience of those who embodied the American spirit of individualism, bravery, strength, democracy, hard work, and fortitude—cowboys and pioneers—at the same time they preserved boys' status as the next generation of American leaders.

Most western ranch schools were either founded or experienced tremendous growth in the interwar period and reflected Americans' nostalgia for its agricultural past, with its simpler way of life, amid the rapidly changing technological advances of the early twentieth century. Thomas Jefferson's ideal of the pioneer farmer as wholesome and all that was good in America had a resurgence in the early twentieth century as moralists confronted American society's new urban, modern problem. Urban youth had lost a connection to the natural world and instead embraced the artificiality of new leisure activity and consumerism. Furthermore, Americans' concern over inherited privilege was heightened in the interwar period when the economic gap between the wealthy and the middle class became pronounced. The ostentatious behavior of the second and third generation of the self-made man caused concern among educators, social scientists, cultural critics, and parents.

Men who had earned the elite status that often accompanied financial success in the "Era of Big Money" from 1896 to 1932 worked tirelessly to preserve it and looked to their progeny to continue the family legacy.[4] Their sons and grandsons, however, often seemed to lack the same work ethic of their forebears, and many blamed their unfettered access to unearned wealth as a deterrent to becoming productive men of character. Fathers and grandfathers who wished for their sons to succeed them in their place of privilege and responsibility sought environments that would shape their sons into men of character who understood the value of self-reliance, hard work, and initiative. Some, like the Heinz descendants, secretly labored in their family's industrial operations over summer breaks during college to prove themselves worthy of leading and sustaining the family dynasty. Many looked to the American West as the best place for shaping boys' characters to prepare them for the rights and responsibilities of citizenship as defined by their gender and class.

Before the United States' entry into World War II, approximately twenty entrepreneurial-minded families opened ranch schools in Arizona, and a few others founded ranch schools in California, New Mexico, and Wyoming. The West was ripe for this new industry after the postwar depression of 1919. While most other industries recuperated quickly, agriculture had a difficult time recovering, forcing many western ranchers to sell their property, equipment, and animals. Persuaded by romantic visions of the West or by the prospect of an adventurous business opportunity, easterners and midwesterners bought ranches with the intent of earning a living through agriculture, while others specifically set out to start dude ranches and ranch schools. Based on promotional material, lists created by states and railroads, and Porter Sargent's *A Handbook of Private Schools for American Boys and Girls*, western ranch schools included the Thacher School, California (1889); Evans School, Arizona (1902); Montezuma Mountain School, California (1911); Los Alamos Ranch School,

New Mexico (1917); Deep Springs Preparatory, California (1922); Mesa Ranch School, Arizona (1922); Valley Ranch School, Wyoming (1922); Fresnal Ranch School, Arizona (1924); Arizona Sunshine School (1927); Foxboro Ranch School, Arizona (1927); Arizona Desert School (1927); Judson School for Boys, Arizona (1928); Orme School, Arizona (1929); Palo Verde Ranch School for Boys, Arizona (1929); Hacienda del Sol, Arizona (1929); Albuquerque Ranch School, New Mexico (1930); M Bar V Ranch School, Arizona (1930); Southern Arizona School for Boys, Arizona (1933); Green Fields Preparatory, Arizona (1933); Remuda Ranch School, Arizona (1933); Jokake School, Arizona (1934); and Desert Willow Ranch School, Arizona (1935). In philosophy and aims, they were remarkably similar to the more established eastern private preparatory schools yet incorporated elements of dude ranching, progressive education, and summer camps to create a unique educational experience for America's wealthier children. Most no longer exist, yet in their pre–World War II heyday, they provided an alternative to the more established Select Sixteen boarding schools in New England and on the East Coast.[5]

Loosely defined, a ranch school was a private, nonsectarian boarding school that offered the benefits of an "authentic" western experience and catered to the elite of the Atlantic Seaboard and Midwest. Sargent first used the term "Western Ranch School" as a classification for a type of private school in the 1928–1929 edition of *A Handbook of Private Schools for American Boys and Girls*.[6] In addition to those categorized by Sargent as a ranch school, this study also includes ranch schools listed as such in tourism literature and self-proclaimed ranch schools. Arizona had a significant number of ranch schools when compared to other western states, most likely because its warm winter climate allowed students to study and participate in recreational outdoor activity throughout the school year. In following editions of Sargent's *Handbook*, the number of Arizona ranch schools listed continued to grow, outnumbering those in all other states. Much like dude ranches, ranch schools were a result of, and contributed to, the burgeoning tourism economy that marketed western authenticity by highlighting the landscape, natural wonders, close proximity to national parks, horsemanship, and relaxed lifestyle. Several ranch schools were established for the specific purpose of serving winter visitors with children, who, because of the length of their stay, needed private schools that meshed with a traditional preparatory curriculum of the Select Sixteen.

Ranch schools varied by the gender and age of the students, whether they accepted day students, and how closely they resembled a self-sustaining preparatory school or whether the experience was more similar to private tutoring at a dude ranch resort. The most prestigious and iconic ranch schools were boarding schools, exclusively for boys, that recruited students independent of their families. In Arizona, these included the Evans School, Arizona Desert School, Judson School for Boys, Southern Arizona School, Mesa Ranch School, Fresnal Ranch School, and Palo Verde Ranch School. Material on the Evans School, Arizona Desert School, Judson School for Boys, and Southern Arizona School seems to leap from archival collections and remain in popular memory, while the latter three have somewhat faded from existence. Greenfields is one of the few schools that currently exist, but from all accounts, it seemed somewhat more insular and self-contained than the others. Founded the same year as the Southern Arizona School, it evolved from an alfalfa farm intentionally but slowly into a school. The Southern Arizona School on the other hand immediately and purposefully replicated existing ranch school practices and joined them in interscholastic polo competitions from its inception. All eight were exclusive to boys who for the most part boarded at the school, had no direct affiliation with a resort or dude ranch, and asserted their primary aim to prepare students for college.

Thacher School in California, Los Alamos School in New Mexico, and Valley Ranch School in Wyoming were clearly on par with the "first-tier" Arizona ranch schools, but were slightly nuanced by their location, founding, and geographic isolation from like institutions. Rarely recognized as such, the Thacher School was the earliest model, but its designation and identity as a ranch school did not take hold until the 1920s. Prior to that, Thacher was simply a preparatory school on a ranch that evolved naturally from the needs of the community and Sherman Thacher's desire for a way to earn a living in California. Los Alamos's most distinctive attribute was its owner's adoption of Boy Scouting as a means of instilling character and providing outdoor and nature study. Valley Ranch School evolved from a dude ranch in order to maximize revenue during the off-season. Dudes enjoyed the optimal summer weather, while boys studied and endured the cold as they attempted to participate in the adventurous activity common to ranch school curricula. In a similar vein, Foxboro Ranch School in Arizona evolved from a summer dude ranch into a year-round school. The existence of the Foxboro was fleeting, and it is not certain how long it operated or whether it was ever in continuous use as a school.

Ranch schools were predominantly for boys, but the Orme School, Arizona Sunshine School, and the Remuda Ranch were coeducational. The Orme School, much like the Thacher School, evolved naturally from a need to educate the Orme children rather than intentionally as a ranch school, and it continues to operate. The Remuda Ranch School in Wickenburg was a prime example of a ranch school centered around a dude ranch and catered specifically to vacationing families. Because the tourist season coincided with the school year, students and vacationers were often one and the same, and the school and dude ranch shared physical space. The Arizona Sunshine School was primarily for younger day students whose parents wintered in Tucson, but it was not affiliated with a resort.

The other exceptions to the exclusively male ranch schools were San Luis Ranch School in Colorado Springs, Hacienda del Sol in Tucson, and Jokake in Phoenix. Founded in 1889, San Luis Ranch School became an open-air school in 1917 and held all of its classes outdoors. Camping and horseback riding were only a slim part of the varied activities offered by this school for girls, which maintained "the best of eastern traditions combined with the freedom and charm of western ranch life." Hacienda del Sol, Tucson's first private boarding school for girls, was founded in 1929 as a college preparatory school that combined the ideals of a ranch school for boys with a traditional female boarding school curriculum. Porter Sargent's handbook stated that Hacienda del Sol was "one of the first schools to capitalize on the new interest in the Southwest as a winter residence."[7] Jokake School for Girls opened in 1934 as an addition to Jokake Inn in Phoenix. The daughter of the Inn's owner, Barbara Evans Ashforth, along with her husband, George Ashforth, started the ranch school for girls, which grew quickly and became an accredited preparatory school. Since it was located near the Judson School, some families conveniently sent their daughters to Jokake and their sons to Judson.

Western ranch schools provide a unique chance to study citizenship, class, gender, and region through institutions that were designed to counteract the problems of inherited wealth and modern urban America by constructing an experience for the purpose of instilling character traits associated with the Old West. The presence of ranch schools suggests an expanded interpretation of the American West in the interwar period that incorporates the growth of tourism but also supports the idea of the West as a colony for the eastern and midwestern elite. Although unique in their use of the West as a physical and conceptual place to achieve the aims of private school education, the schools accepted standards set forth by their eastern predecessors, Ivy League schools, the College Entrance Board, and the Secondary Education Board. In the final analysis, they replicated one of the most important avenues for the transference of elite culture created by the eastern establishment. In the minds of Americans, the cultural geography of the West had the power to transform pampered, effete children into gentleman cowboys who could rightly assume positions of power as adults. Bravery, courage, self-reliance, and initiative—traits associated with the pioneering spirit of the Old West—were the very same attributes advocated by character education reformers as necessary to preserve the nation through the next generation. The West portrayed by ranch schools embodied the moral attributes believed to be lacking in urban America. As a result, the ranch school narrative links the history of education and western history to provide a new interpretation of the West as moral space.

Both children and adolescents attended ranch schools, often independent from their families. By catering to the needs of adolescent boys, ranch schools reflected Americans' fear over this newly identifiable and seemingly growing population. Kent Baxter argues that the construct of this recognizable developmental stage at the turn of the century reflected "broader cultural anxieties that characterized American society." Created in tandem with the rapid changes resulting from urbanization, industrialization, and their related problems, "this new age category came to represent all that was threatening about 'modern life.'" He argues that this demographic group was not really new, but simply more conspicuous in American cities, and from its inception, the "adolescent" was perceived as a threat to be contained through measures of control and rehabilitation. This was most apparent in education reform, which segregated students by age through the creation of high schools, and the rise of the juvenile court system to deal with anxiety over the multitudes of unemployed youth visible on the city streets. This fear and the dilemma of how to best usher these youth into productive adulthood was at first focused on those perceived most likely to commit a crime or become a drain on society because of their inability to enter the workforce.[8] By the interwar period, I argue, economically advantaged adolescents became an equally conspicuous problem as newspaper reporters tracked their outrageous escapades. The resulting crisis of the rich man's son, however, was more dire because Americans depended on this next generation of leaders.

The rise of western ranch schools reflects the predominance of the pediatrician, psychologist, and other child science experts who sustained reform efforts of the Progressive Era by focusing on solving the problems of American families and children in the interwar period. Social science experts sought to exert their intellectual influence not only for the sake of social control, but in order to better society.[9] By focusing on children, a small group of middle-class experts were able to influence children of all classes, giving them a degree of cultural power over the economic elite through shaping the next generation of leaders. Headmasters were prolific in their published diatribes, giving advice on everything from the problem of overprotective mothers, the best ways for preparatory school boys to spend their summers, the value of studying the classics, and the significance of competitive sports, to the problems of modern society generally. Porter Sargent's directory of private schools typically included his lengthy commentary on varied contemporary social issues of modern America. The intended audience included headmasters and parents who could afford to send their children to private school. In widely disseminating their opinions, research, and studies to affluent parents, headmasters and private school educators became moral experts who gained the authority to influence the character of the next generation of leaders.

The fact that so many children attended ranch schools for their health was an important indication that parents followed the advice of scientific experts when it came to the well-being of their children. Doctors advised families with asthmatic children to move to dry, warm climates, and all ranch schools catered to children who suffered from sinus trouble, respiratory ailments, rheumatism, and other health-related concerns that were not the result of communicable diseases. Brochures from the majority of Arizona's ranch schools, including Arizona Desert School, Hacienda del Sol, Judson School for Boys, Palo Verde Ranch School, and Southern Arizona School for Boys, identified the dry climate as particularly beneficial for the cure of certain ailments as one of the many features of their unique schools. Girls who attended Hacienda del Sol and who suffered "from discomforts caused by colder climates or by higher altitudes [would] find complete relief in the dry, warm air of Arizona." An Arizona Desert School brochure noted that it specialized "in the care of those who have asthma, chronic colds, sinus infections or bronchial complications" but was "by no means confined to boys suffering from these difficulties." The dry, sunny desert air was equally "beneficial to boys who need general building up or who must avoid the damp winter climate in other parts of the country."[10] In the era of the "priceless" child, ranch schools existed because physicians advised parents that the desert climate was the best environment for their children's health.

The introduction of the psychology of behaviorism provides an important example of the confusion many parents must have felt as they were confronted with conflicting ideologies about child rearing and nature versus nurture. The idea that humans were hollow shells who could be shaped by their environment and external stimuli, referred to as behaviorism, popularized by John B. Watson's *Behavior: An Introduction to Comparative Psychology* (1914) and *Behaviorism* (1925) and applied to child rearing in his *Psychological Care of the Infant and Child* (1928), contrasted with many elites' belief in social Darwinism. As a generation of child rearing–advice givers adapted the idea of behaviorism to be less rigid in its discipline, environmental manipulation evolved as an important means of instilling habit and behavior. Instead of enforcing habits through rewards and punishments, the environment surrounding children could be altered to prevent the development of a bad habit.[11] Dramatically changing the geographic and cultural environment of youth by sending them to a western ranch school indicated a shift in approach from one that emphasized the inherited nature of certain individuals to become leaders to one that required some degree of purposefully instilling character traits. As affluent families noticed that their sons had less initiative than their forebears who were "self-made," an environment that forced boys to prove themselves appealed to many parents. The Heinz family demonstrated a blending of social Darwinism and behaviorism with the belief that their sons had inherited an ability to succeed that needed to be cultivated in a specific environment. H. J. Heinz had a phrenologist assess the innate leadership qualities of his son Howard, yet also insisted that he cultivate these through hard work by laboring in a factory. Many looked to the pre-1890 American West as the best environment for instilling the traits that created the American spirit of individualism, democracy, bravery, and self-reliance.

Private school educators embraced new social science research ushered in by the interwar child science boon that supported enacting change for the betterment of children and society. The importance of character education in private schools was reflected in the results of a 1928 study that found "the development of character" was the number-one aim of private school education for boys. Robert Danforth Cole proposed to present a "broad, general picture of private secondary education for boys as it exists in the United

States" by examining two hundred private school catalogues.[12] His work provides the context for comparing ranch schools to private boys' schools across the country. After compiling his data, he listed thirty purposes most frequently found and then grouped them into ten main headings. "Formation of ethical character" (85 percent) led the list and was followed by "College preparation" (81 percent), "Health" (47 percent), "Meeting the needs of individuals" (42 percent), "Formation of habits" (38 percent), "Citizenship and leadership" (38 percent), "Providing for non-college students" (30 percent), "Manners and general culture" (25 percent), "Substituting or supplementing the home" (24 percent), and lastly, "Mental discipline" (21 percent). The time period between 1890 and 1940 was particularly ripe for a renewed interest in moral education because of the rapid societal changes brought about by modernization. "More than simply a reaction against modernity," historian Edward McClellan argued, educators sought new methods for preserving traditional values in an ever-changing world.[13]

Character education at private schools resembled the ideologies of Progressive Era character-building organizations like the YMCA and the Boy Scouts. They both emphasized Protestant values; however, character education addressed a sense that the moral guidance of religion had been lost during the Progressive Era when reformers advanced a more secular agenda for social betterment. Both reflected anxiety over the impact of modernization and urbanization on the next generation, but whereas Boy Scouting focused on nonrural middle-class boys, character education was discussed most frequently among educators and private school leaders in particular. Ranch schools and Boy Scouts shared the goals of character building and citizenship; however, the former emphasized individuality and leadership whereas Boy Scouting promoted middle-class aspirations "to mold the rising generation into a cohesive, hard-working citizentry—patriotic, disciplined, and conventional in values." For example, Boy Scouts downplayed unplanned adventure and emphasized group experience. In contrast, a key component of ranch schools was the opportunity for boys to conduct overnight camping trips in small groups independent of adult supervision. Ranch schools sought to instill self-reliance in an effort to cultivate leaders and successors to power, rather than workers.[14]

The experience at ranch schools was largely focused on a traditional preparatory school curriculum but also reflected cultural manifestations similar to those of Boy Scouting and summer camps. The popularity of summer camps reflected a reaction to a culture of a rapidly changing world that valued nostalgic skills of canoeing and cooking over an open fire as representative of a simpler past. There was a sense that youth no longer connected to the natural world and that immersion in the pastoral, rural setting of camps was necessary to preserve American character and values. In her analysis of summer camps, Leslie Paris found that "what the men and women who brought urban children into the woods envisioned was a kind of nostalgic countermodern that conjoined traditional aesthetics and modern sensibilities." Camps were both "an antidote to modernity's ills" as well as "an expression of the latest leisure and childrearing practices."[15] In a similar fashion, ranch school owners depicted the environment of the schools as reminiscent of the "Old West" situated in geographically isolated locations. At the same time, parents were assured that the West was civilized, with modern conveniences of transportation, electricity, running water, and other technological amenities available in the nearby urban centers. Ranch schools provided the experience of a West from the past without the sacrifices of living in a premodern society.

The ranch school narrative is rife with similar paradoxes and ironies that mimic those predominant in American culture during the interwar period. For example, Americans perceived the West as more democratic and less pretentious when compared to eastern and midwestern cities, yet the establishment of these most sacred of all elite institutions contributed to the region's continual transformation. They promoted an emphasis on creating true American citizens, yet most ranch school students' community service was limited to the immediate community through school improvement projects. Civic participation came through the pageantry of the rodeo, which in itself was a constructed ideal of the West. Rather than take advantage of their proximity to Native cultures, ranch school owners isolated students from these living communities and encouraged students to explore Indian ruins and collect Indian artifacts left by prehistoric cultures. The Hispanic heritage of the region was experienced only through trips to "Old Mexico" and the occasional interaction with one of the few Mexican workers employed at a ranch school. As a result, the ideal of Manifest Destiny through the conquest of Native Americans and Hispanics was reinforced in the minds of the elite youth since they experienced these cultures as relics of the past or as workers.

The consumerism of ranch schools diverged from the idea that the West was less tainted by luxuries and wealth than were the urban centers of the Atlantic

Seaboard and Great Lakes region. Progressive Era and interwar-period cultural critics focused much of their attention on ostentatious displays of wealth made more prevalent by the greater availability of consumer durables after World War I, as the traditional American middle-class mentality that valued family life, the work ethic, and moderation gave way to an acceptance of consumption, leisure, and immediate gratification. The rise in consumerism, especially among boys and adolescences, was the antithesis of the ideology of the self-made man that was premised on the nineteenth-century ideal that valued production over consumption.[16] As consumer goods became available to a wider portion of the population, elites sought new experiences, including national and international travel, unavailable to other classes. By sending a child to a ranch school, parents commodified the West, purchasing an experience for their child that was exclusive to those of economic means.[17] Although the ideal of the Old West promoted an authentic "simple life," the purchase of consumer goods was essential to the ranch school experience. Henry John (Jack) Heinz II often wrote home requesting money for a horse, saddle, custom boots, cameras, guns, and ammunition.

Chapter 1 will explore the development of heightened national concern over the problems of the "rich man's son" popularized through periodicals, novels, and film. Ranch schools drew students from affluent families and often established migration patterns of the elite to the Southwest from the Atlantic Seaboard and Great Lakes states. As visitors and permanent residents, they replicated the institutions of the eastern establishment as they invested capital in this developing region. Chapter 2 describes how ranch schools compared academically to their Select Sixteen counterparts and examines the evolution of professional organizations for private school educators who became the voice of expert opinion for parents. Ranch schools incorporated the new emphasis on national tourism as a means of citizenship and progressive education through cultural geography into a traditional preparatory school curriculum. The argument presented in chapter 3 focuses on how owners and headmasters constructed a version of the Old West based on easterners' and midwesterners' expectations that simultaneously provided a rugged environment that was safe and civilized. Chapter 4 links character education and masculinity and describes how ranch schools created an experience designed to transform boys into cowboy gentlemen. Chapter 5 describes the challenges of modern homes and families, the evolution of the preference for the boarding school atmosphere to be homelike, and the significance of women in sustaining ranch schools.

Ranch school wives countered the influence of the cowboy, acting as civilizer on the untamed frontier, and provided a stable atmosphere that seemed to solve the problems of overprotective mothers, parental absenteeism, and other situations that experts had determined were ruining American children.

The West of ranch schools was populated by families who made their living by serving affluent boys who were anticipating their future. Children have largely been left out of western history, but as Elliott West explained in his path-breaking study, children's perceptions as explorers who roamed freely with a greater sense of curiosity provide an important perspective. They were at the center of social and political life as the driving force for establishing schools and other social and cultural institutions for the purpose of transplanting traditions. The true settlers of the West came as families, "determined to build what they considered a proper social order."[18] The history of western education is limited to the pre-1890 period, the "Old West," with the exception of studies that explore the Americanization efforts geared toward Mexicans, Mexican Americans, and Native Americans. Other than these important works, the history of education in the West seems to be dominated by schoolmarms who taught in one-room schoolhouses. The ranch school narrative helps to bring the history of education in the West into the twentieth century. Furthermore, by using class, gender, and race as analytical frameworks to treat the education of elite Anglo-Saxon males at ranch schools as unique, it relieves Native American boarding schools and Americanization schools from their status as "other" or outside of what is standard.

This exploration of ranch schools also expands our understanding of the history of American education and boarding schools. The two most significant developments in private school education during the interwar period were an attachment to regionalism and the professionalization of private school education. James McLachlan's seminal work, *American Boarding Schools: A Historical Study*, focuses on the East and ends in 1920, just when the ranch school story begins. The private schools established in the interwar period that centered on the unique characteristics of a particular region became distinctly American institutions. Most Select Sixteen preparatory schools drew from English precedent with little attention to the local geography or culture. Ranch schools adapted this New England boarding school model to create a unique educational experience that drew from the postwar rise in American cultural heritage tourism. Through travel to uniquely American places, students learned just as much about America as they did about the classics, and in the process became better citizens.

The interwar period is further significant to the history of private schools because they were impacted by the rise of psychology and "child science," which led to the creation of professional organizations specifically for headmasters. Headmasters met at conferences to share their experiences but more importantly to advance what they thought were the solutions to America's most pressing challenges—ensuring that the next generation of leaders had the capacity to safeguard the progress of the nation. A newly created professional group dedicated to extending the boarding school experience to younger students to equip and adjust them in anticipation of attending a college preparatory school indicated their desire to expand their influence on America's affluent families. The study of private boarding schools, ranch schools in particular, focuses attention on character education, which otherwise is subsumed under "progressive education." There was some overlap, but their philosophies and approaches often competed. Whereas progressive education came out of the wider social reform movements of the Progressive Era, character education peaked in the 1920s, resulting from an antimodernist trend that sought to restore morality in American culture and society.[19]

By focusing on children and adolescents from affluent families, the social construction of interwar childhood and youth can be explored uninterrupted by the Great Depression. Although the Great Depression altered the agendas of traditionalists and modernizers, and forced some young people to postpone their dreams, the fundamental social and cultural forces of the postwar era that ushered in reliance on child science and emphasis on peer culture remained intact. The majority of families who sent their children to ranch schools maintained their economic status during the Depression, and "young people from affluent families found their lives relatively unchanged."[20] However, the Depression magnified differences in class, and the visual lessons of poverty on display in public spaces for the gaze of impressionable youth may have affirmed the decision to send a child out West. An Arizona Desert School alumnus remembered vividly his astonishment at seeing "hundreds of men covered with newspapers trying to keep warm on the lower level of the Michigan Avenue Bridge as the winds of Lake Michigan whipped over them."[21] One headmaster used the economic circumstances of the Depression to preach thrift and value at the Valley Ranch School's weekly chapel service. The readjustment of spending, according to Larry Jarvie, "gave people a more exacting sense of values, both economic and intrinsic."[22]

The ranch school story is about how the elite, assisted and influenced by a cadre of experts, dealt with the issue of cultivating the next generation of leaders amid a period of rapid social and cultural change by looking to the West to provide an environment conducive to making men out of boys and instilling character traits many worried were lost by the end of World War I. By the time ranch schools were at their height in the 1920s, the progeny of the industrial capitalists were in the second and third generations. In many cases, the conditions men believed had contributed to their own success were not easily replicated in the very environments family success had created. The story is about people with financial means, doing what they thought was best for their families in a rapidly changing world. Throughout this account, colorful stories of individuals, families, and students enrich this study by adding a personal element to this historical narrative. Oral history interviews of former students combine to give a glimpse into the children's views of the pre–World War II era, showing how this unique experience shaped the adult lives of those fortunate enough to have attended a ranch school. Yearbook and school newsletter articles also provide a youthful perspective of ranch school life and oftentimes demonstrate young people's sophisticated understanding of their place in the world and the expectations of western life in determining their future. In the 1923 editorial for the Evan's School "Rodeo" end-of-the-year summary, three soon-to-be graduates reflected, "Our brief taste of western life, the experiences that we have had, what we have learned of self-reliance,—all will form an important page in the book of our lives."[23]

CHAPTER 1

The Problem of the Rich Man's Son

THE SURNAMES OF STUDENTS WHO ATTENDED RANCH SCHOOLS READ like the *Social Register*. *Arizona Highways* proudly listed the families "who have the means of sending their children to any school in the world; yet in increasing numbers these families, with the whole world of schools to choose from, select Arizona ranch schools." Parents included Dr. Gilbert Grosvenor, William Randolph Hearst, Governor Lewis Barrows of Maine, Governor Robert Perkins Bass of New Hampshire, Mrs. Fred Astaire, U.S. senator Josh Lee of Oklahoma, Albert L. Deane of General Motors Holding Corporation, Dr. Alton Ochsner of Tulane University, Dr. Robert Hutchins of the University of Chicago, and distinguished American journalist Dorothy Thompson and her husband, Sinclair Lewis.[1] The Saltonstall, Roosevelt, Vanderbilt, DuPont, Sperry, Cabot, Heinz, Pulitzer, and Lowell families all sent their sons to the Evans School in Mesa.[2] Judson student Fred Dalzell's parents owned Fostoria Glass. The Upton family, who ran Whirlpool, enrolled their two boys at Judson, and their daughter Judy attended Jokake in the late 1930s.

The expense incurred by families who sent children to western ranch schools, particularly those in Arizona, was exorbitant. In his 1928 survey of American private secondary schools for boys, Robert Danforth Cole found that the median tuition fee was $575. Only 15 schools of the 2,432 he studied charged $1,600 or more; they included Los Alamos Ranch School ($2,400), Mesa Ranch School ($1,500–$1,750), and the Evans School ($1,600).[3] Tuition for the opening term of Arizona Desert School in 1927 was $2,500, which included all linens,

1

blankets, and ordinary medical care. Arizona Desert School students were expected to provide their own horses, although the school would arrange for rent-
ing mounts if necessary. The requirement, or strong recommendation at most
ranch schools, that every student have his own horse indicated that attendance
at Arizona ranch schools was restricted to the upper crust of society. Even
during the Depression, Judson students needed to purchase "western saddles,
with western horses and other western equipment" in addition to the $1,600
tuition fee that included residence in a private room, feed for one horse, laundry, books, and all school supplies. Both the Orme School and the Southern
Arizona School for Boys (SASB) eventually built their own landing strips, since
many of the families had their own charter planes.[4]

At the same time they provided services for their wealthy clients, they attempted to address a persistent American concern over the effects of unearned
or inherited wealth that had become more pronounced in the years leading
up to and directly preceding World War I. What was profound about western
ranch schools was their ability to sustain the perception of the West as a region of simple living, devoid of urban dangers, pretensions, and rampant consumerism, while simultaneously perpetuating one of the most revered of all
elite institutions—the private school. Parents from places like Boston,
Chicago, Cleveland, Detroit, New York, Newport, Philadelphia, and Pittsburgh
entrusted ranch school owners and headmasters to educate and rear their
children with the intent that their youth would earn the privileges of citizenship, wealth, and social standing through immersion in a western environment, thus effectively neutralizing the potentially debilitating effects of being
born into wealth.

Inherited versus earned privilege has been one of America's great cultural
and political dilemmas since its founding. Aaron Burr and other Anti-Federalists
advocated strongly that citizenship in America should not be conferred through
inheritance but rather earned through service.[5] Frederic Cople Jaher, a historian
of the nineteenth-century elite urban establishment, eloquently stated the situation many Americans feared:

Family and group founders had been shrewd, self-assertive, and hardworking
businessmen and politicians, whose triumphant careers affirmed the national
and local commitment to pragmatic activism and upward mobility. Their descendants, who haunted the mansions, clubhouses, and ballrooms of Boston,

Chicago, New York, and Charleston were often contemplative, confused, and despairing of themselves, their class, and their nation.[6]

As each generation grappled with the effects of inheritance on their offspring, they concluded that the self-made person had a greater appreciation for money, citizenship, and cultural status. In an effort to initiate their sons, Boston's Colonial and Federalist maritime merchant families required their sons to serve "apprenticeships on deck or at the countinghouse" and work their way up before taking over the family business. Boston entrepreneur Jonathan Jackson gave his child money and rank, but perceived them as disadvantages because "self-earned property, especially if hard earned—is generally the best spending property with everybody. It naturally induces habits of reflection and economy."[7] New England textile magnate Amos Lawrence asserted his desire to furnish his sons with "facility for getting a living for themselves, but not the means of living in idleness." Fathers valued labor over leisure and personal achievement above family inheritance and did their best to "guard their children against the evils of inherited privilege."[8]

The premise for Americans' concern over inherited wealth was partially derived from an ideal of a level playing field and equal start in life. British philosopher John Stuart Mill articulated a vision for an open society and social progress that was largely adopted by late nineteenth-century Americans in shaping opinion about inheritance. He believed that social progress was only possible in a society in which no individual was precluded from making a contribution. Thus, the "unearned advantage of those who inherited savings of others" created an unfair advantage.[9] As a practical man, Mill believed children should be able to receive a reasonable, but not lavish, amount of property. Transcendentalist Orestes Brownson, editor and chief contributor to the *Boston Quarterly Review*, further argued the idea of a fair start in life for all children and asserted that "the child of the descendant stands in the same relation to the property as any other child."[10]

According to Ronald Chester, a law professor who researched the history of wealth concentration through inheritance, since World War I, the majority of Americans believed "that inheritance is responsible for much of the concentration of wealth that exists in America." An individual's right to bequest or inherit and its impact on society soared to the forefront of American life in 1906, when President Theodore Roosevelt proposed that Congress pass a heavy progressive inheritance tax. Conservative opposition stymied the president's efforts until the need for war funds produced the estate tax of 1916. However, a significant redistribution of wealth left by the deceased faltered primarily because of "ingenious arguments used by the privileged to defend their wealth" and a "strong desire of the majority of Americans to have a chance to 'win big' by inheriting wealth, thus vaulting without exertion above the masses of men." He termed this the "lottery" phenomenon to explain the fascination yet simultaneous disdain for inherited wealth that appears in American popular literature.[11]

Many Americans scorned millionaires, not because they were rich, but because so many of them seemed idle. Fortunes continued to grow despite little active work on the part of the nouveau riche or their children.[12] Two of the most outspoken critics of unearned wealth and its consequences were themselves quite affluent. The views of Andrew Carnegie and Theodore Roosevelt toward inheritance were based on their "firm belief in self-help." Their attitudes were similar to those of most of their contemporary Protestant reformers and were "a defense of individualism in an era when concentrations of personal and corporate wealth" stifled upward mobility.[13] Reacting to a clamor for breaking up huge individual fortunes in 1907, American economist G. P. Watkins wrote, "We have too much concentration of riches. It threatens that equality of opportunity, and that spirit of individuality and self-reliance which are essential to democracy."[14] The theme of the self-made man was echoed by economist Irving Fisher on the eve of the adoption of the 1916 estate tax, and in Harlan Read's book, *The Abolition of Inheritance*, published in 1919.[15] This fortress of concentrated wealth greatly hindered individual initiative because all children were not afforded a level playing field.

Carnegie, Roosevelt, and private school educators were deeply concerned over the negative impact of unearned wealth on the next generation of leaders. Inheriting large sums of money potentially took away the need to succeed on one's own merits and stifled the cultivation of self-reliance. Andrew Carnegie strongly advised against leaving surplus wealth to offspring, believing it often served "more for the injury than the good of the recipients," and argued it was only "family pride which inspires these enormous legacies." He admitted that there were "instances of millionaires' sons unspoiled by wealth, who, being rich, still perform great services to the community" but lamented that "such are the very salt of the earth, as valuable as, unfortunately, they are rare."[16] In a study of some of the wealthy men who sent their sons to St. Paul's and Groton during the Victorian Era, many agreed with the idea that "wealth led to luxury, luxury led to immorality, immorality led to vice, and vice led to the destruction of the Republic."[17] Theodore Roosevelt agreed with his friend Reverend Endicott Peabody, legendary headmaster of the Groton School, that the sons of the rich should be steered toward a career of public service rather than enter the less noble field of business. Theodore Roosevelt believed that a boarding school and Ivy League education needed to counteract the influences of an elite society that indulged in "false and unworthy" standards of "the 400," who dissipated their summers in Newport, Rhode Island, leading lives that varied "from rotten frivolity to rotten vice."[18]

Others shared their views and echoed the need for physical labor as a supplement to education in order to be successful citizens and corporate leaders. As a parent and head of the Heinz Company, Howard Heinz indicated his concern for the work ethic of "college bred men" in a company memo he wrote in 1915. Heinz stated that discipline, thoroughness, and reliability were the key factors in building a strong and efficient organization. Noting his preference for "the practical work in life" over "the teachings we receive in school" to acquire these skills, he lamented that it was "easy to preach from behind the desk—discipline, efficiency and similar things, but it is hard to find men for the firing line willing to work hard, early and late, day in and day out, to obtain these things." "The trouble with most highly educated men," Heinz argued, "is that the details of our work do not interest them very seriously and that they are not contented to work at one job long enough to become a thorough master of it."[19] Howard Heinz worked in his father's factories every summer, commenting that he "put me through the mill. . . . He told me he'd have to be harder on me because I was his son. And I've never ceased to thank him for it. For in that very contact with the man who earns his livelihood by the sweat of his brow, I learned what it means to make the physical effort to gain your wage."[20]

Requiring a son to work his way up into a position of leadership was an important means of discrediting any notion that he did not earn it by his own merit. A 1902 *Cosmopolitan Magazine* article celebrating the Swift family specifically noted that not one of the second generation "ever got a desk through nepotism. Each little Swift, as he reached years of discretion, got four months in the yards with a cattle-buyer, another four with a hog-buyer, another four with a general superintendent, and so on until he was fit to take up executive work." Gustav Swift was described as a "Cape Cod Yankee who bought a steer now and then and peddled the meat from the back of a certain go-cart which has since become famous" for its evolution into the refrigerator car. Upon his death, the meat-packing empire he created "passed without a hitch to the hands of a numerous family, who made it their one objective in life a devotion to its perpetuity." The Swifts did not speculate, indulge in fads, "infest the front page," or have a desire to leave home, but instead worked steadily and calmly to preserve the family business. The author credited the family for its members' dedication to hard work and their lack of ostentatious behavior despite their economic means.[21]

Concern over the moral character of children reared in the grandiose households of the elite was especially prevalent in the interwar years as the gap between the rich and the middle class widened. From 1920 to 1929, disposable income per capita rose 9 percent; however, those with income in the top 1 percent enjoyed a 75 percent increase. A study completed by the Brookings Institute revealed that by "1929 the top 0.1 percent of Americans earned a combined income equal to the bottom 42 percent."[22] Much criticism focused on consumerism and its effects on working-class, middle-class, and wealthy Americans. Daniel Horowitz explored different views offered by household budget experts, social critics, and social scientists who struggled with the "problem of the relation between affluence, morality, and the social order." He defined the post–World War I era as the one when modern moralism began, and he traced the evolution of this ideology from the late nineteenth-century traditional moralist perspective that admonished rampant consumer spending as evidence of lack of self-control. The modern moralists and intellectuals of the 1920s and 1930s supported consumer culture, but they "argued that the purchase of mass produced goods was much less worthwhile than the enjoyment of exciting and enriching experiences." This shift from old to new moralism represented long-term changes in middle-class culture and a preference for a vital liberating American culture—one that was exciting and innovative rather than restrictive and genteel.[23]

Most consumption studies and reports focused on the working and middle classes, with the exception of Thorstein Veblen, who launched a fundamental criticism of the habits of the wealthy beginning in 1891. Veblen broke with the tenet of nineteenth-century moralism that held to the notion that "with increased wealth people would choose moral, elevating, and socializing objectives." Veblen abhorred wasteful consumption and argued that affluence

promoted "exclusiveness." On the other hand, he celebrated machine production and had difficulty articulating alternative ways of spending money. During
the Progressive Era, many Americans believed inflation was a problem caused
by the middle class and their desire for new standards of living. Some blamed
the wealthy for setting a standard of extravagance that Americans desperately
sought to emulate. Social commentators advocated thrift and self-denial while
simultaneously urging refinement, though not luxury, through consumption.
Between 1914 and 1921 the cost of consumer goods doubled. The war and drastic
changes in the economy led those above subsistence level to curb waste and
become more self-sufficient for the sake of patriotism and necessity, rather than
out of a sense of moral responsibility. At the war's end, pent-up demand for
consumer goods led to excess spending. The pinch of inflation, forced savings
in wartime, and envy for workers' increased spending capacity afforded by
higher wages, led the middle class to welcome material pleasures at the same
time they critiqued excess. This pattern continued through the Depression, and
many Americans modified patterns of expenditures so that they could continue
to live as they had in more prosperous years.[24]

By the interwar period, consumerism had become the purview of women.
The economic processes that relieved women of hard labor gave them new
power as consumers. As homemakers, women spent money that their husbands earned. This shift occurred at the same time that new ideas about families and motherhood surfaced. According to Rebecca Jo Plant, author of *Mom*,
"unlike their Victorian forefathers, modern American men would learn to
construct their masculine identity largely in opposition to, rather than in concert with, their mothers."[25] As boys became "men in the making" they were to
emulate their fathers rather than remain tied to their mothers beyond the age
of seven or eight.[26] They needed to develop the skills to earn income rather
than consume. As a dependent with expendable income, the rich man's son was
a natural consumer, a situation that was a potential impediment to his developing masculinity.

Educational experts were extremely prolific on the effects of wealth on
children. According to a professor from Duke University in 1930, there was
"good reason to believe that *wealth and luxury* are no less antagonistic to the
truest moral development than poverty and destitution."[27] Dr. James
McConaughy, president of Wesleyan University, argued that private schools
provided an important service by co-opting the influences of wealth on

children. In certain elite homes, he argued, boys were alerted to their privilege as the "leaders of tomorrow" without the pressure to succeed by one's own fortitude. In this case the "boy does not know how to cooperate, either at home or in the school." Dr. McConaughy believed that "the boy who comes from the family of ten on the wrong side of the railroad track has learned the lesson of sharing co-operatively in joint decisions."[28]

Headmasters, who were largely middle class, shared most Americans' simultaneous concern for the character of children born into wealth and their disdain for pretentious displays of wealth. According to a 1913 textbook-like guide for running boarding schools for young boys, it was of the utmost importance that masters remain untainted by the evils of wealth. The author advised that "the school should pay the master a salary sufficient to provide him with all of the necessities of life and a few of its luxuries, and at the same time to permit his retiring on a modest competency from his savings."[29] The Valley Ranch School paid Philip Cummings a monthly salary of $125 in addition to providing housing, meals, and a horse. In reviewing his budget, he soon realized how quickly western accoutrements chipped away at his income. In his first and second month he had spent $8.50 on a wide ten-gallon hat, $25 on chaps, and $11.50 on pure virgin wool pants satisfactory for riding.[30] Sherman Thacher, son of a Yale Latin professor, first began tutoring students from the East in 1889 in Ojai Valley, California. By the early part of the turn of the century, the Thacher School received at least five applications for every space available, and Sherman decided that the quality of the parents, the boy's character and intelligence, and the geographic distribution of his student body should be his primary selection criteria. He justified the predominance of children of means at his school by explaining, "I have a mission among the over-privileged." According to Thacher's biographer, "If a wealthy parent was dressed simply, drove up in a plain car, and did not mention money, his son stood a good chance of being considered on an equal basis. Otherwise, the school was apparently full."[31]

Cultural critics joined parents, economists, and educational experts to bring the concern of the rich man's son to the forefront of American society through literary articles and novels. *Saturday Evening Post* articles titled "The Burden of Wealth" (1919), "The Generation that Comes Next" (1921), "It's Hard to Be a Rich Man's Son" (1928), and "The Rich Man's Son" (1928), provided countless testimonials from leading experts and philanthropists about the problems of inherited wealth. "The Rich Man's Son," written by Albert W. Atwood and printed in the *Saturday Evening Post*, included several thoughts of his contemporaries on this topic. According to Atwood, "One often hears it said these days that the rich man's most serious problem is his son." He then posed the question, "Will the son be able to carry on his father's business despite the tendency of inherited money to kill the nerve of initiative and endeavor?" Toward the end of his life, Harvard president Charles William Eliot wrote a piece on the advantages of a son from a poor family. The strong young lad of fourteen plowed, harrowed, sawed and split wood, fished, and carried water in order to help his family. The son of such a family "has securities against laziness, selfishness and self-indulgence, and inducements to diligence and helpfulness. He knows from the beginnings of reflective life that he will have to work, that he has his own living to make and that the nature of it will depend on his own efforts." In comparison to the rich man's son, "he is not enfeebled by the pampering that comes from comfort and luxury."[32]

In "The Generation that Comes Next," published in 1921, Irvin S. Cobb directed his attention to the particular plight of youth in the early years of the interwar period. He confessed that his observations of the younger generation were limited to the larger cities of the North Atlantic Seaboard. The "modern handicaps" he observed were not those of "professional lounge lizards" but "the sons of well-to-do and well-bred parents—normal youngsters, or rather youngsters who would be normal if only the times were." These potentially "normal youngsters" had been overindulged, overpampered, and overpetted. To their detriment, "they have not been encouraged to develop a sense of responsibility. . . . Their good manners appear mainly on the top like a veneer of varnish; the veneer of their courtesy seems to be no more than skin deep." The composite character of the male youth in his essay was restless and in constant pursuit of adventure and amusement. "Devices for amusement and occupation which were ample" for the author's generation, "he rejects as puerile and childish." Joy rides had replaced hay rides. Cobb conceded that a modern youth might succeed despite his flawed environment and false standards of values, but if he fails later in life, "no doubt the job will be competently attended to by another boy who was reared among simpler surroundings and disciplined by a surer parental control and hardened by the experience of doing without expensive and luxurious things until he had earned them for himself."[33]

The idea that sons born into wealth were morally disadvantaged was reflected in contemporary novels, including Booth Tarkington's *The Magnificent*

Ambersons (1918), Pearl Buck's *Sons* (1932), and Edgar Rice Burroughs's Tarzan series. *The Magnificent Ambersons* is a story about a family and community in transition from the Gilded Age to the modern era, and is centered on the life of George Amberson Minifer, the only third-generation descendant of Major Amberson. Tarkington makes it clear that, as the major's only grandchild, George was doomed to suffer the problems of a rich man's son from birth. By the age of nine, he "was a princely terror, dreaded not only in the Amberson Addition but in many other quarters throughout the Midwestern community." As the result of his bullying, total disrespect for everyone he came in contact with, and flaunting of his family fortune, everyone in his hometown waited for the day when George would "get his come-upance." By elaborating on his obnoxious behavior, Tarkington demonstrated that it was not jealousy that drove George's neighbors to hope that George would get his due; it was that George lacked character and needed a moral lesson.[34]

Tarkington spends a significant amount of time describing the Ambersons' magnificence, but offers no explanation of how Major Amberson attained his wealth. Nor does George inquire as to how the Ambersons amassed such a fortune. As a result, the author provides no opportunity for the major to instill values of hard work and thrift in his grandson through a recounting of his dramatic ascent to riches. Tarkington depicts the citizens of the midwestern town as descended from early settlers "who had opened the wilderness" and survived on thrift. This pioneer spirit was inherited by sons and grandsons, and "their thrift was next to their religion: to save for the sake of saving, was their earliest lesson in discipline. No matter how prosperous they were, they could not spend money either upon 'art,' or upon mere luxury and entertainment, without a sense of sin." In comparison, the "magnificence of the Ambersons was as conspicuous as a brass band at a funeral."[35]

Throughout his life, George frequently described his preference for "being things" over "doing things," and rather than develop any sense of self-reliance, he structured his entire future on his presumed inheritance and "being" an Amberson. George coasted through preparatory school and an Ivy League university, making the minimum effort with no ambition for a future career, further demonstrating his lack of respect for hard work or the need to prove himself. He mocked and disdained business and professional men and when asked by his love interest, Lucy, what he wanted to be after he graduated, he promptly answered "a yachtsman." When pressed further about what he planned to do for a living, he responded that he has never "been able to see any occasion for a man's going into trade, or being a lawyer, or any of those things if his position were such that he didn't need to." Although he claimed that he expected "to live an honourable life" and to contribute his share to charities and take part in movements, when Lucy asked what kind of movements, he replied, "Whatever appeals to me."[36]

The community continued to wait in anticipation for the day when George Amberson Minifer would get his comeuppance, with some becoming more direct in their criticism of his character. After one Christmas when he has visited home from college, a newspaper article appeared with the title, "Gilded Youths of the Fin-de-Siecle," attacking him directly. "With his airs of a young milord, his fast horses, his gold and silver cigarette-cases, his clothes from a New York tailor, his recklessness of money showered upon him by indulgent mothers or doting grandfathers, he respects nothing and nobody." Tarkington's fictional article concluded with a comparison to the ability and character of those who work, rather than inherit.

> Let us pray that the future of our country is not in the hands of these *fin-de-siecle* gilded youths, but rather in the calloused palms of men yet unknown, laboring upon the farms of the land. When we compare the young manhood of Abraham Lincoln with the specimens we are now producing, we see too well that it bodes ill for the twentieth century.[37]

The emphasis on agricultural work for producing more noble leaders, rather than industrial work, was an important distinction. By emphasizing agricultural work, ranch schools appealed to parents who wanted their sons to prove themselves through labor, but not in an industrial setting, unless it was carefully controlled. Tarkington set his novel in the late nineteenth century, but the fictional newspaper article was strikingly similar to the *Saturday Evening Post* articles that shared the same concerns of the rich man's son.

Tarkington effectively demonstrated that George's spoiled upbringing and reliance on his wealth led him to cling to an ideal of the leisured class that was quickly fading away. His choice to set his story in the late nineteenth and early twentieth centuries allowed him to emphasize the drastic nature of the transition from the Gilded Age to the modern era. Lucy's father represented the extreme of modern life by developing the automobile, providing the perfect juxtaposition for George, who gives constant criticism of the horseless carriage and is convinced it will never catch on. He explained to his mother, "I suppose I'm a little old-fashioned and fastidious, but I'm afraid being a sort of engine driver never will appeal to me. . . . It's exciting, and I'd like that part of it, but still it doesn't seem to me precisely the thing a gentleman ought to do. Too much overalls and monkey-wrenches and grease!" Throughout the novel, George's disdain for any kind of work portrays him as terribly out of touch despite his young age.[38]

George Amberson Minifer eventually got what he deserved, but the ultimate irony was that those who had longed for the day when he would get his comeuppance were no longer around to witness this reversal of fortune. When his mother and grandfather died, George found that the inheritance that was the basis for his entire future as a gentleman philanthropist and yachtsman was nonexistent. Starting from scratch, he found a job as a clerk and student of law that paid a salary of $8 a week. After trying to make do on this pittance, he acquired a job in the dangerous trades that paid $28 a week. One Sunday afternoon he walked to his old neighborhood and "stood before the great dripping department store that now occupied the big plot of ground where once had stood both the Amberson Hotel and the Amberson Opera House." After seeing the old mansion and the site of his mother's house, which had been demolished for a tenement, "he turned away from the devastated site, thinking bitterly that the only Amberson mark still left upon the town was the name of the boulevard—Amberson Boulevard." A few moments later, "his eye fell upon a metal oblong sign upon the lamp-post at the corner" labeled "Tenth Street."[39]

The fate of three sons upon the death of their father as told in Pearl Buck's *Sons* (1932) was no more hopeful than George Amberson Minifer's plight as a rich man's son. *Sons* was the second book in Buck's trilogy of the family of Wang Lung. Buck was born in West Virginia to Presbyterian missionaries and spent most of the first forty years of her life in China. *Sons* is set in China at a time when outside influences began to transform traditional rural isolated communities. Just as Tarkington used generational conflict as a means of demonstrating dramatic cultural changes in a midwestern town at the turn of the century, an important theme of *Sons* was the struggle of three generations of sons and fathers that occurs during a transformative period in China.

Wang Lung was a self-made man. "He had been poor once and a man on the land like any other" but died a rich man, leaving his three sons with great wealth. Each brother "longed for the hour when the inheritance was to be divided, since each had in his inner heart a purpose for which he wished to have his own given him." The eldest brother needed to know how much he would have to support his two wives, children, and "his secret pleasures he could not deny himself." The second brother had "great grain markets" and wanted to use his inheritance to invest and earn more money. "As for the third brother," Buck explains, "he was so strange and silent that no one knew what he wished and that dark face of his never told anything at all." Referred to as Wang the Tiger, the third son became the antihero of the story, as his secret ambition was to become a war-lord. He used his inheritance to build a great army. Wang the Tiger was a fierce but just leader, who could not rob because his father "had been a just and honest man," suggesting that he had inherited his father's character, protecting him from resorting to thievery as he built his empire through conquest.[40]

The eldest two sons began selling off their father's land for their personal ambitions and to support Wang the Tiger's military aspirations to become a king. Upon hearing rumors that the first two sons were to sell portions of the land, Pear Blossom, Wang Lung's concubine, implored Wang the Eldest's first wife to ensure that her master's land remained intact. "My own lord labored all his life to bring together these lands that his sons and a hundred generations might rest upon a sure foundation, and it is surely not well that already in this generation they should be sold." To preserve the land acquired by their father required hard work, to which the two eldest sons were unaccustomed. After surveying his father's land, a wearied Wang the Eldest, who had never experienced "such a day's work as this in his whole life," lamented that "a landlord's life was very hard." Buck described the Eldest as "fat and yellow and loathly." His "flesh hung poached under his eyes" and "his lips puffed out full and thick and pale." While the Eldest's laziness and fondness of teahouses and concubines prevented him from living up to his father's ambitions, Wang the Second displayed reckless ambition for earn-ing a fortune rather than the more wholesome enterprise of farming.[41]

Buck conveyed one of the most prevalent concerns of inherited wealth and of being born a rich man's son. Boys who were spoiled, pampered, and accus-tomed to luxury would not only become lazy, but effeminate. Wang the Eldest's firstborn son epitomized the detriments of the rich man's son. At first he begged his father to allow him to accompany his uncle, Wang the Tiger, in his military conquests, but this turned out to be a momentary passing phase. Upon observ-ing his son, Wang the Eldest became greatly concerned, as he began to see his son for what he had become:

a young man dainty and fastidious and idle, without any single ambition for anything except his pleasure, and his only fear that he was not better dressed and less in fashion than other young men whom he knew. Yes, Wang the Eldest saw his son lying on the silken quilts of his bed, and the young man wore silk to his very skin and he had satin shoes on his feet and his skin was like a beauty's skin, oiled and perfumed, and his hair was perfumed and smoothed with some foreign oil. Yes, he was a lord in a rich man's house, as anyone could see, and none would have dreamed that his grandfather was one Wang Lung, a farmer, and a man of the earth.[42]

By contrast, Wang the Second thought he could prevent his sons from suffering the same fate by making certain that they would neither be spendthrifts nor idle. He planned carefully for each one to have a "few years of schooling to learn to read and write and to count skillfully with the abacus. But he would not let them stay long enough to be held scholars . . . for scholars will not labor at anything." Wang the Tiger, however, thought of the sons of Wang the Second as weak and susceptible to the same fate as his other nephews. His brother was so engrossed in money making "that he never saw his sons at all, nor thought of how they would one day spend as eagerly what he so eagerly gathered together, nor only endured their clerking until he died and left them free so that they need not work."[43]

Wang the Tiger's solution to overcoming the fate of a rich man's son was to become physically robust, brave, and masculine through intensive training as a soldier. Wang the Tiger eventually had a son of his own and "swore that his son should not be like any of" his nephews. His son "should be hardened from his youth up and reared to be a great soldier and he should be taught every sort of skill and he should be made into a man." When his son was six years old, "Wang the Tiger took him from his mother and out of the courts of the women, and brought him into his own courts to live with him. That he did so that the boy would not be made soft by women's caresses and women's talk and ways." The ultimate irony for Wang the Tiger was that his son wanted to be a farmer rather than a great soldier, and in the end, he applied his modern military training to join forces with his father's enemy.[44] While the sons of the first two brothers seemed doomed to the curse of inheritance and wealth, by the end of the book, Wang the Tiger's son was on the path to making something of himself, but ultimately at the betrayal of his father. This Freudian psychoanalytical implication suggested that to overcome the burden of inheritance and become self-made, sons must abdicate their wealth, family position, and claim to succession of the family business.

In *Tarzan of the Apes*, Edgar Rice Burroughs, like Buck, emphasized the idea that a life of wealth and luxury inhibited the development of masculine traits, but he approached inherited wealth and its effect on boys from an entirely different perspective. Rather than portray the downfall of those born into wealth, his tale demonstrated how denial of inherited position and money at a young age developed character, advanced physical ability, courage, rational judgment, and above all, self-reliance. Tarzan, or Lord Greystroke, possessed these traits inherited from his long lineage of brave and noble Englishmen, and they were enhanced by his having to survive on his own in the jungle, rather than diminished by a life of luxury and lack of want. Tarzan was left as an infant in the jungle when his father and mother died after being marooned in Africa. "His life amidst the dangers of the jungle had taught him to meet emergencies with self-confidence" and resourcefulness. He was so extremely self-reliant that he taught himself to read from a child's primer and dictionary he discovered in the tree house once occupied by his parents. Burroughs attributed his literacy to "the active intelligence of a healthy mind endowed by inheritance with more than ordinary reasoning powers."[45]

Throughout the novel, Burroughs provided examples of what Tarzan's fate might have been had he lived the life of privilege that was due him by birth. As Tarzan, the true Lord Greystroke, ate raw flesh of boar and wiped his sticky hands on his naked thigh, his younger brother "sent back his chops to his chef because they were underdone, and when he had finished his repast he dipped his finger-ends into a silver bowl of scented water and dried them on a piece of snowy damask."[46] In comparison to Tarzan, the younger Lord Greystroke is finicky and dainty, much like those described by other authors such as George Amberson Minifer and Wang the Eldest's firstborn son.

In *Tarzan Lord of the Jungle*, published in 1928, Burroughs was increasingly critical of the character of the moneyed elite. One of a series of short stories included in this publication contrasts Wilbur Stimbol, a man who tried to bully his way through the jungle by flaunting his wealth, and Jim Blake, whose bravery, chivalry, and honor ultimately led to knighthood, in the lost city of Nimmr. Although Burroughs does not make it explicit that Jim Blake has money, the fact that he can afford an African adventure certainly implied that he has economic means. Upon his first encounter with Tarzan, Stimbol demands his right to shoot a gorilla that Tarzan sought to protect. He announces that he is "Wilbur Stimbol of Stimbol & Company brokers, New York!" In New York, Paris, and London such a proclamation opened many a door, but it fails miserably in the jungle. He foolishly defies Tarzan's order to leave the jungle and continues his hunt for Simba the Lion. Stimbol's hired men desert him, unwilling to defy Tarzan's command, and he is left to his own resources. Lacking the ability to survive on his own, he nearly perishes. Just as Professor Archimedes Q. Porter's education was worthless to jungle survival in *Tarzan of the Apes*, Stimbol's money is equally useless in *Tarzan Lord of the Jungle*.

Historian John Kasson uses generational struggle as a partial explanation for the context in which Edgar Rice Burroughs created his alter ego, Tarzan. Burroughs was a frustrated man who, like many of his generation, came of age in the 1880s and 1890s and missed out on the great adventures of his father's generation. Compelled to match his father's success, in his youth he had several experiences aimed at this goal. He spent six months out West and attended Phillips Academy in Andover, Massachusetts, but only lasted a semester. His father subsequently sent him to Michigan Military Academy. By the early 1900s, he found himself a white collar worker, married, with two children, trying desperately to make ends meet. According to Kasson, "Burroughs's frustrations were shared by countless millions." He began writing for pulp magazines and eventually found employment as a manager for *System*, a business magazine. "*System* proposed a hierarchy of masculine worth and ability" and frequently explored whether "this hierarchy was due to differences in training and environment or innate differences." The magazine promoted a hierarchical system of leaders and followers with a fascination for the process of selection that distinguished "the exceptional individual from the mass."[47] Nature versus nurture was an important theme for *Tarzan of the Apes*, but by 1928, many realized that unearned wealth took away an important competitive element that allowed for a true process of selection. Stripped of financial resources in *Tarzan Lord of the Jungle*, the man of true masculine character, Jim Blake, rose to the top.

The preceding examples do not allow redemption for children born into privilege. In *The Magnificent Ambersons* and *Tarzan Lord of the Jungle*, George Amberson Minifer and Wilbur Stimbol only begin to realize the detrimental effect of their behavior at the point where they are almost entirely broken down. Furthermore, these narratives pay little or no attention to the role of the father.

In *The Magnificent Ambersons*, the father plays a very limited role in his son's upbringing before his death, and in *Sons* the deceased father is exalted as a self-made man.

Two films of the interwar period portray the plight of the rich man's son, but in both cases, it is the father who intervenes to teach his son a lesson, ultimately leading to a change for the better. The core narrative of *A Fight to the Finish* (1925) and *The Adventurous Soul* (1927) centers on the generational conflict between a wealthy businessman and his son. Both fathers resort to trickery and force their sons into an environment devoid of wealth, requiring them to make it on their own merit.

In the opening scene of *A Fight to the Finish* the title card explains that viewers are observing "The Davis home—where the father lived and the son came to sleep—sometimes." Cyrus J. Davis is a retired capitalist who in the first scene pores over an itemized bill for sixty dinners for $600 and "destruction of glassware and china" for $150 "ordered by Mr. James Davis," his son. Cyrus Davis berates his son to his friend Henry McBride, exclaiming, "This reckless extravagance of Jim's has got to stop!" as he pounds his fist on the desk. McBride responds that it was Cyrus's own fault, declaring that he "spoiled [Jim] with too much money." Davis is inspired by McBride's suggestion that if he had "been a poor man, [Jim] probably would have amounted to something." Cyrus seems to acquiesce and listens to an idea of McBride's, who instructs, "Do what I tell you—and we'll make a man out of him yet!"

The next scene opens with a title card stating, "Jim Davis would have been ashamed to get home any morning before the milkman." Dressed in tails, Jim and six friends appear riding on the back of the milk truck, harassing the milkman, instructing him to "take my friends home, James—and don't spare the steed!" After witnessing this general mayhem and the boys' antics, his father decides to enact McBride's plan. Loud enough for Jim to overhear, one of the pair exclaim, "It's a great calamity—I feel very sorry for Jim." His father's carrying on intrigues Jim, who enters the room. Upon seeing Jim, McBride exclaims, "Your father is bankrupt—he has lost everything!" Crying, his father winks at McBride to indicate to the audience that this is the hoax that is part of McBride's plan. Jim tries to console his father by telling him he will "get a job first thing in the morning." After Jim's departure, the father and McBride congratulate themselves and proclaim, "Bet you a thousand he makes good!" Jim spends several days looking for a job before getting into an altercation with a driver who nearly ran over a woman, Mary Corbett. Unbeknownst to Jim, in this act of chivalry, he has clobbered prize fighter "Battling Wilson." This demonstration of his latent talent leads him to become a fighter. Jim rents a small apartment and trains for a month to fight Wilson. Just before the fight, Jim happens upon his father's game, but decides to honor the contest against Wilson, who is simultaneously plotting to fix the match to ensure his victory. This is a significant aspect of the plot because it shows Jim as a man of honor and integrity, especially when compared to his father, McBride, and Wilson. It is clear that the change in environment brought out his better qualities.[48]

Jim's reversal of fortune lasts just a little over a month, but as a result of his father's trickery, he becomes a better person. The ends justified the means in *A Fight to the Finish*, but the father's scheming in *The Adventurous Soul* led to more drastic consequences. The opening scene is almost identical to that in *A Fight to the Finish*. John Martin, the father, is a "colossus of commerce—whose far-flung fleets had carried his flag and name into every Pacific port," according to the title card. He is seated at a desk in an impressive office, shuffling paperwork, when a "professional blonde" and her lawyer walk into the office. She is a chorus girl for the Baby Doll Revue and is suing John Martin's son, Glenn, for breach of promise. The lawyer proclaims to Martin, "Your son has broken this poor girl's heart—and we're filing suit unless you settle for cash. She's got a $50,000 heart." Martin's son works for his father's firm, but when the lawyer and the chorus girl leave at 10:25 a.m., he has not yet arrived.

In the next scene, John Martin finally corners his son for a business conference at home and angrily lectures him with the familiar language of social critics, captains of industry, and elite fathers who were at their wit's end with their sons. "When I was your age I worked six months for the money you spend in one night." He then declares, "I've been too easy—but I'm going to make a man out of you now—whether you like it or not!" As Glenn skulks away, Captain Svenson, a "two-fisted sea-dog," enters. From a comment he makes to the father audiences learn that they had sailed together on a whaling vessel, indicating that John Martin was a self-made man, or had participated in the ritual activity of learning the business from the bottom up. He tells the sea captain, "I want you to shanghai my son. Make him work—treat him rough—and drill some manhood into him. Turn him over to my branch manager in Valparaiso—and we'll give him a chance to make good down there." The captain responds that he will "give him the same dose you and me swallowed—when we shipped before the mast!" Glenn overhears the exchange and sees his father take out money from a hidden safe and hand it to the sea captain.

Glenn's foil is Dick Barlow, a hardworking shipping clerk, who wants to marry Miriam Martin, Glenn's sister. In contrast to Glenn, Dick wants to travel the world by ship for the chance to prove himself. In a turn of events, Dick is mistaken for Glenn and shanghaied. Dick works hard as a sailor, scrubbing the deck and peeling potatoes, with little complaint, and is rewarded with an office job in Valparaiso. The opening title card to part four explains, "Glowing reports of his son's progress in months that followed made John Martin forget Dick Barlow's sudden disappearance." The father believes his scheme has worked, as in a short period of time, the manager declared that his son, who was actually Dick Barlow, was ready to take over the office. The father's brief period of satisfaction is thwarted by a telegram from the American Consul in Paris—"Your son facing prison term for robbery here stop advise by cable what to do." John Martin suffers a heart attack while holding the telegram, which conveniently falls into the wastebasket. No one knows of Glenn Martin's actual fate, and he languishes in prison for two years. By happenstance, upon his release, Glenn finds his way to Valparaiso and discovers that Dick Barlow has been impersonating him. After failed attempts to bully his way into the position he believes is rightly his, he acknowledges to Dick, "If I had have followed your example my father would have been alive today."[49]

In both films, the means were justified by the end goal of instilling character in sons who were disadvantaged by their wealth. The fathers suffered from their scheming, but in the end, audiences believed that the change in environment brought out the inherent qualities of chivalry, honor, respect, and remorse. Upon realizing that Dick would relinquish his position and planned to take responsibility for the impersonation, even though he did not initiate the circumstances, Glenn refused to let Dick make such a sacrifice. The moral of each story is clear. It was not the rich man's son who was to blame—it was the father's inability to control the son's environment to ensure proper character development.

This theme continued throughout the interwar period and as late as the release of *Girl Crazy*, a 1943 movie based on George Gershwin's 1930 musical. This film made a direct connection to the value of immersion in the American West to alleviate the curse of the "rich man's son." In the first scene Danny Churchill, played by Mickey Rooney, does the town, staying out all night to go to clubs, ride around town in limousines, and socialize with glamorous women in New York City. The next morning, his father, a publisher who own fourteen papers, calls him into his office to let him know he does not approve of his son's activities, which were splashed across the front section of the newspaper. In a most derogatory tone, his father announces his displeasure that Danny is "growing up to be a rich man's son" and that he is "not going to let this happen." Mr. Churchill's solution is to send Danny out West to the Cody College of Mines. He tries to assure Danny that the experience would not be that bad despite the absence of girls at the school and concludes that it "might make a man out of you."[50] The film encompassed parents' fear that children who inherited wealth and status did not recognize the hard work involved in amassing family fortunes and, as a result, would lead indolent lives.

By the turn of the century, the imagined West had many qualities that made it the ideal proving ground for American youth. Western ranch schools became a valued resource for the education of the elite because in the American mind, the West lacked the hindrances of inherited privilege and other cultural and social restraints that inhibited youth from becoming "self-made." Its rugged environment forced adolescents to prove themselves, and cowboys and ranchers served as role models of self-made individuals. The absence of urban conveniences and unwholesome leisure activities ensured that youth would not succumb to the indolence that plagued children of privilege. Ironically, western boosters lured wealthy easterners to their communities by offering the elite institutions they were accustomed to while at the same time creating a perception of the West as a place where the constraints of class boundaries and family lineage could be overcome. Furthermore, by creating an image of the West as devoid of consumerism, the region itself became a consumable experience, available only to the very wealthy who could afford tuition fees, a horse, and the plethora of western accoutrements needed to truly remake oneself.

The writings of Theodore Roosevelt, Owen Wister, and Frederick Remington contributed to the shaping of the eastern establishment's view of the West as "anti-industrial and antimodern."[51] The idea of the West as more democratic, more open, and socially less stratified than other regions of the country was fairly established in most Americans' view. At the end of her transcontinental motor trip in 1916, Emily Post concluded, "I feel as though I had acquired from the great open West a more direct outlook, a simpler, less encumbered view of life . . . in even a short while you feel you have sloughed off the skin of Eastern hidebound dependence upon ease and luxury."[52] One easterner who traveled to the

Southwest in search of health benefits in the earliest part of the twentieth century wrote an account of his experiences that further demonstrated how the Southwest embodied the "social and ethical aspects" of middle-class America. "Men or women whom circumstances, in their former home, would have forever kept below the horizon of recognition, will often, in this ampler air of the West, rise to comparative importance. Competition is not so cruelly keen, and business and social emulation possess a kindlier spirit." He made clear his impression of the West as largely made up of respectable middle-class eastern and midwestern transplants in his glowing description: "The homes of the West are veritable homes, sweet and wholesome; each one a little garden spot where children know the exuberant happiness of youth, and mothers and fathers are not society-mad or business-mad, but lead such natural lives as men and women can live who are neither bound to an endlessly revolving wheel of 'society' nor suffer the blight of poverty."[53]

Ranch schools took on characteristics that parents expected of authentic western ranch life, including the opportunity for ranch work. The theme of hard work dominated Westerns—novels, short stories, comic books, radio programs, and film. According to Jane Tompkins, the Westerns transformed the idea of hard work "from the necessity one wants to escape into the most desirable of human endeavors: action that totally saturates the present moment, totally absorbs the body and mind, and directs one's life to the service of an unquestioned goal." The harshness of the West of the Western promoted the idea of "physical strength as an ideal. It says that the hero is tough and strong, that the West made him that way."[54] The need for boys who were being groomed to assume leadership roles to prove themselves through physical labor had evolved into a rite of passage. Jack Heinz harvested cucumbers in Indiana on his vacations from Yale and worked in one of the company's salt mines after he graduated. A newspaper article heralded the "modesty, common sense and sterling character of the young Mr. Heinz" as demonstrated "by the fact that he has been here working for several weeks and it is only by accident that the knowledge of his being here has become somewhat known." He worked the same schedule as the other workers "in the plant, beginning at seven o'clock in the morning and working until twelve o'clock at night if necessary to get the work done." Those who knew him said "that he has his father's and grandfather's common sense and is not afraid of work just because he is a rich man's son and doesn't have to work."[55]

Private schools used service projects as one method for developing a student's appreciation for his station in life. In a section labeled "Work in relation to sympathy and appreciation" included in his 1920 advice manual, *Moral Education in School and Home*, J. O. Engleman advocated instilling a sense of mutual sympathy among the classes in order to facilitate a democratic society.

> A man may be so wealthy that his son will never be likely to face the problem of having to work with his hands to earn his own living; but if this son works at something, if he learns from actual experience what it means in time, in patience, in energy, in skill, to fashion a vase, or make a table, or hammer into shape and weld the links of a chain, he will likely develop a more wholesome respect and sympathy for his neighbor's son who can do these things better than he, and may perforce be compelled to do these or similar things as long as he lives. . . . In these illustrations we may see one of the moral effects which come from any sort of manual or industrial effort. It gives a basis for appreciation, for sympathy, for understanding, and for rightly evaluating the efforts of those who labor in these lines.[56]

Not all types of work were considered appropriate for boys, however. Educator Horace Holden disagreed with having young boys take part in domestic activities. He argued, "Although boys should be required to keep their clothes-locker in order, their bureaus neat, and their chairs unlitered [*sic*]" it should not "be the policy of the school, unless it is a school of small charges where it is distinctly understood that boys are to share domestic duties, to require bedmaking, sweeping, and the like. Those occupations are very well practiced in camp and military school, but here they are better left to the care of servants."[57]

Most work conducted by ranch schools was solely for character building rather than for actually running the ranch, with a few exceptions. Child science-advice givers connected a need for household chores to the decline of child labor in order to supplement the instillation of a work ethic. Proponents emphasized character development rather than a need to contribute to one's family.[58] Orme School students were required to pitch in with ranch chores that included milking, gathering eggs, picking currants, washing windows, and maintaining the ranch vehicles and machinery. At the Fresnal Ranch School, a group of boys under the guidance of the school electrician learned the skills needed to take responsibility for all of the machinery on the ranch. According to a brochure, "because of their skill and constant vigilance, the school has never been without lights, refrigeration, or water, even for brief intervals. Automobiles are serviced as soon as they enter school grounds." Through so-called Project Committee work, all Fresnal boys learned how to solve construction problems and how to handle tools of all kinds in order to keep up the playing fields and plan new projects. Their work was evident in the form of fences, gates, cattle guards, dams, and small buildings. A brochure stated that "individual initiative is encouraged, and the boys develop a real interest in making repairs and improvements, and in working together."[59]

At most ranch schools, students completed service projects in the form of capital improvement to school property. Manual training at the Judson School consisted of learning the craft of woodworking in the school's shop, which was equipped with a power sander, jigsaw, and band saw.[60] In 1931, boys at the Judson School completed a horseback riding trail on Mummy Mountain and built two adobe buildings.[61] Similarly, the students at the Arizona Desert School built a chapel by hauling rocks to make an altar, pulpit, and seats. Daily chores consisted of carrying water to the chapel birdbath, picking rocks off the polo field, weeding the front-yard garden, and grooming horses.[62] Los Alamos Ranch School alumnus Charles Pearce referred to the required afternoon of "community work" as "humbling work calculated to instill community spirit and to quash anything resembling a superiority complex."[63] Ranch life provided opportunities for students to experience agricultural work, labor on construction projects, and develop some technical skills that would otherwise be omitted from their repertoire of life's experiences. Aside from Orme School and the young electricians at Fresnal Ranch School, most ranch school students did not supplement the labor force necessary to run the schools and ranching operations. Nationally and at southwestern ranch schools, servants took care of laundry, cleaned rooms, and cleaned up after meals. Cowboys and ranch hands performed most of the dirty work of caring for horses, livestock, and crops.

Building a trail, rustic structure, or chapel required physical work and forced boys to rely on their own resources, instilling a sense of personal satisfaction that could only come from persistence and personal challenges, effectively avoiding one of the most prevalent problems facing the rich man's son—laziness. Because many perceived the mythic West as devoid of consumerism, ranch schools could also potentially eliminate the effects of materialism that could lead to boys becoming spoiled. Luxuries, amusements, and consumables were not as widely available in the Southwest, thus limiting temptations for developing the habits of the "rich man's son." This is one of the greatest ironies of the ranch school experience, however, as travel to the American West and a western experience was itself a consumer commodity.

In her analysis of tourism literature launched by the See America First campaign, Marguerite Shaffer argues that during the Progressive Era and interwar period, there developed a national tourism that promoted travel, especially to the West, as patriotic and necessary for American citizenship. With the development of a national transportation system, communication network, mass production, mass distribution, and expanding middle class, "tourism emerged as a form of geographical consumption that centered on the sights and scenes of the American nation." Shaffer argues that by "consuming the nation through touring, tourists would become better Americans," defining tourism as a kind of "virtuous consumption" that depended on a national transportation network, distribution of print media, and the emergence of an economy of leisure as it simultaneously promoted democratic ideals, nation building, and patriotism. Tourism changed the notion of citizenship as "political rights or social identity toward a more limited notion of citizenship" as something that could be purchased through travel. While many middle- and upper-class families could travel across the country, few families—aside from those who lived in close proximity to a ranch school—could afford a ranch school experience, leaving only the elite the opportunity to immerse boys in this ritual of citizenship. In treating western travel and ranch schools as consumption experiences that infused national pride through knowing America, ranch schools offered the children of the elite an important and exclusive claim to citizenship.[64]

The West was not devoid of consumerism, however, and a strong element of materialism was associated with attending a ranch school. Tourist attractions and landscapes became consumables through tourist photography, according to Shaffer. "In order to make sense of the experience in the context of emerging consumer consciousness," she asserts, tourists "needed to somehow objectify their experience" and often did so by purchasing souvenirs, postcards, scenery albums, and other mementos.[65] One Arizona Desert School alumnus continues to hold in his possession his trusty lasso.[66] Harold Park's trophies collected in Wyoming while he attended the Valley Ranch School included Navajo rugs, an Indian grinding stone, and a sun-bleached horse skull.[67] In order to participate in all that the West had to offer, children pressured parents to purchase items necessary for ranch life. At the Evans School each student bought his own horse and gear. Incidentals such as horseshoeing and camping cost an average of $32 a week extra. In a letter to his parents, H. J. Heinz II (Jack) enclosed his Fox Chapel bill for $7.95 and then relayed that he

> bought a pair of cheap but very strong and well-made boots for $15.75. I had to get them in a hurry because I went camping this weekend. . . . I believe one said that my boots might be a Christmas present. I would indeed appreciate that deeply in my present financial slump as it were. The rest of my stuff, bridle 5.00, bit 3.50, brush and comb 1.50, made a total of 24— which I can afford o.k. A saddle is being charged to me, $40.

He then thanked his parents for mailing him his gun with an added point, "More expenses for the shells!" In a postscript line, he suggested his parents give him "a little financial support in the camera line. It would be best to buy one out here I figure. It really would be a good thing to have as there are lots of opportunities to take interesting pictures out here."[68]

The antimaterialist goals of headmasters were counteracted by the influx of gifts sent by parents. Parents continued to spoil their children with extravagant gifts, much to the consternation of at least one headmaster, as reflected in an incident that occurred on Christmas Day, 1930, at the Arizona Desert School. Reflecting on his experience as headmaster, Matt Baird described the students who attended the Arizona Desert School as "the sons of wealthy families of Long Island, the Main Line of Philadelphia, and the Lake Shore of Chicago. They were young, third grade through ninth, who led sheltered lives. Certainly they had never known hunger, and what they asked for they expected to receive, a natural and blameless expectation of their age and background." Baird wrote a letter to their parents requesting that they refrain from sending lavish Christmas gifts because of the economic crisis in the local community. Even so, families sent an extraordinary array of gifts, including ping-pong tables, a billiard table, sports equipment, 1.3 radios per boy, and seven sets of electric trains and track. Disappointed in the boys' lack of enthusiasm for donating duplicate items to a local orphanage, Baird initiated a school service project to construct a chapel for the Catholic and Protestant orphanages of Tucson.[69] In future years, the pupils at the Arizona Desert School entertained boys from St. Joseph's orphanage and the Arizona Children's Home. The orphaned boys brought gifts they had made in their workshops for the Arizona Desert School students, who reciprocated by giving each guest a jackknife and baseball glove. At noon a turkey dinner was served followed by an old-fashioned Mexican piñata and rodeo.[70]

Baird's accomplishment simultaneously attempted to instill some empathy for others who were denied essentials by birth, while breaking down the insular nature of the ranch school experience, if even once a year. The latter achievement was rare among ranch school owners, who understood parents' desire to cultivate insular social networks that were essential to the transmission of culture among those seeking to maintain status and prestige. In her analysis of the Vanderbilt children's cottage at the Breakers, in Newport, Rhode Island, Abigail Van Slyck explains the significance of children in translating economic capital into cultural and social capital. Essential to their parents' drive for social status, children were "dynastic resources" who could establish new connections to enhance social capital. Poor choices, on the other hand, could "expose the family to distasteful and socially damaging connections." American aristocrats had to constantly monitor and manage children's companions to achieve and maintain family position in the upper echelons of society. If a daughter married European nobility, for example, this achieved a degree of distinction otherwise unavailable to even the wealthiest of American family dynasties.[71]

Ranch schools attracted students by listing the names of socially prominent families as references, and of all students who attended the school. This was an important recruitment tool, especially in attracting the attention of the nouveau riche who hoped to gain social standing. In 1928 Robert Danforth Cole asserted:

There are certain parents who have gained a prominent place in the world by dint of their own efforts and without the advantage of a formal or extensive education. They desire for their son's acquaintance with those boys whose families have long had a certain social prominence, and so deliberately choose the type of school which caters to the socially elect. It is this conscious attempt to place boys in certain schools not because of the intrinsic worth of the school, but in the hope of gaining social prestige.[72]

When parents compared schools it was their duty "to learn not just of traditions, leadership, and teaching staffs but about the kind of families from which the pupils come and the consequent atmosphere that your children's associates will create."[73] In its entrance requirements, the Palo Verde Ranch School stated explicitly that "the school is meant for gentlemanly, well-bred boys . . . it wishes parents to be assured that their sons are to associate with clean, normal boys, and that no others will be permitted to remain."[74]

Homogeneous school communities were important to parents who wanted to give their children a competitive edge in life. If children were sent to a private school, they would develop personal friendships, future business connections, and possible marriage ties with families who could help elevate or retain their upper-middle class and elite status. Theodore Roosevelt made important life-long personal and political connections as a student at Harvard and may have used one of them to recruit the son of a friend to attend the Evans School in Mesa. Teddy befriended Richard Saltonstall, "a large, shy boy from the highest ranks of Boston Society," at Harvard in 1876. The Saltonstall mansion on Chestnut Hill became Theodore's second home, and through the Saltonstall connection to another old-moneyed Boston family, the Lees, Roosevelt met his first wife, Alice Lee.[75] Nicholas Roosevelt, Teddy's nephew, attended the Evans Ranch School in Mesa with Leverett Saltonstall in 1909–1910 and kept a photo album to record his adventures. "Lev" was featured in the majority of Nicholas's photographs, indicating a friendship between these two boys whose father and uncle, respectively, had met at Harvard.[76]

Geographic isolation was an important asset toward cultural transmission, creating the insular communities that fostered ties between the children of the elite. The Los Alamos Ranch School was situated in a community of two hundred, composed mostly of staff, students, ranch employees, and their families. The ranch was intended to be self-sufficient and isolated. Mail and supplies that could not be raised on the ranch were brought to the school on the Denver & Rio Grande Western Railroad to a location twelve miles away from the school. The school truck met the train three days weekly. Students and visitors were met in Santa Fe or Lamy and driven to the ranch in the school car.[77] In the remote locations of the desert Southwest, it was difficult for boys to meet girls or other boys who did not attend other socially exclusive private schools. Isolation from the urban centers of Phoenix and Tucson gave owners and headmasters a certain degree of social control by regulating whom students socialized with, where they found entertainment, and when and under what pretext they experienced the West, which assured parents that children would not be exposed to or tempted by the degrading influences of urban America. At Hacienda del Sol, former students remember cactus planted under their bedroom windows. Some speculated that the cacti were strategically placed to keep girls from sneaking out of their windows, or to keep criminals from getting into girls' rooms. However, when asked about this, Jean Porter explained that had anyone left their room, there was really nowhere to go. It was "like a prison. There was nothing up here in the foothills." Porter remembered that once every six weeks or so the girls were escorted into Tucson to see a movie.[78]

The desert Southwest isolated children from urban temptations, and most ranch school owners limited interaction with local residents. The statewide Arizona ranch school community was insular, and students had little exposure to others who were not from their social class. Orme School was the exception to this rule: students attended community social functions on weekends and interacted with residents from Humboldt and Mayer. Boys' ranch schools competed against one another in sports and attended social functions with girls from Jokake and Hacienda del Sol. Students from Jokake School for Girls and Judson School for Boys enjoyed joint social functions including, for example, a spring party in 1938 at Camelback Inn hosted by Mr. and Mrs. J. C. Lincoln. Jokake students were an important presence at the Judsons' annual dinner-dance held each April. In 1938, eleven girls from Jokake were listed as guests and twelve other female guests were categorized "Popular Phoenix girls." According to a Judson student yearbook contributor, the event "was a great success, and without doubt the best party in the history of the school. This was largely due to the beautiful new home of Mr. and Mrs. Judson in which it was held."[79] Girls from prominent families were potential marriage partners for boys, and these sponsored social functions cultivated connections that could potentially join families.

Antebellum northern merchants and bankers recognized the importance of traditional kinship and social connections, and marriage became an important means of widening networks to other cities. Good marriage deals were so important that the "Dun credit reporting agency mentioned them in its assessment of the creditworthiness of enterprises." Merchants were frequently related to each other. In New York, 37 percent of the 163 wealthiest citizens in the 1850s were related, and in 1835, 71 percent of the 79 wealthiest Bostonians had familial connections.[80]

The insular ranch school community successfully matched a few students in matrimony. George Judson Jr. married Patty Dalzell, the sister of a Judson student and daughter of the owners of Fostoria Glass. Los Alamos founder

Ashley Pond's daughter, Peggy, became the first faculty wife when she married Fermor S. Church.[81] Jean Dunn Porter was thirteen at the time but remembers that a seventeen-year-old Hacienda del Sol student named Josephine Smith eloped with a boy from the Southern Arizona School for Boys. Apparently, the girl's parents were quite upset, and it was an important topic of conversation around the school for some time. Josephine's parents came out and "there were frantic meetings" with the headmistress, owner, and Reverend Ferguson over whether or not the marriage should be annulled given that Miss Smith was underage.[82] In this case, marrying the right kind of person was not as important as marrying that person at the right time in one's life. Ranch schools did their best to maintain cultural connections through geographical isolation but were not always able to keep students from transgression. Orme Parke remembers that he and some of his friends sneaked out of their dorms at night and "borrowed" Mr. Judson's car to go to a carnival where they saw "exotic" women.[83]

Financial and social connections to the Atlantic Seaboard and Great Lakes region beyond those fostered by geographic isolation were essential to the initial development and success of ranch schools and in turn bound the cultural identity of the Southwest to these regions. According to Hal Rothman, who describes tourism as a "devil's bargain," the capital that sustains tourism "comes from elsewhere, changing local relationships and the values that underpin them." The Southwest by the 1920s had acquired a "cachet of desirability" sufficient to "draw people and money" to enter into the devil's bargain that forced a "redistribution of wealth, power, and status" and complicated local arrangements with an influx of part-time residents who brought capital from the Atlantic Seaboard and Great Lakes region.[84] Most southwestern communities in the interwar period were eager to garner a share of the western tourism industry and celebrated the influx of the rich and famous who visited and relocated to their states. A 1945 *Arizona Highways* article entitled "Arizona Attracts Many Notables" listed several well-known winter visitors including Dr. Gallup, originator of the Gallup Poll; Vernon Stouffer, president of the Stouffer Restaurants; Leonard K. Firestone, of the Firestone Company; and Franck Hoover, of the Hoover Vacuum Company. The former Mrs. Cornelius Vanderbilt married John Frye, president of TWA, in a desert wedding ceremony held in Echo Canyon. According to *Arizona Highways*, "prominent eastern business men, who originally came out to relax in the sunshine, found themselves devoting much of their time and thought to Arizona and its possibilities after their first visit" and invested in guest ranches, reclaimed abandoned mines, developed citrus groves, and extended their eastern businesses into the Southwest.[85]

Few ranch school families claimed permanent residential status in the Far West as they maintained cultural ties to the more established parts of the country. Although school brochures listed many families' point of origin from locations outside of Arizona, oral history interviews and other sources indicate that most of the aforementioned families owned permanent or semipermanent residences in Arizona. For example, in Judson School for Boys and Jokake School for Girls printed material, both Rodney and Joan Kellogg were listed as being from New York, and Mr. and Mrs. Kellogg were listed as references in promotional material as residing in New York. The 1938 Judson School yearbook mentioned that "Judson School boys were entertained at a New Year's Eve dance given by Mr. and Mrs. Donald Kellogg at their spacious new home near the school."[86] This same yearbook listed Mr. and Mrs. J. C. Lincoln as guests of the school from Cleveland. At first this seems curious, because the Lincolns made Arizona their permanent home in 1934. There are three notable explanations for these inconsistencies. Some families may have relocated to Arizona during the time their children attended the school.[87] In this case, ranch schools had a significant impact on drawing families, not just students, to the West. Secondly, many families owned more than one residence. Lastly, it added to the social prestige of a school to list a family's point of origin to assert connections to the more established regions of the country.

The availability of elite cultural institutions, including private schools, allowed families that considered relocating from New York City, Boston, Chicago, and other major cities to maintain social networks and cultural status at the same time they enjoyed a western lifestyle and warmer climate. In some cases, a family member's poor health prompted families to relocate to the arid Southwest. The Porter family moved to Tucson in 1934 because of the father's arthritis. He had three school-aged children at the time, whom he intended to send to private school. When asked why he did not go to public school, Bob Porter said that it was not because Tucson's public schools were poor—it was just family tradition for children to go to private school. His father went to a private school in Delaware and was proud that he was descended from three New England lines: the Willards, the Halls, and the Porters. Because of tradition and expectations for his children, the opportunity to continue this tradition could have eased any hesitation the family may have had about relocation. Bob attended the Old Pueblo School and Green Fields before going on to the Cate School in California. His sister, Annette, attended the Thomas School, Potter School, and Hacienda del Sol. Willard, the oldest Porter child, went to the Evans School.[88]

Arizona ranch schools also drew from the increasing influx of temporary residents, accompanied by their school-aged children, who spent their winters at a resort. The hassle and length of time it took to travel by train from East to West meant staying for months at a time. If they had school-aged children, there needed to be a place for them to go to school. Jokake School for Girls began on the property of Jokake Inn. The intent of the Remuda Ranch School was to cater to vacationers with school-aged children. According to an undated brochure, "All Arizona ranches cater to children but few ranches have as a part of them a regular ranch school with its own teaching staff. Remuda Ranch School has its own buildings, standard desks and playtime equipment. We believe that Remuda Ranch school children have a better time and accomplish more for themselves than under any other arrangements we have seen so far." A *Miami Herald* article further explained that "the problem of how a family with children can take a winter vacation has been solved in this self-styled 'dude ranch capital of the world.' For Wickenburg boasts a ranch school which not only offers qualified modern educational facilities for periods ranging from two weeks to six months—but provides it in the western atmosphere which is synonymous with utopia in the minds of most children in this age."[89] Old Pueblo School student Jean Culver wrote that she and her brother Jimmy "really live in Cincinnati but mother and dad always spend the winter in Arizona so we are put in school here every year."[90] Of seventeen Judson students enrolled in 1931, four were day students who stayed at the Biltmore with their families.[91]

The Jokake School for Girls and Judson School for Boys, both located in Phoenix, were examples of how ranch schools, fueled by tourism, changed the essence of this southwestern community for tourists and newly arrived wealthy residents. John C. Lincoln, pioneer in the electrical industry, brought his family to Paradise Valley for a winter vacation at the Jokake Inn in 1931. Mrs. Lincoln and their daughter, Lillian, had health problems that the family hoped the dry desert climate would alleviate. During that winter, both sons, David and Joe, attended Judson School as day students. John Lincoln was "so

impressed with the opportunities on the desert that he not only built a home"
on part of his 320 acres of land in Paradise Valley, "but became the owner of
the old East Vulture Mine at Wickenburg, several citrus groves, farms and the
Ajo Power Company," and in 1936 built the Camelback Inn.[92] The family permanently relocated from Cleveland to Arizona in 1934, and although David
and Joe were settled and content at Judson School, Lincoln desperately needed
a school for Lillian to attend. According to David, Lillian may have attended
Judson for a year as the only girl, but both the Lincolns and the Judsons decided that this was not a good idea. George Judson opened the short-lived
Judson School for Girls sometime in the 1930s. It is likely that John C. Lincoln
provided the land for Judson School for Girls since he had purchased a significant parcel at the foot of Mummy Mountain for about $20 an acre when he
arrived.[93] Judson School for Girls closed after a couple of years because it
seems that George, who was extremely adept at running a boys' school, had
little ambition for a girls' school. When the school closed some of its students
transferred to Jokake School.[94]

As a Paradise Valley resident and developer, Lincoln understood the mone-
tary advantages of the tourism industry and the need for private schools for his
own family and the children of potential investors, developers, and tourists.[95]
The Judsons had several financial backers for their school who purchased a
"Certificate of Shares of the Capital Stock" at $100 each. J. L. Borah, Charles F.
Willis, Leslie W. Greer, C. H. McKellips, W. L. Pinney, and Ralph Peterson all
bought five shares each; the O'Malley Lumber Company owned ten shares;
E. W. Steinman and Harry Kay purchased twenty shares each; and George W.
Mickle, who invested $5,000 in the school, owned fifty shares. George Mickle
was the only one of these initial investors listed as a director of the corporation
in Judson brochures from the mid-1930s, and Charles Willis, editor of the
Arizona Mining Journal, was included as a reference.[96] What is notable about
Judson School for Boys' initial stockholders is that many were Arizona investors. Historian Gerald Nash argues that the West was a colony of the East, and
during the 1920s, western financiers laid the foundation for decreased reliance
on eastern banks and foreign investments.[97] George Mickle arrived shortly after
statehood and founded the Pay 'n' Takit, the largest chain of neighborhood markets in Arizona. In 1927, Mickle sold out to Safeway Stores and invested his
millions in creating the Phoenix Title and Trust Company. Mickle changed
business interests and became the model of the successful entrepreneur who

made his fortune in Phoenix, unlike John C. Lincoln, who had earned his fortune in Ohio before investing in numerous Arizona ventures.[98]

Financiers became important members of ranch schools and the western communities that served as their backdrop. Tuition alone did not cover the expenses of running the school, let alone capital improvements. Present-day administrators understand the significance of cultivating donors who come from the ranks of alumni and parents. In the pre–World War II era, when ranch schools had few alumni advanced enough in their careers to make personal donations, parents and Arizona's elite community members were vital sources of income and support and became members of the ranch school community. A 1939 Jokake School yearbook recognized Mrs. J. C. Lincoln for providing the school with chemistry equipment for a science laboratory and several recorded musical selections.[99] At the Los Alamos Ranch School, Philo C. Fuller, a lumberman from Grand Rapids, Michigan, provided financial backing for Fuller Lodge, a kitchen–dining room facility completed in 1928, named for early staff member Edward P. Fuller, the benefactor's son, who died in 1923. Another generous Los Alamos parent provided funding for the arts and crafts building in 1934.[100] Most parents who provided resources to the schools did so because they supported their child's private education. Wealthy community members supported ranch schools because of a personal affinity for the headmaster, the ideal of the school, and a desire to replicate the institutions of the eastern establishment in the West. Parents who sent their children to western ranch schools thus not only invested in their children's future, but in the economic growth of the Southwest.

Because tuition revenue and sometimes capital investment came from the urban centers of the East and Midwest, ranch school owners focused their recruitment efforts accordingly. Several schools had offices in New York. Founded in 1927, the Arizona Desert School was established by "wealthy parents of Eastern children whom they wished to place in the warm, dry atmosphere of Arizona" and had a local office in Tucson and an eastern office in New York City.[101] According to the *Tucson Citizen*, of its twenty-four students, twelve came from New York, three from Chicago, three from Ohio, two from Massachusetts, one from Baltimore, one from West Virginia, and one from Pennsylvania.[102] In 1931 the Judson School enrolled the two Judson sons, three boys from California, three from Chicago, one from Indiana, three from New Jersey, three from New York, one from West Virginia, and one international

student from Canada.[103] Former New York businessman Frederick Fox recruited boys from the families of his friends who lived in the suburbs of New
York for Foxboro Ranch School.[104]

Many owners spent their summers traveling to various eastern and midwestern areas of the country, recruiting students. Russell Fairgrieve and his wife left
Tucson by American Airways in June of 1933 with plans "to meet any of our
boys, their parents or friends along the way." Fairgrieve made arrangements for
conferences in Chicago, New York City, Buffalo, Cleveland, Columbus, and
"elsewhere possible with anyone considering the Southern Arizona School for
their sons the coming year." During the summer of 1933, the Fairgrieves set up
headquarters at the Stevens Hotel in Chicago and the New Yorker in New York
City. Their itinerary included spending four days in Chicago for the Century of
Progress Exposition before heading east to spend most of July and August in
Bridgton, Maine.[105] By recruiting heavily in the urban cultural centers of the
Atlantic Seaboard and Great Lakes region, ranch schools established and main-
tained significant social networks with the East, Midwest, and Southwest.

Ranch schools had much to offer upper-class families who wanted their sons
to avoid the depravities of becoming a "rich man's son" but also needed assurance that the traditional institutions that perpetuated their social status could
exist in the West. Especially in the interwar period, popular media advanced the
perception that it was not beneficial to be reared in an upper-class environment.
Parents did not want their children to act "spoiled" even if their station in life
afforded them every luxury imaginable. Many of the children who attended
ranch schools were the grandsons and granddaughters of self-made men. Their
grandparents worked hard to achieve wealth and status and believed that only
through hard work and some deprivation could one act as a responsible
American citizen. Ranch schools perpetuated western travel as a consumable
experience that was a ritual of citizenship and reinforced the region's economic
dependency on the East and Midwest. As more of the urban upper class and
elite brought wealth and traditional cultural institutions to the West, it changed
communities and the authentic experience they sought. Ranch school communities began to resemble little enclaves of Detroit, New Haven, and Pittsburgh
in the wide open spaces of New Mexico, California, and Arizona.

Most families who sent sons on their own or were semipermanent residents
treated a ranch school experience as temporary, with the intent that their sons
would return to the East or Great Lakes region infused with western character

traits and a greater knowledge of America that would make them better citizens and leaders. This assumption was dependent on ranch schools' ability to provide a quality preparatory experience that would allow entrance into an Ivy League college. Headmasters relied on the same social networks that financed ranch schools and alumni contacts to cultivate communities that superseded geographic distance. The next chapter addresses how they adhered to a traditional preparatory school curriculum and simultaneously introduced elements of progressive education by invoking the spirit of the Old West.

CHAPTER 2

Private School Education in the West

RANCH SCHOOLS HAD A DISTINCT ROLE IN THE PRIVATE SCHOOL INDUSTRY
during the interwar period. Personal and institutional connections to the East
created a social network that allowed students to transfer freely between western
ranch schools and Select Sixteen schools like Choate, Exeter, and St. George and
to gain admittance to Ivy League schools. They were simultaneously impacted by
the progressive education movement as they held true to a traditional preparatory
curriculum with unique extracurricular activities suited to a western lifestyle, designed for the specific purpose of developing character rather than fostering experiential learning. In comparing western ranch schools to private progressive
schools on one end of a spectrum, and the Select Sixteen boarding schools on the
other, the western ranch schools fall somewhere in between. A brochure from the
Arizona Desert School described its curriculum as "based on the accepted traditions of American education, but it combines also some of the progressive features
of modern educational theory and practice, which have been proved sound and
stimulating, and have already been adopted in many of the leading schools."[1]
Ranch schools, with smaller student populations and emphasis on a western lifestyle, enabled educators to provide an experience that was not offered at traditional preparatory schools. Children and adolescents for the most part enjoyed
and appreciated their ranch school education, invoking the words "freedom" and
"relaxed atmosphere" when comparing their western experience to time served at
traditional eastern preparatory schools.[2]

Ranch schools explicitly stated their academic intentions in promotional

37

literature, arguing an ability to prepare students for a college or private school of their choosing. The Palo Verde Ranch School, founded in 1929, stated that "the school maintains the highest standard of scholarship. Thoroughness in preparation of work is required. The loss of a single recitation is detrimental not only to the progress of the student, but to the entire class of which he is a member." Masters supervised evening study hours "in order that the boys acquire regular habits of study." Unsatisfactory work meant that boys spent their Saturdays studying.[3] A 1935 newspaper article featuring the Arizona Desert School made a point of highlighting the school's academic credentials. Test results published by the Education Records bureau showed that the "average achievement of the school is distinctly above that of the thousands of students of the same grades taking these tests the country over."[4] Ranch school owners demonstrated their ability to prepare students for college by joining professional associations that catered to the Ivy League colleges, hiring staff with credentials, recruiting influential and well-known individuals to their boards of directors, and demonstrating a track record of success through their alumni.

In his definitive history of progressivism in American schools, Lawrence Cremin identifies its span from 1876 through 1957 and asserts that from the very beginning it was pluralistic and frequently contradictory. Cremin sought to characterize the movement as broad and much more diverse than its legacy suggests by providing a comprehensive look at several influential progressive educators and theorists. Progressive education was essentially the application of progressive social and political reform to schools. As with many progressive reform movements, progressive education began with exposés published by investigative journalists who alerted the American people to the dreadful conditions of American schools. Using the technique of muckraking, journalists attacked the unhygienic conditions, political corruption, and the ineffectiveness of poorly trained teachers. In the post–Civil War era, education was linked to national progress and "virtually every progressive cause from the 1890's through World War I had their program for the school." Cremin characterizes the inter-war period as fractured and boiled down to a series of simplified ideas including a child-centered focus and experiential learning that ended up defining the movement. Although it never developed a strong statement about its purpose and ideals, a leader of the Progressive Education Association described the aims of progressive education just after World War I as "the fullest development of the individual, based on the scientific study of his mental, physical, spiritual, and social characteristics and needs." The end result was that by the interwar period, it had lost much of its emphasis on social reform.[5]

Cremin cites William James's *Principles of Psychology* (1890), Francis W. Parker's *Talks on Pedagogies* (1894), Edward L. Thorndike's *Animal Intelligences* (1898), James's *Talks to Teachers on Psychology* (1899), and John Dewey's *The School and Society* (1899) as seminal works contributing to a growing body of theory to support pedagogical reform. James's *Principles* and *Talks* directly influenced pedagogy by taking on an "essentially behaviorist outlook." Teachers were charged to "educate heroic individuals who would project daring visions of the future and work courageously to realize them. In a society of such individuals James saw man's best hope for human dignity and progress." John Dewey always saw social reformism as the crux of progressive education, and according to Cremin, Dewey's contribution to what was really progressive about progressive education was to treat the school as an "'embryonic community' that was to *reflect* the life of the larger society" at the same time as it improved it. Dewey advocated for shifting emphasis back to the child to benefit from his "natural impulses to conversation, to inquiry, to construction, and to expression. He defined education as 'that reconstruction of experience which adds to the meaning of experience, and which increases ability to direct the course of subsequent experience.'" Dewey believed schools could cultivate "habits that would enable individuals to control their surroundings rather than merely adapt to them."[6]

By 1915 there was a richness and diversity to the progressive education movement that included physical education, nature studies, manual work, and industrial training. Ideas of freedom for children, greater attention to individual growth, unity between education and life, and democratization of culture and learning had infused public and private schools. By the interwar period the emphasis on child-centered pedagogy ushered in a new emphasis on self-expression in education as well as in art. At the Walden School, for example, there was no attempt to define a syllabus, but the school provided a variety of resources for children to use for exploration and experimentation. Using Dewey's method of problem solving as a means of social change, William Heard Kilpatrick of Teachers College, a leading progressive of the 1920s, emphasized purposeful activity compatible with the child's own goals, to occur in a social environment to facilitate certain ethical outcomes. In *Foundations of Method* (1925), Kilpatrick stated that "the only way to learn to live well is to practice living well" and advocated self-reliance. For many progressive educators in the interwar period, like Kilpatrick, the expressionist, child-centered approach meant teaching "children *how* to think, not *what* to think."[7]

The interwar period was an era of great educational experimentation when progressive education became more closely associated with private schools. Cremin argues it is a misperception "that private schools and the educators associated with them have always been the real pioneers of educational reform," but noted that "some of the most courageous and imaginative pedagogical experiments of the interbellum era did proceed under private auspices, and that these experiments did exert incalculable influence on the larger course of American education." In general, private progressive "schools tended to organize subject matter in radically different ways, to take the life of the surrounding community more immediately into account in the business of instruction, and to enlist more directly in the management and operation of school affairs." Private progressive schools included Baltimore's Park School, 1912; Walden School; City and Country School; Oak Lane Country Day School, 1916; Moraine Park School; Chevy Chase School, 1919; and most notably Lincoln School.[8]

Because it represented the "rich diversity of the movement," Cremin argues that the Lincoln School had the most "influence on the subsequent history of American education." Its founder, Abraham Flexner, organized it around activities in four fundamental fields: science, industry, aesthetics, and civics. Greek and Latin were dropped in favor of the modern European languages. He built a curriculum around "units of work" that reorganized traditional subject matter into activity appropriate to the development of children. For example, a third-grade project captured students' interest in the day-by-day life of the nearby Hudson River to study boats and their place in the history of transportation. The end result was that through an interdisciplinary and hands-on examination of boats as an entrée, students learned history, geography, reading, writing, arithmetic, science, art, and literature. With the exception of the Manumit School launched in 1924 and a few other labor schools, "the clientele was overwhelmingly upper middle class. There was an occasional effort to enroll the children of blue-collar families" but it seemed that "working-class parents were not as a rule willing to participate in radical pedagogical innovation."[9]

Many ranch school owners, headmasters, and teachers were visionary in their approach and succeeded in instituting several aims of progressive education. One of the lasting contributions of progressive education was its attempt "to employ indigenous materials, ranging from the local flora and fauna to locally manufactured products in the course of instruction."[10] Ranch Schools' strong attachment to the study of American regions and locales by immersing students in the local culture and geography replicated aspects of the early twentieth-century progressive schools. The educational benefits and opportunity to develop self-reliance from horseback riding and overnight camping trips, for example, were numerous, and included an element of experiential education. Ranch schools emphasized their ability to offer outdoor activities including horseback riding, camping, and hiking as well as "simplicity of living," a phrase well known among progressive educators as the antidote to the artificialities of the city.

With a solid grounding in traditional preparatory aims and curriculum, ranch school owners, headmasters, and teachers were free to experiment with personal vision that usually employed the cultural and natural resources of the West.[11] At the Fresnal Ranch School, boys gained "an introduction to geology, archeology, and natural history through the interest of the surrounding country."[12] David Wick's interest and educational background in mining combined with Arizona's rich mineral resources enabled him to launch a special course in mining engineering at the Judson School.[13] Shortly after the opening of Fenster Ranch School, struggling artist Ted De Grazia taught classes at the school and painted murals on its walls.[14] De Grazia also taught art classes at Green Fields School. Hacienda del Sol offered a Spanish Club to help students "take advantage of their presence in a locality with Spanish traditions by familiarizing them with the Spanish language and giving them an opportunity to learn Spanish and Mexican songs and to acquire some knowledge of the history and characteristics of the southwestern peoples."[15]

The Los Alamos Ranch School exemplifies the evolution of a school intended to be a model of progressive education through experiential learning, into one that blended this vision with the need to adhere to a more traditional curriculum in order to attract college-bound students. In 1917, idealist Ashley Pond intended for the curriculum of the Los Alamos Ranch School to instruct boys in outdoor education rather than traditional subjects. In his first school folder he wrote that "studying from books is absolutely unnecessary." But in order to elevate the school to that of a college preparatory school, Pond hired an educated staff who transformed his original idea to offer courses in exploration and mapmaking, forestry and silviculture, and mountain works, to a curriculum that prepared boys for the requirements of the College Entrance Examination

Board. In 1918 Fayette S. Curtis, a recent Yale graduate, accepted Pond's offer to serve as headmaster, and in 1921 Los Alamos welcomed Fermor S. Church, a young New Englander who was fresh out of Harvard.[16] Church added advanced subjects like nuclear physics, physiology, and aeronautics to the existing curriculum. There is evidence that students benefited from this scientific study. Los Alamos Ranch School alumnus Stirling Colgate, from Morristown, New Jersey, earned his BA and PhD degrees in physics from Cornell University and became a nuclear physicist. He remembered that after learning that the U.S. Army would take over their school, some observant physics students had recognized Ernest Lawrence among the advance parties sent to the site and guessed that the Army project would have something to do with nuclear physics. Lawrence, who had won the Nobel Prize in Physics in 1939 and appeared on the cover of *Time* magazine in 1938, was familiar to the Los Alamos Ranch School students who studied these advanced subjects.[17]

One of the more significant legacies of progressive reform was the adoption of open-air classrooms. Progressive reformers established open-air schools to benefit urban children stricken with tuberculosis by providing relief from stuffy, crowded, dark apartments. In this respect, ranch schools resembled urban public schools for children from poor economic circumstances, except that parents of ranch school students could afford to send their children to a climate more conducive to open-air study. Using scientific studies that proved fresh air and sunshine were beneficial to children's health, reformers opened numerous open-air schools throughout the country. Open-air schools were largely the result of reform efforts of antituberculosis organizations and public health officials who discovered that fresh air, sunshine, nutritious food, proper rest, and personal hygiene improved the health of urban children who had, or were susceptible to, tuberculosis. The open-air design of ranch schools attracted children and families who were advised by a physician or (prescribed for themselves) to relocate to a drier, warmer climate to relieve suffering from arthritis, asthma, and other respiratory ailments.

The original open-air school opened in Charlottenburg, Germany, in 1904 and was followed by the first American open-air school established in Pittsburgh in 1907, followed by ones in Providence, Baltimore, and Boston in 1908.[18] Government studies showed that in addition to preventing, and sometimes curing, tuberculosis, schools that provided "fresh air and nourishing food" would benefit children suffering from "malnutrition, anemia, chorea, lack of appetite, indigestion, neuralgia, nervousness, chest pains, headaches, heart trouble, impaired nutrition, relaxed skin and muscles, and chronic fatigue."[19] Government officials in 1916 asserted that "children in open-air schools are usually sick or anemic because they have been cheated out of the birthright all children should have—fresh, clean air."[20] The children denied their "birthright" were those of the urban poor, the most likely of American children to contract tuberculosis and other debilitating diseases. Public health officials examined home living conditions and concluded that urban tenement living greatly increased a child's risk for tuberculosis and other diseases. Thus public open-air schools were day schools located in the suburbs, "to avoid the smoke and dust of the city."[21]

In 1917, when the Department of the Interior issued the report on the status of open-air schools, 168 cities in 32 states had public open-air schools for city-reared children with the aforementioned ailments. Ironically, given its severely cold winters, thirteen of these schools were located in Chicago. Budget estimates for establishing open-air schools included the cost of Eskimo suits that could be purchased at Marshal Field and Co. to give children the benefits of fresh air year-round.[22] Either the Eskimo suits were sufficiently warm or the children did not mind the cold because, according to a former assistant surgeon general, "during the coldest days in St. Louis, when the thermometer was below zero, 22 of the 25 children were present."[23] Witnessing the success of open-air schools in improving children's health, authors of government reports began to advocate open-air, or at the very least, open-window schools for every child, since the "benefits to the subnormal child are so thoroughly proven and accepted, why not apply the same principle to the normal child? Why not give it the same advantages?"[24] A few progressive educators heeded the call. Professor and Mrs. Hocking established Shady Hill School in 1915 as an open-air school when they became concerned over the health of their children in cramped, overheated quarters of public schools. Rather than serve the urban poor, Shady Hill catered mostly to the "children of Professor Hocking's Harvard colleagues and a few Cambridge businessmen."[25]

Ranch schools were limited to students without communicable diseases to ensure that they did not earn a reputation as sanitariums. The Palo Verde Ranch school stated that boys "bothered with sinus trouble, asthma, rheumatism, the after-effects of pneumonia, etc., find the dry, mild climate beneficial" but distinguished itself from the public open-air schools for tubercular children by its emphatic statement that the "school is in no way a sanitarium, and boys having communicable diseases are not admitted."[26] The Arizona Sunshine School, founded in 1927, and the Old Pueblo School, opened in 1932 as an outgrowth of the first out-of-door school in Tucson established in 1926, emphasized the healthful benefits of year-round fresh air and sunshine for children. The Arizona Sunshine School for boys and girls from preschool age through the eighth grade held its classes in open-air ramadas where the students could "pursue their studies while simultaneously soaking up sun and tonic air . . . free from the strains of urban life." This school was open to both day and boarding students, but was not for children with tuberculosis or "any communicable disease" and required health certificates from physicians for each student upon enrollment.[27]

Ranch schools promoted the healthful benefits of dry air, year-round sunshine, and warmer climate for all students, healthy or otherwise. The ability to study, play, and explore outdoors contributed to the ideals advocated by progressive educators by promoting good health. Educator J. O. Engleman advocated the study of nature as an excellent character-building activity because children spent time in the "great out-of-doors" and it required physical exercise.[28] The Palo Verde Ranch School stated it was "essentially an open-air school." The school provided "every inducement to be out of doors as much as possible" and described a "climate so warm and dry that classes may be held outdoors, permitting the boys to be in the open the greater part of the day in a climate as nearly perfect as any in America."[29] Rubie Atchley believed that Green Fields' clientele came from families who had visited Tucson and understood that the area afforded a beneficial environment particularly but not exclusively for boys with respiratory ailments. In keeping with the outdoor lifestyle promoted by the school, classes were held outdoors, even in the winter when teachers and students bundled up rather than move indoors.[30] "Life in this climate is beneficial to every boy," Judson school promoters observed.[31] One Judson School student remarked that "the climate cannot be beat anywhere in the U.S.A. Sun all day long, and these kids get the full benefit of it. They are the healthiest lot I have ever seen."[32] The Arizona Desert School stated that not only did Arizona offer a dry climate, but the location of the school was "in a dust-free area" in the foothills of the Santa Catalina Mountains.[33] The parents of a West Virginia boy relayed to their friend that their son would have gone to Deerfield Academy "but the climate wasn't right for him," so instead he went to the Arizona Desert School in Tucson.[34]

Preparing for college remained separate from ranching activity at most

Open-air classrooms were a feature of the Judson School in Phoenix. This image appeared in a 1930s promotional brochure for the school. Courtesy of David C. Lincoln, Phoenix.

western ranch schools. Expansion of extracurricular activity as part of the school program was an important legacy of progressive education, but truly progressive schools integrated learning with practical activity. Most ranch schools required students to study core subjects in the morning, leaving the afternoons free for ranch chores, horseback riding, and sports. At the Los Alamos Ranch School, students rose at 6:30 a.m., assembled for fifteen minutes of calisthenics, ate breakfast at 7:00 a.m., made their beds, cleaned their rooms, and then attended class from 7:45 a.m. until 1:15 p.m. The academic program included English, history, mathematics, science, languages, art, and music.[35] At the Palo Verde Ranch School, boys had three school periods from 8:15 a.m. to 10:15 a.m. and three more periods from 10:30 a.m. to 12:35 p.m. After lunch and a rest period, boys had three hours for sports and outdoor activities.[36]

For some, the ideals of progressive education were in direct opposition to preparing the next generation of leaders because it promoted too much emphasis on the "self," leading to "self-ishness." Alfred Stearns noted that "the teachings of modern pedagogy and the theories so rampant in modern school life"

Reformers established open-air schools for urban children to enjoy fresh air even during the coldest months of the year. Students wore Eskimo suits to keep warm. This photograph shows an open-air classroom located on the roof of the Mary Crane Nursery in Chicago sometime between 1900 and 1920. Goldsberry Collection of open-air school photographs, Library of Congress Prints and Photographs Division, Washington, D.C.

were rife with "catchwords that are so common and so gratifying to a generation immersed in pleasure, seeking material gain, and averse to all things irksome and restraining,—'self-expression,' 'self-realization,' 'self-determination.'" Lamenting that this new educational approach both reflected and reinforced contemporary society's obsession with material gain, self-indulgence, and privilege over "obligations to society as a whole," he pointed out that seldom "do we hear the inspiring words 'duty,' 'service,' 'sacrifice,'" spoken by "those who laid the foundation" of our nation. Stearns advocated the need for service to others by investing one's talents in the welfare of the community. For him, discipline was essential for boys to learn to serve the welfare of the community even if it meant sacrificing personal interest.[37] In reality, John Dewey wanted the same thing—better citizens through education. For him, children needed to learn how to participate in a democracy. For Stearns, who worked with the nation's elite, education meant cultivating the next generation for leadership through a commitment to service, moral character, personal responsibility, and discipline.

Traditional preparatory school curriculum, driven by the College Entrance Examination Board and Secondary Education Board, included classical studies, mathematics, Latin, and English, and remained at the core of ranch school curriculum. The three-hour essay exams were given in June and administered nationwide in test centers. In 1925 the Valley Ranch School was accredited as one of three test centers in the Rocky Mountain states. The Evans School, Fresnal Ranch School, Los Alamos Ranch School, Palo Verde Ranch School, and Southern Arizona School for Boys participated in the College Board examinations at the testing center in Flagstaff. At the Los Alamos Ranch School, seniors had to pass the College Boards in order to graduate, whereas most students only took the Boards if they were required by the college they planned to attend.[38] Valley Ranch School examinations were modeled on the College Boards and used its grading system. Philip Cummings recorded in his journal that "he gave three examinations and the lowest mark was 68 and the highest 88. Our passing grade is 60, based on the like passing grade of the College Entrance Board Examinations."[39] The Fresnal Ranch School proclaimed that its "course is a sound and thorough one which meets all the requirements of the College Entrance Examination Board, and scholastic standards compare with the leading schools in the East. The work in mathematics, geography, history, science, English, Latin, French, and Spanish follows the College Board syllabus."[40]

Their adherence to offering Greek and Latin was an important indication that western ranch schools prioritized the desires of colleges and a traditional model of preparatory curriculum over experimental progressive ideals. Many progressive educators rebelled against the traditional idea that by mastering Greek and Latin, one was considered educated. In advocating for a county normal school to train agriculturally oriented teachers, a Wisconsin newspaper editor asserted that a democracy of culture meant more than access to education. Rather, it needed to transform the very nature of education, to serve broader populations of Americans. Traditional preparatory school educators, however, continued to argue that to be educated and cultured, one needed to study Greek and Latin.[41] In his essay included in *The Education of the Modern*

Boy, published in 1932, Endicott Peabody filled five pages with examples defending the study of the classics and its usefulness and appeal to the "average man." He explained that the "average man" has equally little use in his daily life for mathematics and geometry, but it would be unthinkable to eliminate these subjects from a standard curriculum. According to a Harvard Law School dean, "There is no better way for the student to train himself in the choice of the very word that will fit his thought than by translation from Latin and Greek. Thus he develops habits of analysis, habits of discriminating choice of words, habits of accurate apprehension of the meaning which another has sought to convey by written words, which lead to power of expression and to power of clear thinking." A professor of clinical medicine at Johns Hopkins conveyed his fear that "education is in danger of becoming illiberal" because of a "tendency in the colleges to displace liberal by vocational education." He protested that if humanities subjects were to be neglected, "all human progress would be endangered, and medicine as well as other sciences would suffer." Edward P. Mitchell, editor of a New York daily paper, argued for the maintenance of classical culture in the war against slang and vernacular speech. In the conclusion of his defense of the classics, Peabody quoted his friend, ex-president Theodore Roosevelt, who emphasized, "Nothing makes a man more interesting to himself and others than that wide knowledge of men and life, that wide knowledge of the globe and of man's past and present on the globe, which is given by a liberal or cultural education in which the study of classical literature is an essential element."[42] The inclusion of classical studies in a preparatory curriculum was not only essential to the College Board examinations, but it distinguished a school as one that provided a "liberal or cultural" education as opposed to a practical education.

Between 1900 and 1942, the curriculum of American preparatory schools was closely linked to the requirements of colleges—Harvard, Yale, and Princeton, in particular. In order to control the curriculum, and conversely, the quality of the students who entered these prestigious universities, a voluntary, nongovernmental organization, the College Entrance Examination Board, was organized to create and sustain school standards. From 1900, when it was founded, until 1942, the College Board administered a system of essay examinations that college admissions officers could use to assess students' academic accomplishments but also gave universities, mostly Ivy League colleges, control over preparatory school curriculum by requiring that college-bound students pass the College Board examinations. In addition to paving the way toward a standardized curriculum for college-bound students, the exams also created incentives and standards for teachers, but limited the opportunity for much experimentation.[43] Schools that offered and successfully prepared students for the College Entrance examinations gave them an advantage when it came to attracting students. A mother, writing for *Harper's* in 1926, explained that one of the reasons she sent her daughter and son to private boarding school was that public schools did not prepare students to take the College Board exams. She described several situations where bright students failed because of over-crowded classrooms of forty students and the public high school's need to "take care of the average child."[44]

By the 1920s, several leading headmasters from Select Sixteen schools began to question the emphasis placed on preparing for an exam in lieu of a secondary education. Alfred Stearns of Phillips Andover Academy highlighted key issues facing preparatory schools in a series of essays. He praised a new school near Boston that frankly stated it "does not believe in what has been aptly called the 'storage battery' type of education, nor does it propose to use the week between the closing of the school and the Board Examinations for an intensive tutoring period."[45] This critique was not aimed at the actual exam, but the process that many schools adopted in order for students to pass. Instead of having students cram information in their senior year, W. L. W. Field, for example, advocated a record of ordered progress that provided the foundations for learning and mastery of skills, leading up to the exam. He supported the College Board examinations as a welcome "test of prowess" and an exercise in "resourcefulness for the meeting of crises, for the solution of unforeseen problems, for endurance of adversity, even disaster."[46] This method also prepared students who might not go to college.

The founding of the Secondary Education Board (SEB), the predecessor to the National Association of Independent Schools, reflected the professionalization of private school education and the desire of headmasters to shape the nature of private schools on their own terms. By coming together to define issues specific to private school education, they asserted authority for their own unique piece of American education as distinct from the Ivy Leagues and public schools. In 1925 a group of New England headmasters met to create the Secondary Education Board with the initial intent of standardizing admissions requirements for private schools. Younger students seeking admission to certain college preparatory schools would prepare for the SEB exam to demonstrate a standardized level of proficiency before they could be admitted to the upper grades. The fact that this test's purpose was similar to that of the College Entrance Examination was somewhat ironic; however, it demonstrated headmasters' desire to create and regulate their own standards, rather than serve at the mercy of the Ivy Leagues.

From its inception, the SEB catered to schools in the East. Its premise that the examination be given in a few established centers to avoid having the test "sent promiscuously about the country" left little potential for western schools to participate in the program.[47] According to the SEB president, his goal in 1926 was to establish examination centers in Boston, New York, Philadelphia, and Chicago.[48] At least two ranch schools, the Palo Verde Ranch School and the Arizona Desert School, prepared boys for the Secondary Board examinations.[49] When Green Fields School opened in 1933 it promoted its ability to prepare boys for entrance to prestigious eastern preparatory schools. This intent established the school's premise that each boy followed the course of study of the private school in the East from which he expected to graduate. Green Fields's 1942 alumni list attested to the school's ability to prepare boys for entrance and graduation from Sewickley, St. Paul's, Exeter, and St. James in Maryland.[50]

Over the next five years, the Board found that its secondary goal, to serve as clearing house of private school information, drew more members than the examination program.[51] The Los Alamos Ranch School in New Mexico was listed as a member in 1931, and the Arizona Desert School appeared on the SEB annual list of members in 1936. It was about this time that the organization began to offer an associate membership. Upon receiving a letter from an administrator at an American school in France, the SEB executive secretary proposed the establishment of an associate membership category that he argued would be "attractive for many schools, which at least by reason of their location do not feel that they can gain the benefits of an active membership." Reports indicate that a number of western schools, especially those in California visited by members of the SEB, expressed similar sentiments regarding the fairness of having to pay the full $50 membership fee when they were "handicapped by distance."[52] This idea was propelled into action as the Board gradually realized that less than 50 percent of its members participated in the testing program and that the economic devastation of the Depression caused membership to decline. Thus by 1936, western schools could join as associates and receive the SEB newsletter and annual report for a reduced membership fee of $20.

By 1942, the Arizona Desert School, Evans School, Fresnal Ranch School, Green Fields Preparatory, Judson School for Boys, Russell Ranch School, and Southern Arizona School for Boys were listed as Associate members of the SEB, attesting to a desire to meet standards and participate in national discussions about private school education. As early as 1939, before Green Fields, Judson School, or the Russell Ranch School joined, the number of SEB members in Arizona was exceeded only by those in California, Connecticut, Florida, Massachusetts, New Jersey, New York, Pennsylvania, Illinois, Rhode Island, and Maryland. It is hard to imagine the forty-eighth state, located in the Far West, as having more memberships in the SEB and more private schools than the majority of established states.

Western ranch schools' membership in the SEB indicates the significance of their participation in a professional network that included prestigious private schools from across the nation. Ranch schools had a specific function within this network: they catered to younger boys who would then advance to a college preparatory school, and they acted as legitimate fallbacks for boys who could not attend one of the Select Sixteen schools for reasons of health, family relocation, or unpreparedness. A former instructor at one Arizona ranch school suggested that because they were relatively new and largely tuition-dependent, "ranch schools are often glad to take students expelled from other schools."[53] Theodore Roosevelt's second-youngest son attended the Evans Ranch School in Mesa, Arizona, after he was expelled from Groton for writing a letter ridiculing the headmaster.[54] Others, like Jack Heinz, attended a ranch school for one year, most likely because of his health. A master from Choate wrote Evans a letter of recommendation for Heinz to be admitted to the Evans School. He sent Howard Heinz, Jack's father, a copy of the letter he wrote and stated he wished "it were possible to recommend all boys so unreservedly."[55] The establishment of a reciprocal relationship with Select Sixteen schools enabled boys to transfer freely between them and also enhanced the credentials of ranch schools.

Deerfield Academy in Massachusetts catered to a similar clientele in the interwar period by serving as a safety net for boys unable to continue their education at one of the more elite private schools. Founded in 1797, Deerfield did not draw students from outside of its immediate vicinity until the 1920s, when it became a full-fledged boarding school after a forty-plus-year stint as a hybrid public-and-private institution. It has since evolved into one of the Select Sixteen. Frank Boyden, who was hired in 1902 and served as headmaster until

1968, developed Deerfield's reputation as a "school where students dismissed from rival institutions such as Exeter might save face and begin anew." Boyden's biographer attributed this to the headmaster's preference to reason with and understand boys rather than whip them into shape, which was common practice at other schools that offered little to no latitude for transgressions. Embracing this role, Boyden cultivated associations with other secondary schools that might send their discards to Deerfield Academy. In one instance, a boy's Jewish faith was his principal difficulty at Exeter. An official from Exeter wrote to Boyden that one of their students, "the son of a Jewish rabbi in Denver was required to withdraw from the Academy at the end of the fall. He is slow and diffident and seems to lack somewhat in physical and mental vigor." Deerfield was less sectarian than Exeter, and the boy seemed to thrive in an environment where he was less of an outsider.[56] Limiting the number of Jewish students who enrolled was of particular concern to private schools that could pick and choose among their applicants because those Jews who wanted to attend could also afford to pay and met admissions criteria. One survey found that "nearly 5 percent of Andover students were Jews in the 1940s. The head wanted that number reduced, lest it frighten away his mainly Protestant constituency."[57] Robert Danforth Cole's 1928 study examined thirty-five preparatory schools and found that twenty-four wanted "to know the church preference of the boy or his family, in ten of which the query" was raised to see if the boy himself was a church member. The Peddie School included the frank statement that "on account of its pronounced Christian character this school would hardly be congenial to Hebrews and they are admitted only in exceptional cases." Cole believed that this exclusion was probably carried on to a greater or lesser extent in many schools, though he found no other printed policy.[58] There were at least two Jewish girls who attended Hacienda del Sol and a Judson alumnus recalled that his roommate was Jewish.[59]

Schools like Deerfield and western ranch schools accepted students who were expected to be college-bound, but did not always muster the strict academic and behavioral requirements of the more established and prestigious preparatory schools. Upon his arrival at the Valley Ranch School in 1932, Philip Cummings, a newly hired teacher, discovered that the students "were of the type who have to get into certain colleges because their parents require it, but may take all the [course] work they wish and do as little as they wish. The review of last year's grades were scandalous." By October, one student "confessed his laziness" and Cummings concluded that the boy could not find much to interest him, "and since he has certain means will not do what displeases him, and unfortunately French and, in fact, school in general does not interest him." Despite the fact that most of the eleven Valley Ranch School students were less academically inclined, at the end of the year, two students advanced to Williams College and another had his choice between Yale and Princeton. An important aspect of the Valley Ranch School and other ranch schools was the attention given to students as individuals. Cummings commended the headmaster for taking the time to share with him each student's individual problem. Headmaster Lawrence Jarvie was particularly adept at understanding the boys, speaking to them in their vernacular, and engaging in their games at the same time he "let them know just where he stands with them."[60]

In some cases, the less rigid disciplinary approach of ranch schools led to chaos within the school community. Harry Coderre, a former master at an Arizona ranch school, described an incident involving a student, "R. S.," as "one of the greatest travesties on discipline that occurred" at the school. R. S. had been expelled from other schools and entertained himself by continually breaking school rules. The headmaster and instructors agreed that to participate in the spring vacation trip to Mexico, students must work to the full extent of their ability and keep themselves "free from any disciplinary trouble." R. S. met neither criterion, and faculty informed him that he would not be going to Mexico. Upon hearing this news, R. S. appealed to the headmaster, "broke down, cried, and finally, was allowed to take the trip by the headmaster who did not trouble to inform the faculty of his change of decision." Coderre wrote that "the situation had disagreeable results" as it demonstrated that the faculty possessed no disciplinary power and gave the other students a bad example, since R. S. "boasted of his success."[61] Leniency in discipline might also be the result of a need for tuition-paying customers in an era when children assumed a degree of power as consumers and clients.

Despite greater leniency for what would be intolerable at one of the more prestigious preparatory schools, ranch schools provided an environment that often led to academic success, and schools promoted the individual accomplishments of students and alumni to document schools' academic strengths. *Time Magazine* presented Judson School student Rufus Hayden with the book *Oliver Wiswell* as an award for his high standing in *Time*'s Current Affairs test.[62] Evans School graduates included John Davis Lodge, ambassador to Argentina;

Rodman Paul, western historian, scholar, and California Institute of Technology professor; Leverett Saltonstall, who became governor of Massachusetts and a U.S. senator; and Lawrence Sperry, who developed an aerial torpedo for the Navy during World War I.[63] Green Fields School alumni included Missouri governor Christopher Bond and Texas lieutenant governor William Hobby among its distinguished alumni.[64] Graduates of the Southern Arizona School attended Amherst, Bucknell, Claremont Men's, Cornell, Duke, Harvard, Tulane, Washington and Lee, William and Mary, and Yale.[65] Los Alamos Ranch School student Charles Pearce attended Cornell, and his best friend went to Southern Methodist University. Pearce joined Army Intelligence in 1943 and served for three years before moving to Texas to become a rancher and a published author.[66] Los Alamos inspired other writers including Gore Vidal. Headmaster and school founder George Judson received a letter from one thankful parent who relayed that his son was "really sitting on top of the world," since he was admitted to Williams College, "where he will take a combined course, and, in either five or six years, get a B.A. from Williams and an engineering degree from M.I.T. I don't know what you taught him, but he certainly has built himself up a lot of ambition and has laid out a real schedule for himself as Williams has the reputation of being the toughest college to get into in the country."[67]

The educational credentials of ranch schools' faculty were impressive and further reflected the creation of a social network that included the more prestigious institutions in the Atlantic Seaboard. Brochures and published histories of ranch schools confirmed that headmasters and teachers of ranch schools were a well-educated and experienced lot who had degrees from Ivy League and other well-established universities. Faculties' and headmasters' firsthand experience with traditional bastions of the elite domain gave schools cultural and academic legitimacy. *Arizona Highways* proudly claimed that "the faculties of these schools are served by members who received their own education at some of America's and Europe's foremost universities."[68] According to Cole's study of private schools, southwestern states had a slightly higher-than-average percentage of teachers with bachelor's degrees (62 percent compared to a national average of 61 percent). Seventeen percent had earned master's degrees, and three percent had a doctoral degree. The number of headmasters in the Southwest with advanced degrees was extraordinarily high, with 64 percent of them holding master's degrees compared with a national average of 42 percent (no other region had a percentage greater than 47 percent).[69] H. David Evans, the founder of the Evans School in Mesa in

H. David Evans founded the Evans
School in October 1902 near Mesa,
Arizona, and in 1921 moved the school
to Tucson. Arizona Historical Society,
Nicholas Roosevelt Photograph
Collection—PC 113-AE.

1902 and its branch operation in Tucson in 1921, was a graduate of Cambridge
University and had been the assistant headmaster at Elsted School in England.[70]
Evans faculty included A. D. Carlisle, a Harvard graduate who tutored the sons of
William Randolph Hearst and developed his own system of teaching mathematics, which made it possible for all his students to pass the college entrance examinations.[71] Green Fields history teacher Grace Hammarstrom earned her MA
from Columbia University and had teaching experience at St. Mary's in New York
and the Katherine Branson School in Ross, California.[72] Matthew Baird, headmaster of the Arizona Desert School in the 1930s, was an alumnus of Princeton
and Oxford. James S. Hutchinson, director of the Palo Verde Ranch School, was a
graduate of Stanford University.[73]

The 1935 faculty at the Judson School for Boys included Princeton graduate
Hugh Preston Cox, Yale graduate John Gardiner Bridge, and James B. Felton,
who held degrees from Pomona College and the University of Southern

Matthew Baird (December 1901–
October 1972) served as headmaster of
the Arizona Desert School in the 1930s.
The note on the photograph states that
it is from 1934. Courtesy of David C.
Wilhelm, Denver, Colorado.

California. Felton taught math and history, Cox taught Latin, German, and
Romance Languages, and Bridge worked as the acting school secretary in addi-
tion to providing instruction in history.[74] In 1936, a youthful Yale graduate,
Henry Wick, came to Arizona to teach at the Palo Verde Ranch School in Mesa.
Two years later he joined the staff at Judson School for Boys. Wick left Judson
in 1942 to serve as a captain in the United States Army during World War II.
Upon his return to the States in 1946, Wick and Joseph Blake Field purchased
Judson School for Boys from George Judson. Like Henry Wick, Field gained
teaching and administrative experience at other ranch schools before becoming
the co-owner of Judson. A graduate of Harvard University, Field served as the
headmaster and co-owner of the Mesa Ranch School for thirteen years beginning in 1926.[75]

Headmasters and faculty with degrees from prestigious universities demonstrated the educational caliber of a private school, but, more significantly, they

also indicated a school's ability to provide entryways to important social networks. Teachers, headmasters, and owners who came from the East and Midwest often became permanent residents of Arizona, California, New Mexico, and Wyoming, yet maintained personal and institutional connections from their cities of origin and their university alma matters that developed into back-and-forth migration patterns from East to West. Headmasters recruited faculty from Ivy League universities to the West to teach in ranch schools and sent graduates East for their university education. The Valley Ranch School, and possibly others, used Porter Sargent's Teachers Placement Bureau to staff their schools with educated men who were suited to guide and mentor boys from affluent families.

In his late twenties, Yale graduate Sherman D. Thacher accompanied his ailing brother to Southern California and, having not yet found his life's ambition, decided to stay and cultivate a citrus grove in Ojai, located twelve miles inland from Ventura and forty miles east of Santa Barbara. In 1889 Thacher received a letter from an old New Haven friend, who asked Thacher to take his nephew and namesake for "a year of out door life combined with study in preparation for college." The request was a fortuitous surprise, as he needed the extra money to hold him "until the oranges should make his fortune." News traveled throughout Ventura County that Thacher was willing to tutor, and he received a request from an ambitious fourteen-year-old to join him. Because the boy was unable to pay fees, Thacher allowed him to work on the ranch in exchange for tutoring. Numerous other requests from locals led Thacher to fear that "if he were not careful he would have a school on his hands." Forced to admit that realization of profits from his citrus grove remained in the distant future, Thacher decided to advertise to attract more boys to his ranch with the intent of charging exorbitant fees to make up for the intrusion of youngsters. In the brief description he sent out in 1891, he stated that "the place has not been given the title of school. While it is a school as far as progress in study goes, it is hoped that it will always preserve distinctly the more normal life of a household and ranch." At the end of his letter, he included a list of twenty men, mostly family friends and relatives, who agreed to serve as references. Although he made Ojai his home, "he still clung to family and Yale associations," and according to his biographer, "All his life they were given preference." In 1898 he wrote the Fiske Teachers Agency in New York and specified that he sought men of good character, good breeding, "the manners of a thorough gentleman of refinement," good scholarship, and "a manly acceptance of responsibilities and loyalty to the school." Throughout his tenure as headmaster until he retired in 1931, he only hired teachers from the East, the majority of whom had graduated from Yale.[76]

The curriculum at Thacher evolved naturally based on college entrance requirements, Thacher's own interests, and the cultural geography of Ojai. Since no one college entrance examination was the same in the early years of the school, meeting each student's need was challenging. Thacher was most familiar with Yale's entrance examination and conducted it for the Pacific coast at San Francisco. Thacher's biographer found that "New Haven customs flourished among the sagebrush." There were no organized games on Sundays, and after supper on Sundays, Thacher read from the Bible, followed by the singing of hymns or a guest speaker. As Thacher was agnostic, the Sunday activities are representative more of his cultural background growing up the son of a Yale professor than of any desire to preach. His lectures to students centered on purity as the touchstone of judgment and the basis for all conduct, as he brought his brand of Puritan religion-turned-to-ethics to the West.[77]

Throughout his career he sought to maintain his ideal ratio of students from the East and Midwest in proportion to those from the Pacific coast. By 1902, "of the 140 boys who had attended the school, 58 came from East of Ohio, 31 from the Middle West, and 51 from the Pacific Coast." In order to keep his enrollment at a ratio of one teacher to every five students, he had to become more selective after 1902. His criteria included geographic distribution, quality of the parents, and the boy's character and intelligence. The amalgamation of East and West to Thacher was a significant draw of his school, and in order to continue this tradition, he needed to make sure he had a supply of eastern representatives, giving preference in direct proportion to their proximity to New Haven. His own sons trained for Yale at Thacher, but two of them spent a year under the tutelage of their father's good friend Horace Taft, who started his own preparatory school in Watertown, Connecticut. Thacher must have felt as many parents did that while a western ranch school experience served many important educational and personal development needs, in order to succeed in the rigors of an Ivy League school, some experience at a traditional eastern preparatory school was also useful. As a result, some boys' private school experience included both.[78]

In addition to attachments to certain eastern preparatory schools and universities, ranch schools cultivated special relationships with local state universities. While some students saw their time in the Southwest as temporary, others who believed the environment had cured their health ailments wanted to stay and attend local universities. The Southern Arizona School, for example, could boast that it was accredited by the University of Arizona, and through this rating, SAS graduates were admitted without examination to any of the state universities and to a number of other colleges and universities that accepted students on certificate.[79] When approached by a parent who wanted to prepare her son for admission to the University of Arizona, a university representative referred her to the Southern Arizona School for Boys and the Arizona Desert School. According to a letter written by Laura Judson to her husband, this parent's interest in the Arizona Desert School grew out of the conversation she had with the person at the university who spoke highly of George Judson.[80] Personal relationships between headmasters and university faculty were then, as now, an important avenue for college admission.

Several private schools that emerged in the 1920s distinguished themselves by offering the benefits of immersion in American places, often located in desired tourist locations. Ranch schools benefited from an expanded tourism industry that advocated pilgrimages to distinctly American locations as a requirement of American citizenship. An emphasis on the heritage and uniqueness of place differentiated them from more established private schools, but also reflected a modern approach to preparatory school education consistent with the aims of progressive education as articulated by the Progressive Education Association. John Dewey dedicated a chapter to combining the study of history and geography, advocating the adventure of travel to unfamiliar places. To isolate one from the other made history a series of names and dates, and geography simply "the height of a mountain here, the course of a river there, the quantity of shingles produced in this town, the tonnage of the shipping in that, the boundary of a county, the capital of a state." When explored in tandem through nature study, children learned that "nature is the medium of social occurrences. It furnishes original stimuli; it supplies obstacles and resources. Civilization is the progressive mastery of its varied energies." Dewey advocated treating "local or home geography" as "an intellectual starting-point for moving out into the unknown." Focusing solely on the familiar was, to Dewey, as deadly as rote memorization.[81] Building on a growing tourism industry that sought to celebrate the unique landscape and history of America, ranch schools—and a few

New England schools—emphasized a connection to specific regions of the country. Consequently, the new private school of the interwar period could be touted as an American institution rather than one that boasted of its English origins.[82]

In a 1933 chapel service at the Valley Ranch School, Philip Cummings "spoke on finding our own national background," affirming the significance of understanding America's past to becoming citizens. In order to know America, he suggested people needed to appreciate the early West as "the last frontier; for, indeed, in no other part of the country does one find the first settlers still living, albeit that they are old men. There is strength in this background, as there was in the colonial background of chivalrous Virginia and the South, or in Puritan witch-persecuting New England. There is as much sentiment in the struggle in the ruins of an early trapper's lodge-pole pine log cabin as in the ruins of some of the signorial castles of the Continent." Cummings himself was experiencing the West for the first time and made several observations in a journal that support his understanding of the significance of exploring the remains of the Old West to national identity.[83] In her study of American tourism from 1880 to 1940, Marguerite Shaffer found that the emerging tourist industry "actively promoted tourism as a ritual of American citizenship," and promoters "encouraged white, native-born middle- and upper-class Americans to reaffirm their American-ness by following the footsteps of American history and seeing the nation firsthand." By visiting the sights and scenes that embodied the essence of America, travelers would become better Americans.[84] Boosters, particularly in the West, used the slogan "See America First" to persuade Americans, easterners specifically, to postpone European travel until they attained intimate knowledge of their own country. Charles C. Moore, president of the Panama-Pacific International Exposition, wrote: "I know men who have never been west of Buffalo, New York, yet who go frequently to Europe, perhaps once a year. Such men would become better citizens of this country were they to see the West."[85]

National identity could also be discovered in New England. Deerfield Academy provides another case study of the value of region in preparing boys for college and life. Frank Boyden acquired the advertising services of Bruce Barton, who effectively described Deerfield as a "truly American academy in an authentic New England village." "There is something about Deerfield," Barton wrote, "something that you feel in the corridors of its hundred-year-old buildings, and the atmosphere of its rugged hills. That something is the New England tradition, the presence of the New England conscience." The essence of New England virtue could be absorbed by anyone who attended Deerfield Academy. Those born and trained in New England "have spread across the continent, leaving colleges and white-steepled churches in their wake. They enter cities and rise to leadership. Somehow the granite of those hills has bred itself into their being. They stand firm and yield not. Men depend on them. The stuff which is in them does not crumble; institutions are established on it." He argued that a school can be built anywhere, but "that something that is in those ancient halls" cannot be bought or created. He concluded that "the souls of just men made perfect people its corridors; character covers the campus like a mantle; and the difference between what is right and what is wrong thrusts itself across the horizon as inescapably as Mount Tom. This is the stuff of the New England conscience, America's great asset and greater need."[86]

Deerfield Academy's rise to national prominence in the interwar period coincided with the town's new tourism-based economy, enabling it to construct an identity based on the values of the New England character. Boosters asserted the region's significance to the nation by emphasizing the role of its cultural geography in producing native-born citizens who demonstrated initiative, worked hard, and persevered in the aftermath of the 1704 French and Native American raid on English settlers. In continually reconstructing the local history, largely defined by that singular tragic event of 1704, Deerfield residents explored what it meant to be a New Englander and worked to preserve what was unique about its character through publications, lectures, and its museum. Local historians credited their Puritan forefathers with planting "the seeds for what would grow into the fruits of modern liberty and freedom of conscience." Deerfield's ancestors received "admiration for their character as much as the specific principles they espoused." They were pioneers who conquered wilderness, "confronted frightful adversity, did not flinch, and set to work." Michael Batinski paraphrased a speech delivered by local historian George Sheldon who, on the two-hundredth anniversary of the 1704 raid, explained the impact of historical events in shaping the New England character:

"It was the meeting face to face of the sterner aspects of nature and life, . . . the suffering and the death, . . . the dangers of the new land" that made the New England character. It was the founders' "progressive manhood" that enabled them to turn "wilderness into gardens." That "sturdy manhood of the early days" provided both "a lesson and an inspiration" for today. Succeeding generations inherited these hardy traits of character; equipped with such moral fiber, they had turned this town into an "Eden."[87]

Deerfield Academy's reliance on New England character instilled through the region's cultural geography paralleled western ranch schools' dependency on a constructed ideal of the Old West for cultivating better citizens through an exploration of national identity.

Since the foundation of the curriculum had been established on traditional standards of preparatory school education, students were able to negotiate between the North Atlantic Seaboard or Great Lakes region and the West throughout their academic careers. Many migrated back and forth well into adulthood and retirement. Ranch school students had the rare opportunity to experience temporary geographic and cultural separation from established social expectations of children of their class and region with the assurance that they could return at any moment. Children who understood their experience in the West as temporary could embrace the role-play of being a westerner, with the protection that they were and always would be part of the eastern establishment. For some, a western ranch school was a fallback for the more prestigious Select Sixteen boarding schools. In this respect, western ranch schools perpetuated the idea of the American West as a safety valve and place of renewal for boys who had difficulty in the more established regions of the country.

Classes and study periods prepared students for college, but it was the extracurricular activities and experience living in the West that were intended to provide life lessons, as advocated by progressive educators. Sherman Thacher's biographer aptly pointed out: "To the parental question about what he did at school no boy would ever answer, 'I studied and went to classes.' On the contrary, there would probably be no mention of books but only of those things which make life worth-while in the eyes of a normal boy."[88] Boys experienced and explored the western region through extracurricular activities and immersion in this particular geographic region. Tourism promoters and travelers themselves perpetuated an ideal of travel within the United States, especially to the American West, as a necessary experience for citizenship. Although they were the antithesis of John Dewey's vision for democratic schools that transcended the boundaries of class, ranch schools became a destination for pilgrimages of citizenship. Once the business of preparing for college entrance tests was addressed, headmasters sought to satisfy other educational objectives by maximizing the cultural geography and imagined pre-1890 West. The result was that children and teenagers enjoyed their ranch school experience, and headmasters prided themselves on knowing that they were cultivating self-reliant, responsible citizens and leaders who embodied the spirit of the American West.

CHAPTER 3

Constructing the West

IMMERSION IN THE CULTURE AND ENVIRONMENT OF THE AMERICAN
West was an important part of the ranch school experience. Ranch schools
constructed experiences for boys based on a mythic West, set in the least
settled part of the region, and boasted of their ability to transform youth. By
the 1920s, travel to the American West was an accepted antidote to the problems of the "rich man's son," having established a track record of transforming young men born into privilege, who sought the opportunity to prove
their self-reliance, rise to physical challenges, and demonstrate an aptitude
for rugged individualism. A key element of the western ranch school experience centered on accepted ideals of southwestern landscapes that included
wide open spaces providing the illusion of a rugged, sparsely populated
environment. Brochure photography evoked the spirit of the Old West by
featuring students dressed in cowboy attire riding horseback, southwestern-
style architecture, and interior spaces decorated with Native American art.
Ranch schools resurrected certain aspects of the Old West—the agrarian
paradise that had forged the American spirit of individualism and democracy as antimodern, antiurban, and antitechnological—for the dual purpose
of preparing boys for college and assuming the responsibilities of masculine
citizenship. At the same time, promotional literature assured parents that
the Southwest was civilized, safe, and located near urban conveniences. The
result was that ranch school students experienced a rugged yet protected
version of the Old West through geographic isolation, restricted encounters

with indigenous cultures, overnight camping trips, and other ranch activity intended to cultivate self-reliance.[1]

Accounts of the benefits to be gained by experiencing the American West generated by boosters, pioneer societies, and social commentators were seared into the American mind by the time educators and entrepreneurs began to establish ranch schools. The Fresnal Ranch, for example, was established in 1924 when two eastern boys who "lacked the vigor to succeed" traveled west in search of renewal. Soon others ventured to the Fresnal Ranch until it "became a place for those who wished to regain their strength and courage to carry on with life."[2] According to a fellow Judson student, in just eight months, "Teddy" from New Jersey had developed such a "healthy glow and sturdy look" that the author wondered whether his sister "would know him when he goes home."[3] Theodore Roosevelt, Owen Wister, and Frederick Remington publicized their transformation into masculine role models through extended travel to the American West that included ranch work, hunting, and roughing it in sparsely populated wilderness areas that lacked urban conveniences. Dude rancher Struthers Burt commented on a lesser known "handsome son of a well-known New York family sent west as a supposed drunkard; he surprised everyone by developing into a shrewd and sober cattleman."[4]

Americans' expectations of the West were based on mythic, pre-1890 ideals perpetuated by promotional literature, boosters, pioneer reminiscences, travel journals, dime novels, and Western movies. Nineteenth-century landscape paintings; articles and stories included in periodicals like the *Atlantic, Collier's, Harper's, Scribner's,* and *McClure's*; turn-of-the-century Western dime novels; Westerns; and twentieth-century tourism publications, including *Arizona Highways,* coupled with a nostalgia for the past, led to the creation of an idealized West. The West seemed untainted by the Civil War, in comparison to other regions of the country, providing individuals as well as the nation the chance for renewal in the aftermath of tragedy.[5] Urbanization and industrialization sparked an interest in a past and a region that was more direct, simpler, and more easily understood. Tourists and promoters, anxious about modern urban-industrial society, reinforced an ideal of the West as the embodiment of American democracy, freedom, friendliness, and community. The West of the American imagination was a land of farmers, ranchers, cowboys, and friendly Indians who were connected to the land, in stark contrast to half of the American population who lived in alienating, crowded, sterile cities.[6]

However, by 1893 the Old West of the American imagination that shaped the character of ranchers, cowboys, and pioneers had disappeared, according to Frederick Jackson Turner. Early twentieth-century Americans traveled west to claim what was left of a vanishing way of life and in search of affirmation that this was indeed untrue. In her cross-continental motor trip in 1915, Emily Post lamented upon arriving in Omaha, "Where, Oh, where is the West that Easterners dream of—the West of Bret Harte's stories, the West depicted in the moving pictures? Are the scenes no longer to be found except in the pages of a book, or on a cinematograph screen?" In traveling west of the Mississippi, she expected to see "ranches, cowboys, Indians, not little cities like sample New Yorks."[7] A few Hollywood Westerns poked fun at easterners for mythologizing the West, indicating that the irony was openly presented in popular culture. In *Wild and Woolly* (1917), Douglas Fairbanks plays a son of a railroad magnate who goes to Bitter Creek, Arizona, to promote a railroad spur. He expects a "town infested with outlaws, gamblers, and dance-hall girls." Understanding his disappointment and desperately wanting the railroad spur, the citizens attempt to transform their tiny town into the West of his dreams. "They put up clumsily spelled 'authentic' signs for the saloon and hotel" and plan a fake railroad holdup and Indian raid.[8] In her reflections on the field of western history, Patricia Limerick found that "long involvement with the commercial, intentional mythologizing of the West as a place of romantic escape and adventure" is a common characteristic of western places. This mythologizing has "given the region a particularly heavy dependence on the uncertain industry of tourism and on the effort to meet the expectations generated by this myth."[9] Ranch schools not only "proved" to easterners and midwesterners that the best of the Old West still existed, but afforded the chance for their children to take part in a western experience. The Orme School summer camp program, for example, promised the city-reared child the chance for "dreams of the Old West" to come true.[10]

In constructing an image of the American West of the interwar period as open and maintaining several characteristics of the Old West, yet simultaneously settled and safe, ranch schools benefited from a trend set in motion by Buffalo Bill Cody's Wild West show and post–Civil War era boosters. Buffalo Bill's Wild West show provided audiences "adventure in a safe, secure context" by portraying the West as vanishing, yet not quite vanished. In large part this was accomplished by featuring American Indians who participated in the

reenactment of several battles where Euro-American settlers emerged victori-
ous. Their very presence demonstrated that elements of the Old West still existed, but since their subjugation was affirmed through pageantry, the audience
understood that Native Americans no longer posed a threat.[11] Historian David
Wrobel explored boosters' efforts to portray "desolate frontiers as settled regions, rich in culture, and devoid of danger and privation" in order to attract
permanent settlers and investors. While booster text reflected visions of western
prospects, pioneer reminiscences published during the same time period
brought the past of the rugged conditions of the West to the present.[12]

In his journal from his year as a teacher at the Valley Ranch School, Philip
Cummings frequently described the landscape and its remnants as being from
a bygone era, in a place that was now safe for the civilized populations.
Cummings wrote, "Every day I rejoice more and more that this has become
wilderness area of the first class, and that no individuals of undesirable class
may come and settle, nor more ranches be established, and no game ruthlessly
slaughtered. This will keep the region unspoiled." In another entry he grappled
with what he saw as a constructed experience of dude ranches that tried "to
present a few of the things which the East expects of the West, even when na-
tives would normally have no such customs or costumes," and his desire to "feel
the old and real west." He then proceeded to convey his delight at coming "face
to face with the real west in some local tradition" when he and Henry Larom
came across the ruins of a homestead. Larom proceeded to tell him about an
event that had occurred at the site around 1890, involving robbery, murder by
gunshot, escape, vigilantism, and revenge. Cummings wrote, "these may not be
parlor tales, but they are true pictures of this valley in the early days." To
Cummings, the Old West was violent, but all that remained from this bygone
era were the physical remnants and memories to be safely enjoyed by tourists
and newcomers.[13]

Promotional literature stressed that the West was a desirable and acceptable
place to live by highlighting the prevalence of churches, schools, and modern
amenities. At the same time, it had to assure readers that aspects of the Old West
existed, even while its rougher elements were under control and posed no real
threat to visitors. In a 1902 Santa Fe Railroad brochure, Whitelaw Reid,
American journalist, politician, and diplomat, deflected readers' concerns about
moving across country to the Far West in his response to the brochure's question, "Is it a place fit to live?" Arizona boasted "two transcontinental lines of

railway, with numerous feeders; it has fast mails, and rival telegraph lines, and is throbbing with the intense life of the splendid West." Phoenix and Tucson had "ten thousand inhabitants or more," and each city had "electric light, telephones, trolley cars, plenty of hotels, banks, book stores, good schools, churches, an occasional theatrical performance, sometimes a lecture or a circus, often a horse race, and, in the spring, a thoroughly curious and interesting 'fiesta.'"[14] Furthermore, he explained, "The man who goes to any considerable Arizona town with the ideas of the Southwest derived from novels, or from 'The Arizona Kicker,' will be greatly mystified. He will find as many churches as in towns of corresponding size in Pennsylvania or Ohio, and probably more schoolhouses." Acknowledging that visitors could "find plenty of liquor shops, too, and gambling houses, and dance houses," there was no need for concern for "disorder unless he hunts late at night for it." He further attested:

> During my winter there I did not see a single disturbance in the streets, or half a dozen drunken men, all told. Mining men and an occasional cowboy certainly had quarrels, sometimes in the disorderly quarters at night; and there were stories of the use of the knife among Mexicans; but the visitor who went about his own business had as little trouble as on Broadway or Chestnut street. The Pima and Maricopa Indians, who are encountered everywhere, have been friendly with the whites for generations, and there isn't an Apache within some hundreds of miles.[15]

Most ranch schools were situated far enough from metropolitan areas to convince easterners and midwesterners that the expanse of the Old West still existed, but the schools remained within a reasonable distance of the modern urban convenience to which the students were accustomed. Arizona Desert School overlooked Tucson and combined "the advantages of being near the conveniences of civilization with the advantages of living in a remote and unspoiled part of the country."[16] The Arizona Sunshine School was "only seven miles from downtown Tucson, just off a main road—[its location] makes communication with the city simple, preserving at the same time the secluded peace of the country." The school emphasized that the "unique advantages of the peaceful desert setting and climate nourish development free from the strains of urban life."[17] When H. David Evans purchased the land for his Tucson school in 1921, its location in the Tanque Verde area at the foot of the Rincon Mountains was far out in the open country. Directors George Harper and Captain Russell B. Fairgrieve carefully selected the site for the Southern Arizona School for Boys in the foothills of the Catalinas, twelve miles northeast of Tucson, described as a "delightful little city, whose past is filled with the romance peculiar to the Southwest," but whose residents also enjoyed every modern convenience.[18]

The portrayal of the American West as a promised land of opportunity was in part fulfilled by emphasizing education. Claims of more money spent per capita on education and images of impressive school buildings contained in promotional literature assured readers that the post-1890 West was not only settled, but culturally advanced. Wrobel suggests that this preoccupation with schools indicated an attachment of value to the future of western places.[19] After World War I, the National Park Service increasingly emphasized the educational value of the parks, partly in reaction to attacks against their protected status. By 1925 the National Park Service advocated more than the enjoyment of scenic beauty. Visitors would learn "about history, geology, botany, archeology and biology" and ultimately, "the character and spirit of the nation," which elevated the cultural status of tourism. Narratives disseminated by tourism promoters reflected an emphasis on education, as several "assumed a scientific tone" in documenting their observations.[20]

Ranch schools were the institutional blending of tourism and education, already set in motion by boosters, the National Park Service, and dude ranches. As preparatory schools, they were also the bedrock of civilized society and provided important economic benefits to the region. *Arizona Highways*, the state's magazine created by the Department of Transportation to promote road trips to the Grand Canyon state, featured several articles on Arizona ranch schools. In September 1939, an article explicitly connected ranch schools to the state's economy: "Arizona owes its gratitude" to the founders "who have developed these schools to the best in the nation." Investors contributed "hundreds and hundreds of thousands of dollars . . . in the plants and properties of these schools. Around these schools have grown up an important industry, the beneficial effects of which are felt by the whole state." The introduction to this article rumored that "it has been said that half of the ranch land in southern Arizona is now owned by former students of the Evans School."[21] Both the Southern Pacific Railroad and the Tucson Chamber of Commerce marketed Arizona's ranch schools, further suggesting their importance to the development of western tourism. Two tourism pamphlets published by the Southern Pacific that listed guest ranches along rail lines in Arizona, California, New Mexico, Nevada, and Texas featured Arizona's ranch schools.[22]

Tucson citizens and city officials consciously entered into the winter tourism market in the 1920s, in an effort to stimulate the local economy. A major thrust of the city's tourism campaign highlighted Tucson as a healthy place for families. The Tucson Sunshine-Climate Club commissioned the McCann Agency of Los Angeles to attract "people of means" who could afford to spend an entire winter season in southern Arizona. In one advertisement, the McCann Agency addressed the concerns of eastern parents by proclaiming, "Here is the place, Mothers, for your pale, inactive children." The ad further noted that all schools would accept students at any time and that "a season in Tucson . . . will bring big appetites and fill frail little bodies with glowing health and energy—the heritage of every normal child." Several other associations joined the efforts of the Sunshine-Climate Club, including the Arizona Polo Association. This group spearheaded the effort to stage the La Fiesta de los Vaqueros in 1925 and sought national attention for Arizona as the "winter capital of Polo."[23] Tucson ranch schools both supported and benefited from these initiatives.

Just as tourism promoters had to balance the image of the West and ranch schools as civilized, yet rugged, they needed to emphasize the health benefits of the region at the same time they dispelled the idea that the Southwest was a place for sick people. Brochures from the majority of Arizona's ranch schools, including Arizona Desert School, Hacienda del Sol, Judson School for Boys, Palo Verde Ranch School, and Southern Arizona School for Boys, identified the dry climate as particularly beneficial for the cure of certain ailments as one of the many features of their unique schools, at the same time that they carefully explained that no children with communicable disease would be admitted. In their history, Fermor S. Church and Peggy Pond Church emphasized that Los Alamos Ranch School, "in addition to being college preparatory, was a health school."[24] This did not mean that Los Alamos was a school solely for children with illness, but like many ranch schools, Los Alamos touted its ability to promote the health of all children—those with and without afflictions.

Ranch schools evolved, practically and conceptually, from dude ranches, building on their strategies for creating "genuine" encounters with the Old West. Dude ranches provided middle- and upper-class educated Americans with the opportunity for extended, immersive, instructive experiences in the rugged environment of the West. Ivy League–educated easterners enjoyed hunting and western hospitality on dude ranches beginning in the late nineteenth century. In his seminal work on dude ranches, Lawrence Borne found that "dude ranching had developed in the late nineteenth century from four major sources: hunting parties, remittance men, the scenic appeal of the West, and ranches, which added their own type of appeal and which provided the hospitality to accommodate visitors." Rothman distinguished early dude ranch guests as those seeking "authenticity," wanting "to touch and feel as part of understanding the mythic West and the human past" beyond the experience of viewing western landscape from train windows. They were typically wealthy and wanted access to archaeological sites, scientists, paleontologists, and anthropologists to help them understand the antimodern world. By 1930 dude ranching had become a rite of passage and a means of class identification.[25]

Shortly after the first official dude ranches appeared, the largely all-male hunting clientele evolved into family travelers and boys traveling alone. Dick Randall, who founded the OTO Montana Dude Ranch in 1898, expanded his operation in 1910 to accommodate hunters' families. Some of the men sent their children to the ranch in the summer while they and their wives went abroad. In Jackson Hole, Wyoming, Princeton graduate Struthers Burt tried an interesting experiment at his Bar BC dude ranch by building a separate ranch for children called the Little Outfit. Burt was from a wealthy Philadelphia family and excelled in dude ranching because of his keen understanding that a dude ranch was not a cow ranch and that success was "predicated on affiliation with the East." On the contrary, Charles C. Moore was a westerner who developed contacts in the East as a student attending Lawrenceville preparatory school and the University of Michigan. Moore brought his classmates to his parents' ranch in Wyoming to enjoy hunting and camping. In 1906 Moore opened a boys' camp at his parents' ranch and recruited teenagers from the East. As the number of these campers increased, his idea evolved into dude ranching for children. Because of his contacts in the East, he was able to provide references to assure parents of his credentials.[26]

In 1915, Princeton alumnus Irving H. "Larry" Larom and Yale graduate Winthrop Brooks conducted a significant experiment at Valley Ranch, another dude ranch in Wyoming. They purchased a homestead that became the destination of many eastern visitors and later specialized in summer pack trips for boys. When they recruited Julian Bryan, a fellow Ivy League alumnus, to the project, they acquired contacts at three prestigious eastern colleges; Colgate,

Princeton, and Yale, which in 1922 facilitated the transformation from a vacation experience to boarding school by establishing the school's academic credibility. Brooks and Bryan remained in the East, while Larry lived on the ranch and became the headmaster and director of the school. Larry hired men from Harvard, Princeton, Penn State, and the University of Illinois to teach classes. Mornings were reserved for classes while afternoons were spent in outdoor activities including riflery, polo, horseback riding, trapping, fishing, mountain climbing, and football. All-day rides and weekend pack trips were standard activities. The school expanded quickly and graduates attended Princeton, Yale, Harvard, and Dartmouth.[27]

Ranch schools located in the Southwest were also connected to dude ranches, but it was more typical for those in Arizona, especially, to evolve from and cater to the newly established vacation resorts of the 1910s and '20s. Arizona ranches appealed to guests for many of the same reasons as dude ranches in Colorado, Wyoming, and Montana, with the added benefit of year-round sunshine to attract winter visitors, including families with school-aged children. The southwestern ranch resorts offered a wider variety of activities by building tennis courts, swimming pools, and golf courses that were seldom offered in the western states that were further north. These newer, year-round establishments caused some confusion as to what actually constituted a dude ranch. An important distinguishing feature of a dude ranch, according to Borne, was that the ranches were actually family-owned homes where dudes came as paying guests of the family.[28] This aspect of Arizona ranch schools, coupled with the emphasis on western activity, horses, and landscape, affirms that they were more like dude ranches than resorts, despite the fact that many boasted tennis courts and resort-like accommodations.

The Southwest's desert climate allowed students to attend school in optimal weather and provided families the opportunity to travel with their children. Several Arizona schools attributed enrollment to the guests of nearby resorts. Rubie Atchley, cofounder of Green Fields School in Tucson, "once said that her school might never have succeeded in the early years if it had not been for the Arizona Inn, where parents and grandparents first became so enchanted by the desert as to decide to send sons and grandsons there."[29] The significance of ranch schools to Arizona's tourism industry was recognized by the Works Progress Administration in the Maricopa County description of the Arizona Writers Project. Under the subtitle "Guest Ranches and Private Boarding Schools," the author explained that "because of the large number of winter tourists who visit the county, and the famed Sahuara desert areas, there has been established a number of well-known Guest Ranch and Private Boarding Schools" and included Jokake School, Judson School for Boys, and the Remuda Ranch School as examples. The primary purpose of the Remuda Ranch School in Wickenburg, "dude ranch capital of the world," was "to keep all students up to the work of the school from which they came." The school's clientele were the children of the guests of Remuda and its neighboring dude ranches.[30]

School-aged children who accompanied their parents on extended winter vacations to Phoenix attended the Judson School for Boys and the Jokake School for Girls. Of the seventeen boys listed in the 1931 edition of the *Rattler*, published by the student body of the Judson School, three of the younger boys, two of them from Chicago, lived at the Biltmore and attended as day students. One Judson student lived at Jokake Inn that same year.[31] The Jokake Inn had its own preparatory school, but it was only for girls. The Jokake School for Girls, founded by the daughter and son-in-law of Jokake Inn's owners, shared many of the resort's amenities, including the pool and stables. The Inn's winter tourist season ran from January through March, which gave the school exclusive use of the facilities during the other five to six months of the school year. Ranch schools were an important amenity for long-term winter visitors at the same time that they affirmed the economic and cultural promise of the region.

The typical entry to a child's western experience was by train, and railroad companies included ranch schools in their promotional material.[32] Even when families made extended stays at a nearby resort or ranch, the school year often did not coincide with the family vacation, and most students traveling from the East and Midwest traveled alone. Students gathered at train depots in New York City, Pittsburgh, and Chicago to begin their western experience. In his autobiographical account of his experiences at the Los Alamos Ranch School, Charles Pearce recalled vividly waiting at the Chicago station with several other students. "An authoritative voice ordered all L.A.R.S. boys to assemble under the school banner. It was time to board the train."[33] Jack Heinz "had a great time" entertaining himself on the train with seven other Evans School–bound boys. The group "set up on the club car for hours at a time playing the phonograph" and alone he "did quite a bit of reading, both good and bad." The boys slept in berths "and various places" and went to sleep as late as about 12:30 a.m.[34] John Donaldson remembered boarding the train at Grand Central with thirty other students bound for the Arizona Desert School in Tucson. The boys were accompanied by one member of the faculty and met several other students in Chicago. John remembered that during this stop, "we went to the Chicago Athletic Club and went swimming." He also recalled that he was on a lower berth: "I looked up after two days and there were Ocotillos." A group of Arizona Desert School alumni chuckled when one alumnus noted that Carl Tucker Jr. traveled by private car, and teased that "he wasn't allowed in with us."[35] Rather than focus on landscape, these adolescent passengers' attention was on social connections with peers and the relative freedom that independent travel afforded.

Although travel by rail was the most practical means of transportation, it deprived ranch school students of an immensely important aspect of the pioneer experience. In studying pioneer reminiscences created in the 1880s through the early twentieth century, historian David Wrobel found an emphasis on hardship, partially through recountings of the journey itself. The Old Pioneers commonly equated their trials and tribulations to their identity and claimed to be true westerners, contrasting their experiences to the "modern comforts and conveniences of the safe, tamed, new West." Reminiscing pioneers geared their accounts as object lessons for younger generations who they believed should know the harsh conditions overcome by the older generation of pioneers who laid "the foundation for their present comforts." The Pullman car served as one of the starkest contrasts between "the demands of the past with the luxuries of the present" and "became a stock symbol of the comfort and ease that made it so difficult for the members of the present generation to appreciate their pioneer predecessors."[36] Some ranch schools were located in remote enough places to give students a small taste of the Old Pioneer experience. The distance from the train depot to the Valley Ranch School in Wyoming and Los Alamos in New Mexico required a similar endurance of its young passengers who made the last part of their trek by wagon on underdeveloped dirt roads. Students who attended ranch schools in Tucson and Phoenix, however, were greeted by the headmaster, faculty, and sometimes the in-residence cowboy, who drove them by automobile the short distance from the train depot to the school.[37]

Traveling by train with modern conveniences, and arriving at one's destination with few stops, denied ranch schools students the hardships of the pioneer journey, but may have relieved the sense of being so far away from home and assured children's safety. At the same time, because students had little

Los Alamos Ranch School was the only ranch school included in Louise Dunham Goldsberry's comprehensive survey of open-air education. She published her report in 1921 and "all but a very few" of the photographs were assembled in 1913. The caption on the back states: "Main building to the right, commissary and shop to left. These boys were out to scatter the oats . . ." Goldsberry Collection of open-air school photographs, Library of Congress Prints and Photographs Division, Washington, D.C.

opportunity to experience a sense of geographical transition, the insular nature of travel by rail reaffirmed the feeling of spatial and cultural distance from the urban centers of the Atlantic Seaboard and Great Lakes region. Arizona Desert School alumnus Howard Bremond remembered "the first impression I had of Arizona—we got into Benson, and I looked out the window, and it was quite a shock." When prompted by a fellow alumnus to explain what he was expecting—"Dancing girls in a saloon? Was it the desert scenery?"—Bremond answered that it was the difference in the landscape and described it as "sort of drab."[38] Emily Post, who in 1915 journeyed by automobile from New York City to California, found that traveling by automobile was somehow more authentic than by train, commenting that taking the Pullman "carefully preserves for you the attitude that you started with!" Because southwestern geography was prominently featured in Westerns, paintings, and literary descriptions as exotic lands and distant places of the Old West, passengers might have felt as though they had transcended both time and space when experiencing the landscape for the first time.

Photography of the Southwest's natural landscape was a prominent feature of ranch school promotional literature and demonstrated that wide open spaces, devoid of human contact, still existed. According to Jane Tompkins, the "desert is the classic Western landscape, rather than the rain forests of the Pacific Northwest or the valleys of California, because of the strange message it sends. . . . Fertility, abundance, softness, fluidity, many-layeredness are at a discount here." The vast open space of the southwestern desert landscape was in extreme opposition to the urban East and Midwest. This space gave the feeling of limit-less possibility and promise, "a tabula rasa on which man can write, as if for the first time, the story he wants to live."[39] It was not until the late nineteenth and early twentieth centuries that tourists developed an appreciation for the natural geography of the desert. At first they scorned the land because of its dissimilar-ity to eastern and European geography and had difficulty finding the language to describe what they saw. In time, easterners and Europeans found the Southwest to have "the most authentic claim to aesthetic merit in all of the United States." It was so unfamiliar that it became charming. To the wilderness lover, "the desert sometimes seemed a last refuge, especially before airplanes and air conditioning made it a suburb of the metropolis." Interest in southwest-ern landscapes and ancient ruins appealed to Americans' search for a unique national culture. Geological and ethnographic discoveries of the 1880s proved that America had its own cultural and natural resources that rivaled Europe's in terms of its antiquity and significance to human progress. Western landscapes, celebrated by See America First promoters and exalted at the Panama-Pacific International Exposition of 1915, represented the "true" America at a time of reactionary patriotism sparked by the European war. Exhibitors showcased sub-lime, scenic, and extraordinary natural landscapes of the West that insinuated both the promise of progress through the nation's abundant natural resources, at the same time they inspired awe for its pristine, vast, open spaces that had the potential to provide sanctuary for overworked Americans.[40]

Educators echoed promoters' zeal for the value of unspoiled landscape to civilization. In an essay subtitled "What is Civilization?" educational philoso-pher and author of the annual *A Handbook of Private Schools For American Boys and Girls*, Porter Sargent, praised civilizations that protected their land by

Judson School for Boys, opened in 1928, was located at the base of Camelback Mountain in Paradise Valley, Arizona. Courtesy of David C. Lincoln, Phoenix.

sustaining a "soil conserving culture" and criticized "western peoples" for waste and destruction. Because white America's ancestors were originally nomads, Sargent argued, we "are not yet thoroughly fixed to the soil." Throughout the essay he admonished cultures that abused nature, asking, "Who is civilized? We westerns take a beautiful place of prairie land or a lovely cove on an estuary and make a slum of it, and a cesspool,—a romantic valley with cascades and water-falls, where Indians have fished for centuries, and make it a mill town."[41]

The staunch proponent of progressive education firmly believed that environment had a significant impact in shaping individuals and expected his readership to conclude that cultures that protected the natural landscape and lived in harmony with nature were more civilized. Nathaniel Shaler, dean of the Lawrence Scientific School, made similar assertions in "The Landscape as a Means of Culture," published in the *Atlantic Monthly* in 1898. David Teague summarized that Shaler "suggested that Americans learn to see their continent as an aesthetic resource rather than an economic resource." Shaler stated that "the habits of civilized life tend to separate men from the charm of the world around them" and called for readers to consider "the art of appropriating the landscape" by advocating "landscape as a means of culture." Teague argues that Shaler's article and others published between 1890 and 1910 in journals like the *Atlantic Monthly, Century Illustrated, Harper's,* and *McClure's* set in motion the idea that "people who could appreciate the difficult, strange, and weird landscapes of the desert could do so because they were more 'civilized' than other people."[42]

Ranch school owners capitalized on the new appreciation of the Southwest desert and the emotional appeal of unspoiled environments by including visual images of the landscape in promotional brochures. Just like Frederick Remington's paintings, the landscape imagery used in ranch school brochures served as a background for human activity, but never depicted the spoils of human impact. When there was evidence of human activity, it was either buildings that were created using natural materials or students engaged in activity that evoked the ideal of the Old West, before there was concern that natural environments could potentially be spoiled by extractive industry. Photos and accompanying text convinced easterners that ranch schools provided an "authentic" Old West experience in the unspoiled expanse of the American desert. Photographs showed boys in cowboy attire amid wide open spaces, giving the impression of a pre-barbed wire ranching experience. A Southern Arizona School for Boys brochure proclaimed that "Southern Arizona is Nature's Wonderland . . . a great unspoiled playground." The accompanying photograph depicted a small stream flowing through terrain dotted with palo verde trees and sagebrush. "Nearby cottonwood trees lend their lower limbs for tree-houses and a few secret caves are known to some explorative minds," the owners told potential students.[43] Photographs of various Tucson schools depicted Old Spanish-style buildings surrounded by cacti with rugged mountains in the background. The Arizona Sunshine School, Old Pueblo School, Judson School for Boys, Southern Arizona School for Boys, and Foxboro Ranches showed students in western attire riding horseback through pristine desert scenes complete with saguaro cacti and other flora. A full-page photo of "Evening on the Desert" at the Palo Verde Ranch School in Mesa displayed the silhouettes of saguaro cacti against a desert sky.[44]

Many students embraced the sublime beauty of the desert, and authors used romantic prose to convey its significance and their awe and appreciation. A Jokake student described the Arizona landscape as "an eternally fascinating place to ride in. Its quiet beauty, impossible to describe in words, fills one with

(*left*) Evans School Boys on horseback look up in awe at a cactus, c. 1909–1910. Nicholas Roosevelt's photograph caption states: "Giant Cactus at Salt River Indian Reserv." Arizona Historical Society, Nicholas Roosevelt Photograph Collection—PC 113-AB.

World's Largest Sahuaro Cactus

(*right*) "World's Largest Sahuaro Cactus." Text on the back of postcard states: "Having stood unchallenged for years as the world's largest cactus—over 200 years old, 43 feet tall, with 52 branches—this fine specimen of Sahuaro was seriously damaged in a recent storm; and now Arizonans are searching for a 'new champion.'" Lollesgard Specialty Co., Tucson. Courtesy of author.

a feeling of peace and reverence which sinks into the minds of our little groups as they turn towards the sunset, and home again."[45] In his article on the falling of the world's largest cactus, located in Phoenix approximately one-half mile east of the Camelback Inn, reporter for the Judson School's Gopher World Ted Simmons wrote on February 25, 1940: "This one time proud king of the desert was said to be at the ripe old age of six hundred years when it fell. If this is true the cactus was here two centuries before Marcos de Niza came to Arizona in 1539."[46] Promotional material, especially that associated with the See America First campaign, repeatedly connected the landscape with American history, to encourage national travel as a means of "knowing" America. In this particular student's mind, human history and natural geography were intertwined and provided the author a means of conveying the significance of the age of the cactus to fellow students. It also suggested an understanding of America's natural resources in terms of progressive history and American exceptionalism. The Spanish empire failed to conquer the Southwest or tame its natural resources, and the cactus survived for centuries, demonstrating the superiority of America's natural resources to European cultures.[47]

By emphasizing the Southwest's open, premodern landscape, promoters sought to demonstrate that this experience would isolate children from the immoral influences of America's cities. At the same time, they linked landscape and region to a unique lifestyle that was the antithesis of the harried, fast-paced Northeast. An *Arizona Highways* article described how "life at an Arizona ranch school is the life of the west—the life of the open range, the friendly, hospitable life of easy and charming informality."[48] Students' attire emphasized the "informality" of western life, complementing the desert scenery and southwestern style of architecture. Instead of the standard eastern prep school uniform, students adorned themselves in jeans, chaps, cowboy hats, and Mexican serapes. At Foxboro Ranches, "boys and guests" wore "the simple, practical cowboy outfit consisting of blue-jeans, boots and sombrero."[49] Orme students liked to wear "the costume of the Arizona cowboy about the ranch—'Levi's' (blue denim pants), blue chambray or bright-colored cotton flannel work shirt, heavy work shoes for daily wear; cowboy boots for riding; cowboy hat." An Orme School brochure even advised that "these articles are best purchased in the West, and it is suggested that parents allow the Directors to buy them for the students in Phoenix."[50] Similarly, the Fresnal Ranch School suggested that "the following equipment necessary for Ranch life can be far better purchased in this country: 1 pair cowboy riding boots. 1 pair chaps. 1 cowboy coat. 4 pairs blue denim trousers. ½ dozen inexpensive blue cotton shirts. 1 cowboy hat. 1 sleeping bag."[51] Ranch schools not only enriched owners financially, but put money into the pockets of everyone who was in the business of providing western accouterments.[52]

The selection of southwestern tourist sites highlighted by ranch school brochures demonstrated a celebration of the region's natural wonders at the same time they showed the potential of the region for economic development through technology. Typical of post–Civil War and early twentieth-century booster campaigns, hope for a postfrontier future coupled with a longing for the frontier past played an important role in creating western identity.[53] See America First promoters justified this contradiction by promising to preserve sublime landscapes "while opening up all land not designated as 'scenic' to development" and encouraging the "benefits of progress without suffering the ill effects that had corrupted the East."[54] An illustrated map, described as "a real cowboy's version of the country surrounding Foxboro," depicted the Foxboro Ranch School at the center of a multitude of tourist destinations, including the Kaibab National Forest, the Grand Canyon, Navajo Country, the Painted Desert, and the great copper mines in the Verde Valley.[55] The Palo Verde Ranch School boasted its proximity to the Tonto National Forest, the rugged Superstition Mountains, Indian ruins, ancient forts, and the "fabulous Lost Dutchman Mine."[56] Students at the Southern Arizona School for Boys could take deep sea fishing trips to the Gulf of Lower California or motor over the famous Apache Trail to Roosevelt Dam, Phoenix, and other attractions.[57] Listing human-made marvels in concert with natural wonders perpetuated an idea of the Southwest as both preserving its natural heritage yet benefiting from advanced technology. By attending a ranch school, the next generation of leaders experienced the landscape of the Old West that had shaped American character and studied the ingenuity of mines and dams that gave promise to America's economic future.

Ancient Indian ruins, considered part of the natural landscape, provided an important educational opportunity for ranch school students and a selling point for promoters. The discovery of the first cliff houses in southern Colorado and northern New Mexico in the late nineteenth century proved the presence of ancient cultures in North America that rivaled if not superseded the European classical heritage. Americans "had discovered a dignified history that they could use for their own cultural needs."[58] Ranch schools highlighted ancient Indian ruins and the opportunity to gain firsthand experience in learning about America's ancient cultures. A Judson School for Boys brochure proclaimed: "Arizona, youngest state in the union, is the site of the oldest indigenous civilization in this country."[59] During the 1930–1931 term at Judson School for Boys, students planned and built a museum "to serve as a suitable place to house all prehistoric relics found on many of their camping trips."[60] For a nominal fee, Hacienda del Sol provided instruction in archaeology through its contacts at the University of Arizona.[61] The Southern Arizona School for Boys advertised its proximity to a "Pit-house Indian Village." Brochure photos depicted prehistoric pottery carefully displayed on a table covered by an Indian rug and showed boys excavating pots from an archaeological dig.[62] In retrospect, one Los Alamos Ranch School student reflected that "[There were] . . . many little ruins around. . . . we excavated a little . . . very ignorantly."[63]

A couple of these sites, located on or nearby ranch school property, turned out to be significant to the archaeological community. Don Everitt, former English and Latin instructor and academic advisor, and assistant headmaster of Southern Arizona School from 1937 to 1970, conveyed his fascination with "the environment of the school, especially by the fact that there was an ancient Indian ruin on the school property" and took care to document the context of the artifact finds. Eager to look for artifacts, Everitt investigated the ancient Hohokam village. At least one pit house had already "been dug into by a former student, William Neil Smith, who later did notable research among the Seri Indians of northern Mexico." Everitt persuaded a group of Southern Arizona School boys to help with the work of excavating another part of the village in lieu of tennis, football, calf roping, or horseback trail rides, for their daily two hours of physical activity. Working with Everitt, Southern Arizona School boys uncovered the walls, floor, fire pit, postholes, and storage bin of a Hohokam pit house. The group also uncovered the squashed bottom of a large olla and found pottery pieces to reconstruct the pot with only three gaps, "which we filled in with plaster of Paris." Everitt "uncovered two burials: one was a handful of cremated bones all by itself and the other was another collection of bones under a small inverted pot about the size of a cereal dish" at Pit #2. Dr. Emil Haury at the University of Arizona Archaeological Department examined the bones from under the "cereal dish" and "from pieces of the skull estimated the bones to be that of a girl about eighteen years old." The only other significant discovery was made by student Russell Scheidler, who uncovered the only whole pot ever found at the site. The ten-inch-tall pot with red design was eventually stolen from the school, and over time the pot from Pit #1 collapsed from handling. The Fenster School that took over the buildings and grounds of the former Southern Arizona School for Boys owns the little cereal bowl–sized pot that covered the bones.[64]

Practicing amateur archaeological excavations, hunting for petroglyphs, touring Native America museums, and collecting artifacts were the primary avenues for ranch school students to learn about Native Americans. Arizona ranch schools also benefited from university experts who visited and delivered lectures on Hopi and Navajo Indians. For the most part, pre–World War II school curricula isolated students from living Native American communities and treated Indian culture as something from the distant past, reiterating that the Southwest was civilized and safe for youngsters unaccompanied by adults. R. E. Souers, founder of El Coronado Ranch School, stated that "there is in the heart of every adolescent boy a deep seated longing . . . to live and know an outdoor life. To go west. To ride a horse over mountain trails! To sit on a high [ground] at sunset, as Apache Chiefs once did."[65] This statement portrayed the Apache as a culture from the past, rather than a living community. The Page Company's See America First travel guide series published between 1912 and 1931 highlighted ancient Native American ruins to celebrate Indians as "quintessentially natural," embodying the "simplicity and self-sufficiency of preindustrial living" desperately sought by disaffected urbanites. At the same time, the presence of ancient Indian ruins conveyed American progress and glorified conquest.[66]

The use of representations of Native Americans to guide children toward a more noble, pure, and natural way of living had precedent with Indian play, popular in the Progressive Era. Historian Philip Deloria argues that Americans "used Indian play to encounter the authentic amidst the anxiety of urban industrial and postindustrial life" and demonstrates how Boy Scouts of America leaders Ernest Thompson Seton and Daniel Carter Beard sought to create modern American character in children, but differed in their views of Indians as appropriate role models. By the late nineteenth century, Seton developed an organization called the Woodcraft Indians where potentially delinquent boys camped on his estate, listened to Indian tales, made Indian costumes, and played nature study games. Beard, who believed that children learned Americanness by re-creating pioneering experiences, formed the Sons of Daniel Boone. While

Nicholas Roosevelt included photographs of "The Indian Team" and "Indian at the Bat" in his 1909–1910 album that commemorated his adventures at the Evans School. He noted that the students at the Evans School sometimes competed against Indian teams, indicating contact with Native Americans through sports competition. Boys on both teams wore baseball uniforms rather than western attire. Arizona Historical Society, Nicholas Roosevelt Photograph Collection—PC 113-BQ.

Beard "tended to shunt Indians into a mythic frontier past," Seton believed Indians represented authenticity and natural purity. Critics of Seton pointed to images of Americanized Indians as representing the "new savagery of the modern. Coded as drinking, tramping, and laziness, Americanized Indians were powerful examples of the corrosive evil of modern society," according to Deloria. Seton's complex modernist/antimodernist use of Indian play eventually lost favor within the Boy Scouts of America as well as with the broader public, and he was ousted in 1915.[67] Beard's emphasis on a mediated experience based on ethnography and third-person accounts of Indian life and culture persisted and was evident in ranch schools.

Philip Cummings was an avid collector of Indian relics and became fascinated with the burial rituals of the Sioux. While visiting friends over the Christmas break in Pierre, South Dakota, he spent an inordinate amount of time conducting research on the topic at the State Historical Society. Because of his interest, he was invited out to the Indian school and he recorded: "The Indians are still new enough to me so that I get a decided reaction out of riding along with an old warrior in the back seat." On the one hand, he was in awe of the ancient tribe and related his own ancestry to theirs in the forming of the nation by noting that his mother's family "were in Massachusetts and Connecticut (the Webster family) as early as 1647. After all, I come next after the Sioux in the tribe of Americans." On a subsequent visit to the school, he toured each grade and noted how the children were "subject to regular inspections as to the cleanliness and personal hygiene." He "asked the school nurse about the Indian morality and she said that, among the full bloods not in frequent contact with the whites of poor and riff-raff classes that hang around the reservations, they are of high moral tone."[68] Even with his keen interest in the history of the Sioux, he did not seem to be bothered by the fact that the purpose of the school was to acculturate them by ridding children of their traditions. His question about their morality spoke to the contradictory nature of the American West and its Native peoples. Its past was superior and worthy of study, but the living cultures were still feared and needed to be contained.

Native Americans bordered the geographic spaces occupied by ranch schools, and owners did their best to control interaction between the children of the elite and the subjugated people of the Southwest. Tourism operators faced a similar dilemma since the opening of the Southwest to Anglo-American visitors in the late nineteenth century. The Indians who appeared at train stations to beg for money and sometimes alcohol were a far cry from the noble Indians portrayed by James Fenimore Cooper and disappointed early travelers. New ethnographic studies in the late nineteenth century helped to foster an appreciation for Native Americans that changed tourists' minds. As the result, promoters recruited Native peoples to their resorts, national parks, and other travel destinations, but always in controlled ways that celebrated their crafts and performances. By the time of the opening of rail lines to the Grand Canyon in 1901, Native peoples' presence added to visitors' southwestern experience, and they became a sought-after commodity.[69]

Jokake Inn owner Sylvia Evans recalled how guests enjoyed their frequent interaction with Pima and Apache Indians and how their presence added to the western ambiance of the Inn:

> The Pima Indians who made our baskets and pottery became regular visitors to the Inn. So colorful were their calico dresses they first chose to squat near the front door hoping to sell to our guests. Later we allowed them to build a wickiup near the Inn gate where they could house and sell their wares. These

warm, simple people were an important part of the scene in the dirt-street village of nearby Scottsdale. Every Saturday many Apache and Pima Indians brought their wagons pulled by the Indian ponies into Scottsdale and camped for a day under the mesquite trees. The women with bright calico skirts, velvet jackets and braided hair nursed their babies and chatted. The men gossiped while waiting to get groceries or sell their fine crafts.[70]

The Pima Indians enhanced the landscape of the Inn and offered guests consumable goods as an important part of the southwestern experience. Oftentimes the reality of the daily life of living Native Americans was too raw for the new residents of Phoenix, resort guests, and certainly unchaperoned children. Sylvia Byrnes, daughter of Jokake Inn owners, recalled that earlier in the history of the community, "the 'very proper' people of Scottsdale had started the practice of hanging men's pants on the nearby trees each weekend, since it was customary for the Indian men to arrive in town wearing only a loin cloth."[71] Native peoples greatly enhanced tourist and student southwestern encounters as long as owners could shield guests from any interaction that would jeopardize their ability to convincingly convey the region as safe and civilized. When sending their children to private schools, elite parents sought to isolate their children from what they considered the less desirable populations of cities, and may have equally disdained and feared the culturally diverse populations of the Southwest.

Chance encounters with Native peoples outside of traditional tourist venues provided ranch school students a rare and memorable experience. Charles Pearce recalled his enthusiastic anticipation for a trip to Ojo Caliente, a hot spring up toward Taos, New Mexico. Apparently the spring had a long history of use by Native Americans even "way before Spanish times." According to the headmaster, a treaty stipulated that "for all time Indians could bathe at the hot spring with no charge." Pearce remembered "the whole idea of treaties and Indians was exciting . . . real Wild West stuff. We kids speculated about the possibilities all the way up." As the boys hollered and splashed around the spring, an Indian emerged from the locker wearing a headband. "We kids fell silent and simply stared. The Indian stared back. . . . Our Indian turned out to be a college graduate from San Juan pueblo. We laughed and quizzed him about Indian life. He laughed and asked what reform school we came from. We had a heck of a good time." Pearce wrote that "boys from L.A.R.S. had made many trips to the [San Ildefonso] pueblo—to see the dances and to buy Maria's famous pottery."[72]

Judson School students often ventured on horseback to the Pima Indian reservation in Scottsdale, but most schools in the Tucson area were located a far enough distance away from tribal communities that chance encounters were unlikely. During their trips to Sonora, Mexico, Arizona Desert School boys often took excursions to the Gulf of California to Puerto Libertad, a fishing village of Seri Indians. The students' interactions were memorable, but played into stereotypes and fears. The boys fished and caught yellowtail, mackerel, and cabrilla that they gave to the Seris. The Seris sold the fish to truckers for pesos and liquor. According to alumnus David Wilhelm, "Within hours after the fish had been sold, the Seris would get stinky drunk." On one occasion, they apparently were so drunk that they burnt down their village of thatch shacks. "They were so poor," remembered Wilhelm, "that they would sit around our campsite at our dinner time and eat any scraps that might be left over—including orange peels."[73]

Living Mexicans and Mexican Americans were almost equally absent from ranch school communities, although there was evidence that people of Mexican descent worked at ranch schools. For the most part, however, students experienced Mexican culture through school-sponsored trips to "Old Mexico," or unknowingly embraced elements of Spanish Colonial and Mexican heritage by wearing serapes and *chaparejos*, or "chaps," through the architectural designs of their schools, and by participating in rodeos (translation in English is "round-ups").[74] Wilhelm remembered riding with a Mexican cowboy during a trip to Sonora, Mexico. "Neither of us could speak the other person's language," and they rode the entire day in silence. This did not seem to bother him as he recalled "it was just like riding the range and being a cowboy on my horse." At night, the boys slept on cots on an open veranda and "were lulled to sleep by the guitar playing and singing of the enlisted men of the Mexican Army."[75]

In a listing of faculty and staff for the Los Alamos Ranch School, several people have Spanish surnames, including Manuel Diaz, employed as a master; Lupe Herrera, who was a cook; Adolfo Montoya, who was the head gardener; and Jose Montoya, employed as a cook's helper. Benceslado Gonzalez was the camp cook for the Los Alamos summer camp; his family homesteaded on a nearby mesa before the turn of the century. From the same account of Los Alamos written by one of the headmasters, Indian and Spanish-American houseboys appeared to be employed at the school.[76] In the 1931 edition of the *Rattler*, a yearbook-like publication of the Judson School that summarized the academic year, a combined profile for "Mariano and Katherine" was included at the end of the booklet, with a photograph of brother and sister who appeared to be of Hispanic descent. Mariano is referred to as "industrious" and "cheerful in his work." In the 1935 edition of *El Conquistador*, a publication similar to the *Rattler*, "Marianno and Katherine" are listed under faculty. Marianno kept the "school grounds and the corrals in ship shape condition" and his sister Katherine was a domestic servant. "In addition to his duties as a yard man," according to the author, "Amigo has hurled 'em over the plate in several of the old men's baseball games." The use of "amigo" was absent from the other descriptions of faculty and students, suggesting that the author's use of this term indicated Marianno's ethnicity in addition to a sense of informality lacking from the other profiles. In both publications, Marianno and Katherine are the only two who do not have surnames listed, and all of the other staff and faculty are referred to predominantly as "Mr."[77] The informal address and description indicate that ranch schools students learned to treat Mexican people much like recent immigrants in the Northeast and Midwest—as laborers and domestic servants.

Although Native Americans and Mexicans were consistently absent from these insular ranch school communities, their presence via art was an important part of the attempt to create a southwestern ambiance. Owners' dedication to incorporating southwestern motifs into every aspect of the schools' architectural and interior design further helped to "authenticate" the western experience that families expected, and distinguished them from the institution-like facilities of eastern prep schools. For example, the Palo Verde Ranch School for Boys featured a rustic interior scene complete with Indian rugs covering its floors.[78] Most of these interiors were a hodgepodge of art, crafts, motifs, and even costuming that inadequately reflected any one Native American community or Hispanic heritage. At the Jokake Inn, Sylvia Evans and her friend Lucy Cuthbert dressed their first staff member, a Mexican boy named Emmanuel Corral, "in a striking red velvet Indian jacket, white slacks, moccasins, concho belt, Indian jewelry and a red band around his head." As business increased, more "costumed Mexicans were added to the staff." This bizarre combination of cultural clothing worn by staff was also reflected in the decor of the Inn. According to Sylvia Evans, "we furnished and decorated the . . . adobe desert home in a blithe mix of cultures because 'it would be so colorful and pretty.' We persuaded Pima Indians to make all of our pottery; used Indian Kachina dolls, painted the walls with Mexican designs, hung red peppers on the patio, tie-dyed table cloths and napkins to use with painted tables and chairs from Mexico." The owners admitted that this style was not "typically Indian or typically Mexican but certainly it was typically 'Southwestern.'"[79] In other words, what constituted authenticity in terms of unique aesthetics and cultural design to the Apache, Navajo, Pima, and Mexican communities had little relevance. What mattered was what tourists thought "authentic" southwestern decor was supposed to look like. They were not looking for realistic displays of culture.

For all of its shortcomings, the southwestern and western interior décor popular in the interwar period conveyed the sense of informality that had become one of the region's most appealing attributes. The rustic interiors of ranch schools and affiliated resorts perpetuated an image of the West as less formal and pretentious in comparison to the Gilded Age interiors of the elite of New York City, Chicago, and Pittsburgh. Ranch school interiors were more homey and less conspicuously ornate, making them more American. By the late 1920s, Hollywood's nouveau riche created palace-like homes that included exotic foreign imagery or emulated the tastes of European aristocrats. Western film star Will Rogers, because of his mixed Cherokee and Scotch Irish ancestry, tended to identify "the frontier with the making of a mestizo republic rather than an Anglo-Saxon republic rooted in racial exclusion." His estate in the Santa Monica hills "was rooted in vernacular of a multicultural people" and "represented a vastly altered approach to consumerism and abundance." Indian and western traditions mixed to form an interior space in Rogers's home that lacked any air of conspicuous consumption, similar to the interior spaces of ranch schools.[80]

The exterior architecture of ranch schools, featured in photography amid wide open desert landscapes, was designed specifically to enhance each school's ability to convey a sense of western authenticity. The exterior architecture of most Tucson ranch school buildings was primarily of the Old Spanish style. This style of architecture did not become popular until the 1920s, when westerners gave up the idea of trying to "mold the history of the West into the nearest representation or equivalent of the East and of Europe that seemed possible with the materials at hand."[81] This transition in resort architecture from a European model to one that met turn-of-the-century tourist interests symbolized Americans' reliance on the Southwest landscape for a representation of national culture. As a result, "architects took their cues from the surrounding environment, rather than pretending it did not exist." In the new construction of buildings like Old Faithful Inn (1903–1904), El Tovar Hotel (1905), and Hopi House

Singing Cowboy Songs in the Patio
Southern Arizona School
Tucson, Arizona

The buildings of the Southern Arizona School for Boys, like most ranch schools, featured southwestern-style architecture. Arizona Historical Society, Main Photograph
Collection—PC 1000, image #15537.

(1905), "buffalo heads, Indian artifacts, and grand log palaces replaced the
French chandeliers, Italian fountains, and English manor houses of earlier decades."[82] The Mission style in California and the Pueblo style in the Southwest
received wide exposure from San Diego's Panama Pacific Exposition of 1915.
Intent on illuminating San Diego's past, exposition planners hired Bertram
Goodhue of New York, who had recently written a book on Spanish Colonial
architecture.[83]

By the time Arizona's ranch school developers hired architects to construct
schools, the Old Spanish style was the accepted norm of southwestern authenticity. The Arizona Desert School "like the old Mexican ranch houses" was
"built around a big patio," carefully planned "so that the sun reaches every
room."[84] Codirector and owner George Atchley personally constructed adobe
dormitories for Green Fields boarders.[85] The original Pueblo-style buildings of
the Southern Arizona School for Boys still exist on the campus of what is now

Fenster School, Tucson, 2002. The Fenster School, established in 1944, took over the campus of the former Southern Arizona School for Boys (SASB) in 1973 and has preserved the original adobe buildings. In the main room, visitors can view branding irons created by SASB students. Courtesy of author.

the Fenster School. "Hopi House," the main building at the Southern Arizona School for Boys, contained a "huge stone fireplace on one side and an immense plate glass window" opening onto a gorgeous view of Sabino Canyon. "This large living room has beamed ceilings on which Hopi Indian characters have been painted," and it boasted a "large number of Navajo Indian rugs and blankets and the Hopi Indian pottery which were selected from the Indian reservations in northern Arizona." Over the years, graduating seniors designed their own personal brand, which they sizzled onto wood ceiling beams.[86] The name "Hopi House" was familiar to early Grand Canyon visitors who stayed at this faux pueblo–inspired design by Mary Jane Colter, built in 1905. It too displayed Hopi and Navajo art and housed Hopi people who made crafts for tourists, while Indian laborers were invisible to visitors.[87]

Other ranch schools used authentic and replicated historic structures to convey the Old West. Valley School in Wyoming affirmed its legitimacy through its historic structures:

Few ranches still preserve the old sod-roofed cabins of the early days, but here you will find several of them,—built in the early 80's and creating an atmosphere of "hominess" and informality that only time can produce. They are the original homestead cabins of Jim and "Buckskin Jenny" McLaughlin, built of huge cottonwood and fir logs, hewed out by hand, and the keystone around which the ranch has grown in the past sixty years.[88]

Perhaps reflecting the growing national interest in Western movies, the Orme School in Mayer built its own frontier town. "Main Street, Orme School, U.S.A." featured building facades reminiscent of Tombstone, Jerome, and many other Western ghost towns. A photograph showed a horse hitched to a post and surrounded by four lounging Orme students. The buildings in the background housed the senior shack, a general store, barbershop, and post office. "It's also the spot for pausing for a cold drink after a ride," the caption assured potential students.[89]

Affiliation with an actual ranch enhanced the sense of authenticity. Historically, ranching in the West involved livestock, preferably cattle, wrangled by cowboys on horseback. Without livestock, a ranch was simply a farm, and since agricultural activities took place in every region of the country, it lacked the mystique of western cattle ranching. Real cowboys herded cattle—they did not farm alfalfa, even though in the twentieth century, more westerners earned their living in agriculture than in cattle. Cowboys had transformed into ranchers by the interwar period but "cowboy myth reinforced the masculine occupational identity of raising beef even as the reality shifted from nomadic all-male herders to men and women together on family ranches."[90] Even in the absence of actual cattle and/or livestock, ranch school owners hired cowboy ranchers to care for students' horses in an attempt to provide an "authentic" experience that reaffirmed what easterners expected of the West. Many schools were not affiliated with working ranches, but still touted their ability to offer a western experience through their other amenities and activities. For example, although Judson School for Boys was not housed on an actual ranch, it highlighted its proximity to many great cattle ranches, where students could develop a natural interest "in all rodeos and cowboy sports."[91]

The real-life experiences of cattle ranchers demonstrated the economic difficulties of providing an "authentic" western ranch experience. Despite the romantic images of the cattle industry projected by dime novels and popular

Orme School, Mayer, Arizona, 2002. The architecture of the Orme school resembled a town in the Old West. These historic buildings still remain, reminding current students of the school's connection to the past. Courtesy of author.

literature, western cattle growers were saddled with fluctuating prices, shortages of credit, animal diseases, and harsh weather that could seriously affect their livelihood. The postwar depression of the early 1920s devastated southwestern cattlemen. The price for cattle dropped from $14.50 per hundredweight in 1918 to $6.00 per hundredweight in 1922 while overhead and expenses remained the same. Between 1919 and 1925, thousands of cattle ranchers were forced to sell their stock, land, and equipment. Increasingly, western cattlemen turned to the federal government for help. High on its list of priorities, the National Cattlemen's Association wanted new grazing policies and access to federal lands through leases. Until the passage of the Taylor Grazing Act in 1934, Congress was unresponsive to the latter demand, although many ranchers continued to graze animals on federal lands with little government retribution.[92] It was no coincidence then that so many eastern and midwestern entrepreneurs established dude ranches and ranch schools in the late 1920s.

Ranch schools that had connections to an actual ranch highlighted this important western attribute in their promotional literature. The Southern Arizona

School for Boys in Tucson occupied historic ranch land rumored to have been part of a large Spanish land grant. Thomas Gonzales owned a ranch on the land in the early part of the century and then sold it in 1916 to pioneer rancher Charles DeBaud. When DeBaud in turn sold it in the early 1930s, the land was divided, and part of it became the Southern Arizona School for Boys while another portion became the famous Double U Guest Ranch where the movies *Arizona* and *Billy the Kid* were filmed.[93] Green Fields Preparatory School for Boys, established in 1933, was located on the Circle Double A Ranch, nine miles from Tucson. "Double A" stood for George and Rubie Atchley, who purchased the property and established the elite boarding school. Alfalfa grew on the grounds, inspiring Rubie Atchley to name the school Green Fields. A 1940 Valley Ranch School promotional booklet asserted its authenticity by stating "the ranch is a business concern that has been operating as a legitimate hay, grain, and stock ranch for almost sixty years."[94]

The Foxboro Ranch School grew out of an effort to save the Latham cattle ranch from financial ruin. In 1922, Frederick Fox purchased the struggling ranch one hundred miles north of Phoenix, range rights, and cattle for $2,000 cash. Fox, who had moved to Arizona from New York seeking a cure for his asthma, knew nothing about cattle ranching. He hired veteran rancher Frank Gyberg to manage operations and returned to New York to resume his business. During his four-year absence, cattle prices continued to slump. Fox returned in 1926 with the idea of turning the ranch into a school for boys. He envisioned "a school without books," dedicated to improving the bodies as well as the minds of his students. Foxboro opened for business in the summer of 1927. Because of its affiliation with an actual working ranch, Foxboro could claim that "there is nothing artificial or 'put on' in and about Foxboro Ranches. It is a consolidation of a number of mountain and valley ranches."[95]

The Fresnal Ranch School in Tucson advertised the opportunity for boys "to take part in all of the activities which keep cowboys busy in this country—riding fence lines, hunting for young calves and colts, driving the herd at roundups, throwing, tying down, and branding calves in the corral . . . on one of the largest ranches in the West."[96] Some Arizona Desert School boys developed an interest in "bee culture, the cactus honey of Arizona being justly famed." This same school proclaimed that it was "a real ranch, and consequently affords a wide range of constructive interests." In addition to the traditional cowboy ranch activities, these boys also had the "opportunity to learn about chicken and horse raising." The school owned a small herd of beef cattle that grazed nearby, but nothing indicates that boys had much involvement with this aspect of the ranch.[97] At the Evans School in Mesa, boys cleaned out the stables and performed other chores. Meanwhile, Evans purchased 420 acres of land in Tucson, where he built corrals, barns, and shops. He fenced off 250 acres of pasture for cattle, sheep, hogs, milk cows, and turkeys. Evans took an active proprietary interest in the ranch operations, hoping to make the school as self-sufficient as possible. By 1923 he was somewhat successful in providing enough meat and milk to feed students and staff. He raised barley and alfalfa on a dozen large fields irrigated by several wells and a spring that rose at the upper end of the ranch.[98]

The founding of the Los Alamos Ranch School in 1917 illustrates both the close connection between ranch schools and dude ranches as well as the complex realities of combining ranch activities with a preparatory school. Ashley Pond came west as a boy to be reinvigorated by the thin, fresh air of New Mexico, as had many others suffering from lung diseases. Pond "lived among cowboys working on ranches, fell in love with horses as well as the beauty and ruggedness of the landscape, and concluded that this was the sort of life that would equip a boy to take on the responsibilities of manhood." His first attempt to found a boys' school was in 1904, near Watrous, New Mexico, but his vision for the school was washed away in a flood. Supported by automobile manufacturers from his hometown of Detroit, Pond subsequently founded a dude ranch, the Pajarito Club, in Pajarito Canyon on the eve of World War I.

Pond finally realized his dream of instituting a ranch school when he purchased a nearby homestead owned by his ranch manager, H. H. Brooks. For the first two years, the school operated as a sort of combination cattle and guest ranch, with tutoring and camping expeditions on the side. An article in the *Santa Fe New Mexican* on June 28, 1917, described Los Alamos ranch as

one of the completest and most up-to-date practical farming plants in New Mexico . . . 400 acres growing beans, corn, oats, alfalfa, barley, and other crops . . . a large irrigated garden supplying plenty of fresh vegetables . . . half a dozen cows keeping the milk room well-stocked with milk, buttermilk, butter and cheese . . . a crop of 100 calves expected . . . pens full of litters of young pigs . . . large, modern barns, corrals, three or four cottages . . . horses for the boys to ride, cattle they may learn to rope, cliff dwellings to explore, mountains to climb, fish to catch eight miles away just across the divide.[99]

The year 1918–1919 turned out to be disastrous for the school's cattle ranching operations. Albert J. (A. J.) Connell, hired by Pond to run the school, described the winter as "the worst in history in this part of the country according to government records and the oldest Indians. . . . We have lost over 10% of our cattle because snow has covered our winter range since October. We have had to buy hay at frightful prices to save what we could of our herd." Not long after this experience, Connell decided that the school should take priority over ranching operations and felt great relief when the cattle were sold in 1922. Connell and Pond also found that inexperienced boys were a handicap rather than a help when it came to the work involved in the care of livestock.[100]

The most authentic of the ranch schools in the sense that it provided children with a working ranch experience was the Orme School. At least one young author realized the value of attending a school at a "real" ranch. In describing the Circle V Bar Ranch for the 1939–1940 yearbook, Sherman Bloomer made the distinction that "it is not a dude ranch. It is a cow ranch and a school."[101] The school began in 1929 when founders Charles and Minna Orme decided to educate their children at home rather than transporting them twelve miles daily to a school in Mayer. The county offered $10 per student each month in place of a transportation allowance to pay the teacher's salary, and in exchange the Ormes agreed to provide room and board. One year after establishment, it became known as the Orme Ranch School. In the 1930s, Orme students came from several sources. They were children from neighboring ranches, the children of the Ormes' friends and relatives, and asthmatic children from the East. From the establishment of the school through its duration as a working ranch, students were required to pitch in with ranch chores that included milking, gathering eggs, picking currants, washing windows, and maintaining the ranch vehicles and machinery. During the Depression, everyone, including cowboys, teachers, and students, worked in the carrot patch after school. The Ormes continued to run ranching operations along with the school until the two business ventures separated in 1962.[102]

Whether it was a working ranch or not, every ranch school employed an "authentic" cowboy who supervised actual ranch operations, taught roping, led horseback-riding trips, and/or implemented rodeo performances. In reality, the abandonment of open-range grazing after the hard winter of 1886–1887 made the nomadic cowboy obsolete, an icon of the Old West. Ranch school owners, however, found men willing to step into the role of cowboy and perpetuate the idyllic western image. After he founded the Evans School, H. David Evans bought Tex Barclay's 3-R Ranch at the base of the Superstition Mountains and hired ranch foreman Slim Rucker as a faculty member. Rucker doctored horses, hauled hay, cooked chili for camping trips, and ran the work squads.[103] The Jokake School employed three cowboys to manage the stables and enabled each girl to have her own horse.[104] Some ranch school alumni seemed to remember the cowboys employed at their school more so than the majority of their teachers. Jean Dunn Porter who attended Hacienda del Sol described the school's wrangler, Jack, as "a leathery old soul from the West; a John Wayne type."[105] Orme student Diane Frazier provided a description of Mr. Null, who was a cowboy at the school, for the 1939–1940 Orme School yearbook:

At the ranch we have an old cowboy, a real cowboy you know, not one of the kind you find in a magazine. He is around eighty and still goin' strong. The first time you are likely to see him is when he is riding from the east or west pastures. You rub your eyes and look again. He looks as if he and Sweetheart, his horse, had stepped down from a pedestal in a park in Phoenix. He looks like a statue cast to honor the cowboy of yesterday, the only difference is that he is a living one. He goes around in his old pants and jacket, wide brimmed hat, and a pair of brown boots.[106]

Recreational activities, similar to those of dude ranches, were further essential to promoting a ranch school as uniquely western. In comparison to eastern preparatory schools, sports and weekend outings were geared toward individuals or small groups and patterned on the natural activity of cowboys, with the goal of cultivating self-reliance. Horses epitomized the Old West and horseback riding was an important aspect of the ranch school experience. "Life on a cattle ranch means life in the saddle," the Orme School explained to potential summer camp students.[107] In her analysis of Westerns, Jane Tompkins found that "there are certain things you take for granted . . . sage-dotted plains, the buttes, the town with its false fronts, sandy main street, saloon, livery stable, cowboys in jeans and ten gallon hats. And horses: in town tied to the hitching rail, being ridden by a single rider outlined against the sky. . . . In the background, in the foreground, in the margins, at the center, horses are on the screen constantly, seen in every conceivable attitude." Tompkins noticed that the gradual appearance of horses, "first in dime novels, then in major best-sellers and in films at the beginning of the twentieth century coincides with the disappearance of horses from daily life." Horses symbolized American nostalgia for a rural past before cars, telephones, and electricity.[108]

Horses were a significant and exclusive asset of western ranch schools that gave children the opportunity to participate in rodeos and play competitive polo.[109] Because equestrian experience was relatively unique to western ranch schools, the idea that horses belonged to the West was further transfixed in the minds of children and young adults—especially those who had attended both a traditional preparatory school and a ranch school. Sherman Thacher believed that "boys learn more from their horses than from their teachers," as they provided a natural form of manual training. Grooming, feeding, and exercising horses instilled responsibility. On the first day of his arrival at the Evans School, Jack Heinz wrote his parents that he "didn't do much except unpack and get settled altho' I did spend considerable time trying to find a decent horse" and found one that "handles well and won't die in his tracks." He explained to his parents that "the boy who owned him last year does not want to sell him even tho' he is no longer at the school so he wants to rent him. He wants no money for the rent so that all I have to worry about is feeding and the school pays for that so——! Not a penny does it cost me, and if I discover a better one later on I can buy him and let this one go." In subsequent letters Jack told his parents that he named his horse "Sapolio, nicknamed 'Sap'—my horse and I, well I guess!"[110]

Ranch school students rode horses on camping trips, participated in rodeos, and wrangled cattle on horseback. "Much of the active ranch life" at Foxboro was centered "round the horse and rider," and "the opportunity to see and take part in the interesting phases of the cattle business is offered during the roundups and other work," the school's promotional literature announced. Rancher Frank Gyberg, who had served in a cavalry unit during World War I, loved to train campers in cavalry maneuvers. Foxboro campers, however, preferred rounding up cattle and branding colts. A brochure asserted that "each guest is given a horse for his very own; between the two there grows a bond of fellowship which furnishes a pleasant memory for all time."[111] Even younger students at the Old Pueblo School made horseback excursions in the Catalina foothills every Wednesday and Friday and learned from an expert cowhand how to handle a horse.[112] Horses were incorporated into the Los Alamos Ranch School graduation ceremony. The ten students in the 1938 graduating class "came riding two by two from the corrals" and "rode straight and tall, proud as only boys can be." After dismounting from the horses, the western pageantry of the graduation ceremony continued when the graduates marched to the steady solemn beat of an Indian drum.[113]

Camping trips on horseback were an integral part of the ranch school experience. Judson boys were encouraged to take weekend-long camping trips into the nearby mountains. Older boys, with camping experience, planned and carried out short unsupervised trips to the McDowell Mountains, Indian Ruins, cattle ranches, and irrigation and diversion dams.[114] At Palo Verde Ranch School, "week-end camping trips are an outstanding feature of the School's outdoor life. . . . This vast area of desert and mountain country, broken by arroyos, sandy washes, and deep canyons, is admirable for camping."[115] Students at the Evans School in Mesa developed skills in riding, mule packing, and camping. Organized camping trips included a horseback trip over the entire northern portion of the state, and other field trips that centered on archaeological sites and Indian reservations. Because Flagstaff was still in 1907 the only place between Denver and the West Coast where students could take college entrance exams, Evans bought a camp on the outskirts of town and for six weeks prepared students for this important test. Instead of traveling by automobile to the study site, students journeyed by horseback for ten days.

Public displays of horsemanship, such as the rodeo, became symbolic of what westerners believed eastern tourists expected from the West and were an important event in the lives of ranch school students. By the 1920s, "the rodeo seemed to be in many a Western town only the most climactic feature of a system of pageantry in which not only the 'cowboys' but the whole population acted." Beginning in 1925, the citizens of Wicksburg, Arizona, reenacted the Days of '49, while in Tombstone, the Helldorado celebration "provided tourists with a basically pulp novel and movie version of the wild West of the 1880s, complete with stagecoach holdups, lynchings, and dances." Participation in this western public ritual immersed ranch school students in the past and present of the American West. Historical pageantry as a form of civic celebration reached its high point during the Progressive Era, according to historian David Glassberg. After World War I, historical pageantry became "more closely associated with antimodernism and the use of tradition as a bulwark against modernity." This sort of historical imagery was an essential element for communities to forge a sense of identity and common history.[116]

Western rodeos were a means of community participation for tourists, and every Arizona ranch school used rodeos to immerse students in the Old West. Arizona's ranch schools and dude ranches developed in conjunction with an antimodernist trend in America, and their pageantry reflected nostalgia for the Old West. The students at the Orme School built their own rodeo arena in 1950, the year the Orme Ranch Roping Association was founded. Cecil W. "Doc" Pardee, a charismatic rodeo contestant, assisted with staging a rodeo for Foxboro campers.[117] Students at the Arizona Desert School hosted a public rodeo each year to display their horsemanship skills. In 1934, approximately 250 Tucsonans observed students participating in a quadrille, a pony express race, straight rails, polo, a junior equipment race, pig sticking, and jumping.[118] Even the girls' schools emphasized horseback riding and public displays of horsemanship. Hacienda del Sol offered daily horseback riding in the afternoons, and like their male counterparts, girls rode in the annual Rodeo de Los Vaqueros parade. An author for the 1939 Jokake School for Girls yearbook wrote that "every Monday, Wednesday, and Friday a small group of bantering girls in gay shirts and kerchiefs may be seen eagerly hurrying down to the stables at Jokake." One hour was spent working on the drill, and during the second hour, the girls rode in the desert. The Jokake drill team performed at the Arizona State Horse Show and hosted its own meet at the school.[119]

The Evans School's Vaquero Cup Contest was an interesting display of horsemanship that modified actual ranch activity for the purpose of performance and competition. Each spring, Mrs. C. W. Dempster of Chicago presented the cup in memory of her son, Wesley. According to a student account in the 1923 issue of the *Cactus Needle*, "The prettiest event of past contests—the jumping on and off a horse while at a lope—has been discontinued for the simple reason that the horses are cow-horses and have been trained to stop short, when the rider jumps off." In its place the school devised a pack race that the students found "most amusing." Each contestant started from inside his sleeping bag and had to get up, put on his hat and boots, saddle and bridle his horse, pack his bedding on a second horse with an assistant to help in throwing up a stirrup hitch. "He must then race over a distance, determined by the judges, and finish with pack, horse, and hat—not to mention himself, in good shape."[120]

Judson School for Boys, Paradise Valley, Arizona. Courtesy of David C. Lincoln, Phoenix.

In addition to western riding, eastern riding and polo were included in school activities, emphasizing the supreme importance of horses at ranch schools and the curious blending of an elite cultural tradition with that of the mythic Old West. The Arizona Desert School, the Evans School, Palo Verde Ranch School, Judson, and Southern Arizona School for Boys practiced polo in preparation for interscholastic ranch school competitions. Judson School offered polo, in addition to tennis, baseball, basketball, croquet, and golf. Polo was the chief competitive sport at the Southern Arizona School for Boys, where in 1934 the owners added a regulation-sized polo field to the campus.[121] The Evans School in Mesa introduced polo in 1931, along with tennis, swimming, and skeet shooting. This was an important shift from the school's previous emphasis on solitary camping trips.[122] Headmaster Jarvie devoted an entire chapel service at the Valley Ranch School to the history and theory of polo, much to Philip Cummings's delight. He noted in his journal, "I am learning much about polo, and yet have no ability or shrewdness at the game. The aim of this practice is to get used to hitting the ball and not the horse, as the latter move on the live quadruped might have disastrous consequences."[123]

Polo players at the Arizona Desert School in Tucson in the mid-1930s. Left to right: John Donaldson, Henry Thompson, David C. Wilhelm, William Havemeyer. Courtesy of David C. Wilhelm, Denver, Colorado.

Polo in general was dangerous and the environmental conditions of the dry desert landscape made it more so. The Arizona Desert School polo field was a "dirt field that had a slope from north to south, covered with stones, and not quite rectangular in shape." Former student David Wilhelm explained, "It was a little tough on our ponies' legs and the dust was a little tough on the players' lungs." Boys from the Arizona Desert School took camping trips to the Kibbey Ranch in Sonora, Mexico, and "played polo with and against the Mexican army team . . . on a dirt skin field that was so dusty you almost had to wear goggles to keep the dirt out of your eyes." Mr. Kibbey, the ranch owner, died during a game, when his horse and another collided, pinning him under his horse. This tragic event occurred right in front of Wilhelm, but did not deter his interest. At the age of 14, he was rated by the United States Polo Association at "one goal." This was a rare accomplishment for someone his age.[124]

Polo was a natural sport for ranch schools because it relied on horses that were already essential to ranch life. British remittance men, younger sons of nobility who received an allowance, introduced polo to southeast Montana and northeast Wyoming in the late nineteenth century. Traditionally, polo served to bond members of an elite subgroup; however, Michael A. Amundson found that in Wyoming, polo players consisted of "a curious blend of expatriates" and locals. A New York publisher visiting England in the 1870s took note of the game, which had been introduced to British cavalrymen stationed in India. From its introduction to Americans, "it was associated with the wealthy." By 1902, U.S. cavalrymen throughout the West played the sport at various military forts. Owen Wister wrote about his experience of attempting to learn the sport in Colorado Springs and raised the question as to "whether western polo was as class conscious as the eastern game."[125] The Arizona Polo Association, organized in December 1924, spearheaded the La Fiesta de los Vaqueros, hoping that it "would rank with the Calgary Stampede, Pendleton Round-Up, and Cheyenne Frontier Days as a major western rodeo event."[126] As equestrian sports, polo and rodeo were popular among Tucson ranch owners until the 1930s, when polo lost favor. The University of Arizona had a polo team from 1919 until 1933 and played 137 matches during this period. One historian suggests that "polo, unlike rodeo, was a non-work related leisure sport and was deemed unsuitable by Tuscsonans as both spectator and participant recreation."[127]

In comparing the activities of southwestern ranch schools to those of the Select Sixteen, it becomes apparent that ranch schools chose activities that defined them as western while at the same time meeting the universal aims of private school education. Schools like Groton, Phillips Exeter, Andover, St. Paul's, and other elite New England institutions toughened boys' character through contact sports like football, boxing, and ice hockey. Rowing was popular because it required strength, endurance, and cooperation among peers. Football especially "was a cure for aristocratic malaise."[128] Robert Kennedy was quoted as stating, "except for war, there is nothing in American life which trains a boy better for life than football." The primary goal of these activities was to prepare boys for a strenuous life as political leaders. They "were parts of the process whereby boys were enjoined by headmasters not to be satisfied with 'being' but to strive to 'do' and 'become.'"[129] In other words, through sports competition, boys learned the rituals of the self-made man despite their aristocratic heritage.

Ranch schools immersed boys in the strenuous life as well, but rather than emphasize football, ice hockey, boxing, or rowing, boys and young men rode horses, played polo, wrangled cattle, and camped outdoors. At the Fresnal Ranch School in Tucson, its brochure made it clear that "horseback riding and rifle practice are the main sports of the day, and impromptu football or baseball is organized among the boys."[130] With the exception of the Los Alamos Ranch School and Valley Ranch School, ice hockey was not an option because of most ranch schools' location in the Arizona desert. Boys at Los Alamos played football, but usually not in the same competitive fashion as the New England schools. The distance between potential competing schools was too great, and there may not have been enough students of the same age to form a viable team. By the fall of 1940, Los Alamos had reached its peak enrollment of forty-seven boys all aged twelve to eighteen, more students within a more defined age bracket than in any of Arizona's ranch schools. Polo thrived at ranch schools because of its emphasis on the horse, its compatibility with the small number of students at ranch schools, and its appeal among the elite.

In addition to immersing students in a constructed version of the Old West, ranch schools encouraged each student to be an active participant rather than a spectator. Jack Heinz's letters to his parents from Choate described going to football games, but he never mentioned participating in any recreational activities. His immense enthusiasm for finding a horse upon his first day at the Evans School and the positive tone of his letters reflected what many men-in-the-making must have experienced upon the discovery that ranch schools emphasized sports and recreational activities that were available to all. David Wilhelm had a similar experience in his transition to Phillips Andover Academy. He tried out for club football but was "slow and small" and "needed a horse." Since he could not skate and did not want to swim in the winter, his only choice was wrestling, which turned out to be "the worst sport I have ever had the privilege to compete in." In the spring he went out for tennis and was more successful.[131]

Rather than replicate the character-building sports activities of the New England preparatory schools, ranch school owners provided the same benefits using the unique and distinctive cultural and geographic benefits of the American Southwest. In order to appeal to parents, ranch schools had to assure them that the more violent and uncivilized aspects of the Old West were under control, but at the same time they emphasized that the environment that had shaped the character of pioneers still existed. The cultural experience of ranch school students evolved out of the tourism industry of the 1920s and was purposefully crafted to imitate what easterners expected of the Old West. Much like dude ranches, the built environment of ranch schools reflected a new aesthetic for southwestern architecture that blended the contemporary and historic artistry of indigenous people, hunting lodge interiors, and Spanish Colonial design. Western activities that revolved around horses helped to provide a sense of authenticity at the same time they provided boys the opportunity for exploration, largely on their own, with the intent that this would foster "self-reliance" and other character traits associated with the "strenuous life" that parents and educators worried had been lost on modern youth.

CHAPTER 4

The West as Moral Space
Character, Citizenship, and Masculinity

RANCH SCHOOLS PROMISED TO MAKE MEN OUT OF BOYS BY IMMERSING them in the masculine environment of the Old West and instilling the character traits associated with the gentleman cowboy. Headmasters felt that organized religion and the home had failed boys in their task to provide moral instruction, and responded by focusing on the development of Christian character through masculine virtues in the crucial years when boys prepared for college. In the interwar period, masculinity and character were intricately linked, and in many cases, they were one and the same. The West was well equipped to cultivate masculinity because "no place has been so consistently identified with maleness—as the region imagined as the American West."[1] Overnight camping trips, Spartan living, and physical tests enabled boys to prove their manhood, bravery, and self-reliance as they prepared for their roles as future leaders and citizens. Allowed to experience a form of constructed savagery through hunting, using firearms, and roughing it in the great outdoors, boys relived the evolution of American civilization by reenacting the experiences of pioneers. As a result, at ranch schools headmasters and boys accepted a curious blend of civilized Christian virtue and savagery as an ideal means of character development. One Judson School student aptly conveyed this blending of manners and ruggedness and the value of his ranch school experience in a fictitious letter to a potential parent: "This school would be the place for that offspring of yours. It would make a man out of him, sure. . . . By the end of the year their education has included everything from becoming real cowboys to holding tea-cups."[2] Through an acceptance of masculinity as equal to moral virtue, ranch schools developed the popular conception of the West as moral space.

In the absence of the influence of church, Stearns believed that private schools and headmasters must fill this void if modern youth were to exhibit the character traits that had built Western civilization, and he dedicated a chapter of *The Challenge of Youth* to addressing the failure of church and home to instill morals and character in boys. "For centuries religion has exercised its potent influence on youth, checking baser impulse, restraining from the evil and unworthy deed, strengthening in the moment of temptation, and always calling into expression and fuller control the best and noblest in human character," Stearns reflected, arguing that modern youth was not "irreligious," but rather unresponsive to "cold dogma and forbidding creed." "To-day that influence has been sadly undermined," according to Stearns, who believed that "in the lives of our youth" religion "has ceased almost wholly to exist" and "has been steadily relegated to the scrap-heaps of the past."[3] Others made similar observations and launched a movement for character education in public and private schools to compensate for the failings of Church and home to instill moral instruction.

Character education as a movement was difficult to define, so instead experts created lists of behaviors, traits, and moral codes in an effort to describe the outcomes educators should expect. Robert Danforth Cole lumped manliness, Christian character, loyalty, integrity, courage, nobility, moral culture, piety, virtue, truthfulness, unselfishness, honesty, responsibility, and worthy purpose under the rubric of character. Boys demonstrated character through obedience, cleanliness of life, good habits, purity of thought, acceptance of responsibility, self-control, and self-reliance. In 1917, William Hutchins outlined the following "ten laws of right living" in the "Children's Morality Code": self-control, good health, kindness, sportsmanship, self-reliance, duty, reliability, truth, good workmanship, and teamwork.[4] Headmaster and owner George Judson directly linked character, citizenship, and masculinity in an editorial for the 1938 Judson School for Boys yearbook:

In this period of rapid social and political changes, or we might say, this period of chaotic conditions, there certainly is a need for men of strong bodies and active minds. Men of clear thinking and unselfish purpose have many difficult problems to solve in our present civilization. . . . The primary purpose of this school has always been the development of our boys into men of responsibility and leadership. . . . Let us dedicate this school to a future of even more useful service in developing a finer type of manhood.[5]

In stating that the chief aim of character education was to turn "boys into men of responsibility and leadership" by equipping boys with a "finer type of manhood," Judson spoke directly to the needs of elite youth in the interwar period by linking character and masculinity.

In the late nineteenth and early twentieth centuries, men proved their masculinity and rights to citizenship through military service, sports, or self-reliance in the American West or a similar rugged environment. Historian Kristin Hoganson argues that an important motivation for the Spanish-American War and subsequent Philippine-American War resulted from a void felt by a generation too young to fight in the Civil War, who needed some way to prove their manhood in order to gain political legitimacy. Jingoists and imperialists believed that belligerent overseas policy was a means of reinvigorating American men through war, to reinstill "manly character supposedly exemplified by soldiers." In aiding Cuban fighters, American men would learn to be less self-interested, a recent character flaw noted in upper-class men that was the result of materialism and wealth. Support for war or actual military service helped wealthy men from the Northeast overcome the perception that they "put comfort above national honor" and that a life of luxury "debased their manly character."[6]

World War I gave the following generation the chance for masculine redemption, but the negative physical and psychological effects detracted from its valor. Instead of a proving ground for manly courage, it was "a site for the technological ferocity of military machinery." By the interwar period, commercialism and corruption took sportsmanship out of sports. In essence, the same technological and commercial forces that caused men to seek military action and sports as a means of filling a void, negated them. Although the frontier had vanished in 1890, according to Frederick Jackson Turner, it was reinvented as simply "the outdoors"—America's last open space and proving ground for American manhood. Novelist Arthur Train predicted in his 1918 description of a family impacted by the war that "there will be a new movement toward the ever-vanishing frontier, a setting westward in search for wider ranges, for life in the open-air."[7] Ranch schools resurrected enough of the Old West to argue that boys still had the opportunity to reenact events and develop the skills that had made men who traveled West masculine. As war proved to be an unpredictable means of achieving masculine virtue, ranch schools provided a viable option for boys whose parents could afford the experience.

In his 1938 editorial, Judson advanced the proposition that masculine men from the elite classes would be the saviors of civilization as national leaders. Decades earlier Theodore Roosevelt argued this very same point, advocating that privileged boys needed to be cultivated into leaders of civic affairs in order to assure the progress of the nation. Roosevelt epitomized the combination of Victorian manliness with the notion of twentieth-century masculinity and depicted ranchers, like himself, as possessing character traits of personal bravery, hardihood, and self-reliance while also embodying the "virtues of upright civilized manliness" by being shrewd, thrifty, and patient.[8] By sending boys west, parents immersed them in an environment that allowed them to experience the influences that had transformed Theodore Roosevelt from an urban, pampered, effeminate easterner into the quintessential male role model of the turn of the century.

Ranch schools incorporated several principles of social Darwinist thought into the myth of the West to construct an experience that allowed ranch school students to experience "savagery" with the intent of making men out of boys in order to become eligible for citizenship rights exclusive to their class. G. Stanley Hall (1844–1924), educator, psychologist, and founder of Clark University, was the first to identify adolescence as a distinct phase of one's life and articulate a solution to the fear that overcivilization was endangering American manhood. Applying social Darwinist ideas to his pedagogical philosophy, he believed education was the key to its revitalization. To succeed, education needed to cater to an individual's natural abilities, which Hall largely defined by evolutionary thought, and its subsequent constructs of race and gender. Parents and educators needed to encourage Anglo-Saxon boys to explore savagery in order to "develop the strength to be both virile and civilized as men." Hall's method rested on his theory of recapitulation, the belief that by re-creating millions of years of evolution in one's lifetime by allowing boys to experience ancestral savagery before they entered adulthood, or the civilized self, boys would become immune from civilization's effeminizing tendencies.[9] In other words, he found a way that men could be both their inherent savage selves (in adolescence) and become the rightful inheritors of society's privileged position as the civilized race. Only middle- and upper-class Anglo-Saxon males were at risk of overcivilization. Other economic and racial groups had not reached the same level on the evolutionary scale as had America's native-born Anglo-Saxon elite and were, therefore, exempt from these problems. Although many attacked or misunderstood Hall, Theodore Roosevelt demonstrated his support for him in a letter agreeing that "the barbarian virtues" could keep civilized boys from becoming effeminate "milksops": "Over-sentimentality, over-softness, in fact washiness and mushiness are the great dangers of this age and of this people. Unless we keep the barbarian virtues, gaining the civilized ones will be of little avail."[10]

Frederick Jackson Turner's "Frontier Thesis" and Hall's recapitulation theory are similar in linking the development of masculine traits in boys to the evolution of American character in the West. Turner argued that the frontier was "the meeting point between savagery and civilization." The American frontier enabled society to return to primitive conditions and evolve into something distinctly American.[11] Just as boys carried with them the barbarian experiences of their youth as adults, Turner argued that frontier society "loses its primitive conditions, and assimilates itself to the type of the older social conditions of the East; but it bears within it enduring and distinguishing survivals of its frontier experience."[12] This evolutionary process created the American character, just as Hall's recapitulation theory produced masculine men. Both relied on immersion in a primitive environment to produce a superior form of civilization.

The popularity of *Tarzan of the Apes* illustrates how masculinity, race, and class were inextricably linked in the American mind. The story of Tarzan also illuminates how assumptions about race, class, and masculinity helped to popularize western ranch schools. Edgar Rice Burroughs's *Tarzan* first appeared as a serial in 1912. It was published as a book in 1914 and sold 750,000 copies by 1934. "Tarzan's perfect masculinity" stemmed from two factors: "his white racial supremacy, inherited from his civilized Anglo-Saxon parents, and his savage jungle childhood with primitive apes. . . . Tarzan's civilized 'blood,' combined with his savage training," made him invincible.[13] Tarzan was not only white, but the son of highly bred, intelligent nobility. To further elevate Tarzan's masculinity, Burroughs created characters who epitomized the character flaws of overcivilized men. William Cecil Clayton, Tarzan's first cousin who shared his bloodline but not his masculinity, represented the intellectual dandy Tarzan could have become had he not been raised by apes.[14] Tarzan exemplified the beneficial predictions of G. Stanley Hall's recapitulation theory. This popular story also illustrated the importance of place to the formation of masculinity. Burroughs constructed Africa as a savage place where a white male could prove his superior manhood by reliving the primitive, masculine life of his most distant revolutionary forefathers. After his exploits in the West, Roosevelt used his hunting trips in Africa to enhance his masculine image.

The masculinity lessons implied in the story of Tarzan are present in the narrative of western ranch schools. If one were to substitute the name "Vanderbilt" or "McCormick" for "Greystoke," and "Arizona" for "Africa," the stories are similar. In theory, Anglo-Saxon, upper-class parents could create ideal masculine men by sending boys into the desert to experience a constructed primitive savagery, as advocated by Hall. This sort of primitive savagery, combined with heredity, could potentially produce a superior male, like Tarzan, who was physically capable of overcoming other races, but whose genetics ensured that he remained "civilized." Not only did the theories make sense to the early twentieth-century public, but the making of a masculine hero in Theodore Roosevelt was living proof. Roosevelt personally endorsed these schools by sending his son and nephew to the Evans Ranch School in Mesa. Photos of Roosevelt appeared in a Foxboro School brochure with a quote from his biography that attested to the benefits of ranch life. The brochure explained the summer ranch school's ability to offer "to boys of college and prep school age and their friends and relatives the sort of experience which fits them for the more serious business of winter months, such as prepared Theodore Roosevelt for the strenuous political career known to every American."[15]

By invoking the mythic West to achieve the aims of character education, ranch schools extended the idea of the American West as moral space. In *The Mythic West*, historian Robert Athearn explained that the winning of the West was based on an idea that the moral toughness of individuals prevailed in the unknown wilderness. Descended from hearty Anglo-Saxon stock, western immigrants brought with them desirable inherited character traits and a disdain for the corruption of big business, urban government, immigrant masses, and everything else that endangered American values. The West was a proving ground, a sort of real-life experiment of the survival of the fittest. Athearn stated that "this quality of natural superiority, nurtured in the unpolluted atmosphere of virgin land, was regarded by some observers as part of a distillation process that had produced the American spirit, which their eyes saw as true Americanization." The American West was "the best hope, because that part of the nation contained the last authentic haunts of the original American ideals, the distinctively American social philosophy." Athearn suggests "one characteristic that strikes all newcomers to the West is that of space and mass, and invariably it has some effect upon them." This vast space is what "molded the character" of westerners, and some claimed it was what made them "broadminded."[16]

Frontiersmen, according to Frederick Jackson Turner, personified democracy, individualism, freedom, coarseness, strength, acuteness, ingeniousness, materialism, exuberance, and optimism. The Turner thesis supported the idea of the West as moral space by arguing that the primitive environmental circumstances that American pioneers had to overcome resulted in the creation of the democratic ideal. At first, the "wilderness masters the colonist. . . . He must accept the conditions which it furnishes, or perish. . . . Little by little he transforms the wilderness, but the outcome is not the old Europe. . . . The fact is, that here is a new product that is American." This process instilled individualism, which in turn promoted democracy. Turner repeatedly referred to individualism and democratic values as direct outcomes of the frontier experience in "The Significance of the Frontier" and in some of his later essays.[17] These descriptive words bound the West with the goals of character education.

The idea of the West as a moral space was also reflected in popular culture and educational discourse. Author Owen Wister helped to perpetuate the virtuous character traits of westerners in *The Virginian* (1902) by making a hero out of the American cowboy who blended chivalry with rugged individualism and ingenuity. Born and reared in an upper-class eastern family himself, Wister gained his sense of self from a trip to Wyoming. In an essay called "The Evolution of the Cow-Puncher," published seven years before *The Virginian*, Wister argued that the cowboy was a lineal descendant of the Anglo-Saxon knight-at-arms. "The rugged outdoor life of the West brought out the latent courage, heroism, and toughness of his kind."[18] The myth of the cowboy, popularized by dime novels, Wild West shows, and novels like *The Virginian*, came to symbolize the moral character traits of honor, physical prowess, and rugged individualism.

These virtuous traits, combined with Protestant themes of progress, suffering, and the work ethic, appeared in Western films. William S. Hart entered filmmaking in 1914 from a career as a Shakespearean actor on Broadway. Disillusioned with the morals of city life, he brought to his films the Protestant work ethic he had grown up with in the West. Developing a unique camera style

to show the environment of the western frontier in "all its stark reality," he created a physical presence of the landscape that overwhelmed and threatened the
hero. "In the midst of this natural world, Hart's characters were portrayed as
emissaries of Christ on earth, dramatized by the Lord appearing over his head
and titles quoting scriptures."[19] The Westerns of the 1930s were the only genre
that attempted to discuss religions, and those that did not directly portray
Mormons or Quakers used "the tension between Puritanism and the softer
U.S. tradition—call it deist, or Unitarian, or Arminian—where progress westward comes from the fruitful collaboration between benevolent God and men
who naturally know right from wrong." A-Westerns like *The Big Trail* (1930)
portrayed nature as healing and divine, and rather than celebrate heroic individualism, incorporated traditions of Christian faith by making sure the hero's
personal mission coincided with public good. In a lengthy soliloquy, John
Wayne emphasized the sublime morality of western landscapes that linked tall
trees to the gates of heaven. As depicted in the movies, the process of going west
and suffering for the sake of progress was in and of itself a kind of religious
experience.[20]

The heroism and bravery of pioneers seemed particularly useful to educators. A 1920 advice book entitled *Moral Education in School and Home* makes
several references to the value of the western story in the teaching of moral
education. Author J. O. Engleman included *The Virginian* in a list of approved
books to satisfy adolescents' "natural longing for the portrayal and history of
the emotional life of men and women." The author advocated the teaching of
history as a method of character building through patriotism. He argued that
the American narrative was one of

> growth in unity and in numbers, of fighting Indians, felling forests, making
> constitutions, establishing churches and schools, organizing territories,
> carving out states, surveying land and establishing boundaries of township
> and farms, crossing rivers and mountains and plains, pushing ever west-
> ward, overcoming nature, and fighting and building mile by mile and foot
> after foot, from the Atlantic to the Pacific.[21]

What he defined as an "American" narrative is largely what historians today
would refer to as the legacy of conquest. Experts in character education stressed
the importance of the tendency toward "hero worship" in modern youth and

urged preparatory masters to "help them choose the right one and to stimulate them toward reaching their goal."[22]

Heroic tales commemorating the experiences of early pioneers abounded as pioneer societies and remembrance groups began recording their hardships and accomplishments. Spurred in part in reaction to the perceived closing of the American frontier, they were fueled by nostalgia and an intense interest to share their morality tales with future generations in an effort to counteract the demoralizing influences of affluence, new consumer goods, and leisure activity. Pioneer societies held reunions, delivered speeches at celebratory events, and documented their experiences to preserve their legacy, but also to provide "an object lesson for younger generations that had not experienced the rigors of frontier life." In 1922 Elisha Brooks recorded his experience as a child who traveled from Michigan to California with the intent that "a sketch of his struggles in his wild pioneer days—thrown as he was entirely on his own resources, and armed only with a resolute will that broke down all barriers—might rouse a spirit of emulation in many youth now drifting into useless manhood." Similarly, booster, author, and frontier journey reenactor Ezra Meeker sought to preserve the pioneer legacy to teach later generations "lessons of industry, frugality, upright and altruistic living as exemplified in the lives of the pioneers." At seventy-six years of age, Meeker left his home in Washington state in 1906 to travel across country in a prairie schooner, dedicating pioneer monuments along the way. When he stopped in cities, reporters often contrasted "the picturesque appearance of Meeker and his prairie schooner outfit" to the hustle and bustle of urban life.[23] Although ranch school students traveled by Pullman car rather than prairie schooner, camping trips, life in the rugged Southwest, and geographic isolation provided an important glimpse into the hardships that created these American heroes, with the intent that the students too would benefit from the moralizing influences of pioneering.

In part, the West demonstrated its ability to affect character by its track record of transforming individuals. Theodore Roosevelt, Owen Wister, and Frederick Remington had been transformed from effeminate easterners into masculine role models. Much to his surprise, as a newly elected New York state assemblyman, Theodore Roosevelt discovered that despite his intelligence, competence, and real legislative successes, no one took him seriously. Daily newspapers lampooned Roosevelt as the quintessence of effeminacy and humiliated him by nicknaming him "weakling," "Jane-Dandy," "Punkin-Lily," and "the exquisite Mr. Roosevelt." Understanding the power of public image, "he knew that his effeminate image could destroy any chances for his political future." In response, he constructed a powerful, male identity for himself in the terms of a western adventure story. In 1883, Roosevelt purchased a South Dakota cattle ranch for $40,000. The financial risk turned out to be a politically "brilliant step to transform his image from effeminate dude to masculine cowboy," as biographer Edmund Morris has pointed out.[24] For Owen Wister, the West was a place of "physical well-being and emotional rebirth, a place where it was possible to heal old wounds, forget old wrongs, recover strength, and start again."

There were countless other testimonials to the ability of the environs of the American West to rid individuals of debasing character traits and turn men into successful gentleman cowboys. Harold Bell Wright, who once preached moral virtues from a pulpit, went west and "preached clean living, the purity of the wilderness, and the moral values to be mined in this new treasure trove." In *When a Man's a Man* (1916), Wright portrayed a "wealthy easterner who abandoned the artificiality of a decaying society to seek a wholesome life" in the West.[25] Ranch school brochures highlighted success stories that students themselves observed and recorded. Before it evolved into a full-fledged ranch school, the Fresnal Ranch was established in 1924 when two eastern boys who "lacked the vigor to succeed" traveled west in search of renewal. Soon others ventured to the Fresnal Ranch until it "became a place for those who wished to regain their strength and courage to carry on with life."[26] According to a fellow Judson student, in just eight months, "Teddy" from New Jersey had developed such a "healthy glow and sturdy look" that the author wondered whether his sister "would know him when he goes home."[27] H. David Evans articulated a more inspirational transformation, as he believed "that life in the West, with its vision, distance and colour, could kindle a boy's imagination, and leave him that ethereal spark which might at any time burst into flame."[28] The Palo Verde Ranch School in Mesa promised that "the spirit of the Far West stimulates the youths' imaginations, a great factor in keeping the boys interested, well, and happy."[29]

Outdoor activities like camping, hiking, and horseback riding facilitated physical transformation that was essential to character and masculinity. The object of the Palo Verde Ranch School in Mesa was to "combine a thorough education for the boys with the development of a strong and efficient body by means of outdoor living."[30] The healthful aspect of outdoor activity was particularly important in the battle to save boys from effeminacy. In the first half of the twentieth century, to be sickly was to be effeminate. Ranching activities created strong, healthy bodies as evidenced by numerous role models. Roosevelt described himself as a weakly asthmatic before his triumphant experience as a rancher in Montana. Sixteen-year-old Thomas D. Cabot arrived in Mesa in 1914 to attend the Evans School. At the time, he was undersized, frail, and too immature to enter Harvard even though he had already passed the entrance examinations.[31]

The focus on physical development, especially on weight gain, reflected scientific views on child development. Critics of the Horatio Alger novels noticed an emphasis on the relationship between potential for success, character, and physical beauty. The pseudosciences of phrenology and physiognomy informed a "correlation between the physical and the moral."[32] Weight gain was an important indicator of improved health according to the Department of the Interior, which boldly stated, "gain in weight is perhaps the best single index of a child's physical progress and condition."[33] At summer camps, leaders' efforts to physically transform children centered on weight gain, which also served as a means for campers to assess their own transformations.[34] In his exhaustive research, G. Stanley Hall documented physical growth as an indicator of the transformation from childhood to adulthood that characterized adolescence. In tune with scientific and cultural ideas about youth, ranch schools also kept track of students' height and weight. At the Judson School for Boys, a Phoenix physician called at the school once each week to carefully record each boy's weight and physical condition.[35] A Southern Arizona School for Boys brochure actually listed weight gain per student by month and touted that weight gain as ranging from 6.5 to 15.5 pounds over the course of the academic year. Ranch school owners used data in their promotional literature to prove that their school provided healthful benefits that included regular habits, good food, and climatic advantages that accounted for the boys' physical growth.[36]

Popular culture figures offered examples that physical strength could be achieved, not just inherited, giving a son of privilege the chance to earn respect by building himself up, literally. Eugene Sandow was the "perfect man," possessing remarkable strength and a sculpted physique that in the 1890s represented a new ideal of the male body. He "shrewdly insisted his strength was not a gift of nature but an attainment strenuously earned." Born in Prussia to parents of modest means, he constructed an identity for himself through his muscular physique and showmanship to become a symbol for what all men could achieve, regardless of social class. Similarly, Angelo Siciliano at age sixteen was a "ninety-seven-pound weakling" who, within a few years, performed as strongman "Charles Atlas" at Coney Island and then on the vaudeville circuit. By 1922 he won acclaim as "America's Most Perfectly Developed Man."[37] At least one Judson School student acknowledged that Atlas's physique represented the highest achievement in muscular strength. Eugene (Barney) Judson was described as follows: "Our little Petty, although his name may not suggest it, is really a very muscular individual." One of his ambitions was to rival Charles Atlas, "and in time he most probably will."[38] Through determination and will, boys had the capability to transform their bodies into statuesque physiques to make themselves into men of strength, confidence, and command.

The most important character attribute of the West was the ability to develop "self-reliance." This term was used frequently both to describe the spirit of the West and to define those traits that made men masculine. Literature generated by ranch schools referenced character education within the context of the mythic West and especially highlighted "self-reliance." Located in the foothills of the Baboquivari Mountains, formerly the headquarters of one of the large cattle ranches of the Tucson district, Fresnal Ranch School was a place

> where a small group of boys falls heir to the traditions and the country that made the American cowboy the symbol for self reliance and courage. Western life is not only endlessly fascinating to boys; it develops physical and intellectual capacities untouched by the regulation school routine. Its essentially useful though adventurous activities, in boundless open country, are closely related to the American ideal of initiative and independence.[39]

Describing the western attributes of the school, especially its "informal, easy-going fashion," Fresnal visitor Hermann Hagedorn wrote that "personalities and characters are being shaped here."[40]

The supreme importance of self-reliance to boys' success as future leaders was illustrated by Henry Cabot Lodge, a contemporary of Roosevelt who shared his views on imperialism, masculinity, and the development of sons. In reflecting on his own missteps as a father, Lodge understood that he and his friends had hindered his eldest son's ability to act independently by going to great lengths to assist George, nicknamed "Bay," an aspiring poet, by bombarding "magazine editors with his poems" and exclaiming that his was the best work since Shakespeare. Bay's reliance on his father and his father's friends prevented him from succeeding on his own merit. Brooks Adams warned Bay's mother that "he must cut free from" older men, to have the "ideas and independence of his own time." Edith Wharton commented that this genuine sympathy and desire to assist kept the poor boy "in a state of brilliant immaturity." Although Henry Cabot Lodge was among late nineteenth-century imperialists who lamented being denied the opportunity for military valor because they were too young to fight in the Civil War, when Bay was determined to enlist, Lodge protected him by arranging for Bay to serve as a midshipman in the navy, assigned to his uncle.[41]

Bay married and had two sons of his own, but died in 1909 before they reached maturity. Henry Cabot Lodge took an active interest in his grandsons and was most likely responsible for sending John Davis Lodge, Bay's second son, born in 1903, to the Evans School in Mesa. Nicholas and Archibald Roosevelt had already moved on from the school when John would have attended, but perhaps they attested to the usefulness of the school in cultivating self-reliance and masculinity. John would have been too young to serve in World War I, and his grandfather would have had every reason to believe that the boy would not soon have another chance to prove his masculinity through military action. The advertised purpose of the Evans School in Mesa was to teach boys "self-reliance, independence and initiative," and H. David Evans sought to put "strength into the fibre of the effete East" through the simplicity of daily living in Spartan quarters and the absence of servants. He believed this was a healthy environment for energetic boys experiencing for the first time the need for and satisfaction of self-reliance.[42] According to one Evans School alumnus, this experience prepared him for other masculine tests. A pilot during World War II, he was shot down over Burma and made his way back to safety alone through hostile territory. He credited his school solo camping experiences as the deciding factor in his survival.[43]

The Evans School in Mesa, founded in 1902, was the first of Arizona's ranch schools and was clearly the most primitive in terms of its living arrangements. Nicholas Roosevelt included photos of the rows of tents that consisted of living quarters and the primitive shower in his scrapbook. Quite assuredly, Nicholas was used to an indoor shower, a porcelain tub, and the privacy afforded to boys of his standing. It must have been a shock for him to learn that the dilapidated

Evans School in Mesa, Arizona, c. 1909–1910. Earlier ranch schools were more rustic to better promote "simplicity of living," whereas those established in the 1920s and 1930s were more resort-like. Arizona Historical Society, Nicholas Roosevelt Photograph Collection—PC 113-X.

wooden structure, resembling a run-down privy, was a shower.[44] As later schools opened in the 1920s, living conditions improved and usually consisted of furnished rooms shared by two boys. This could be the result of the shift from the southwestern desert as uncharted territory to the perception of Arizona as an ideal resort environment. Instead of requiring boys to live in tents, schools invoked the ideology of the rugged West through overnight camping trips and other tests of bravery, fortitude, and physical strength. They cultivated masculine traits by providing outdoor recreation, oftentimes in contrived, or real, primitive conditions. By experiencing western life as exemplified by several masculine heroes—cowboys, frontiersman, and hunters—boys participated in a form of constructed savagery through hunting, using firearms, and roughing it in the great outdoors.

Boys understood and appreciated the degree of freedom permitted at western ranch schools. In reflecting on the 1923 school year, one Evans student wrote that the school was unique because "instead of simply preparing for college," it was "a preparatory school for life." His main example of this distinction was "that boys are encouraged to go off for week-ends, instead of being discouraged or forbidden." This blessing was "the result of two happy circumstances," according to the author: the "splendid opportunities for camping in the mountains surrounding the school and the fact the there is little or no trouble to get into." Permission of the director was required, "but after this is secured, the fellows concerned are at liberty to plan and execute the undertaking as they will."[45] In his comparison to other preparatory schools and the lack of weekend privileges, the author was most likely referring to schools on the Atlantic Seaboard, since many students who attended western ranch schools tended to migrate back and forth. Weekend trips meant excursions into urban areas where there was "trouble to get into." Any dangerous circumstances that boys might encounter camping in the desert—wild animals, snakes, dehydration, horseback riding in general—tested boys' bravery and skill. The ability to overcome these hazards demonstrated self-reliance and courage. Urban trouble—alcohol, prostitution, gambling—was effeminate and degenerating and the only way to overcome urban dangers was to avoid them.

Overnight camping trips in the great Southwest were ideal for cultivating self-reliance among pampered city-reared boys. According to one Judson student, "camping trips are among the most desirable and most enjoyable experiences in a boy's life. There is something about eating food cooked over an open fire, stretching out on a bed roll under the stars and meeting Nature face to face that makes a boy more of a man."[46] The environment itself was still mysterious and daunting when compared to the New England and midwestern landscape of boys' homes. Sparsely populated and somewhat barren, the natural landscape of New Mexico and Arizona could be intimidating, especially for novices. Boys as young as twelve years of age went horseback camping in groups of two or three and often learned by trial and error. Shouldering responsibility for one's own mistakes was an important character-building lesson that was conveyed to Valley Ranch students by headmaster Jarvie when he lectured "it was human to make a mistake but criminal to repeat it." According to the March 1923 edition of the *Cactus Needle*, a publication of the Evans School, the success of the weekend camping trips was dependent "entirely on the boys, as a master joins them only at their invitation. If the boy who is engineering the trip is unfortunate enough to take ten pounds of bologna and forget the bread and matches—well, the chances are that he will never make that mistake again."[47] David Wilhelm described how he and his friends at the Arizona Desert School loaded a packhorse with food, bedding, and cooking equipment to trail up Pima Canyon in Tucson. Upon arrival, the boys had to build a corral for the horses and set up camp before exploring the area. They cooked their own food, baking bread in a Dutch oven. On one occasion, their horses broke loose from the "inadequate homemade ocotillo corral." The boys had to walk back to the school in 2 ½-inch heeled cowboy boots to retrieve the horses, return to the campsite, and repack the equipment before departing the site for good. They "learned that walking in high-heeled cowboy boots produced blistered feet so we best build a better corral the next trip."[48] Boys who mastered horseback riding and survived dangerous situations earned the admiration of their peers. Jack Heinz described his friend, "Tennessee" Morison, as "a wonderful horseman. He not only knows how to ride but can train and break in a horse. In fact, he knows his 'oats.' . . . We were going up a hill when suddenly 'Ten's' horse reared up on his hind legs and fell clean over backwards. Tennessee just managed to scramble out from under him before he hit or else he would have been squashed."[49]

Preparation alone made boys understand the magnitude of the adventure, and many must have looked forward to these experiences with both fear and excitement. Los Alamos alumnus Charles Pearce learned how to pack a horse and could "throw a solid diamond hitch—one that would hold fast over the rough mountain trails that led into Valle Grande." He recalled that "for many days—even weeks—the pack trip was looked forward to with eager anticipation, for the experience was viewed as a sort of test of one's manhood, a dropping back into the days and ways of the early pioneers." In his reminiscence of the four-day pack trip, Pearce invoked the West of the American imagination to describe his adventure. "One often felt like the first human ever to set foot in the area," he explained, "until, that is, traces of an old Indian camp or a blazed tree reminded one that he was indeed a latecomer on the scene." The boys encountered evidence of wildlife from the "hysterical wailing of the coyotes" as "friendly music."[50] Overnight camping trips enabled boys to exercise a leadership role that distinguished the ranch school experience from what they might encounter on similar excursions through the Boy Scouts, for example. The requirement to lead a trip was indicative of the distinct goals for character traits based on social class. The Woodcraft Indians, founded by Ernest Thompson Seton, promoted a return to nature to cultivate self-reliance and at the same time instill a devotion to a tribe to "counteract the selfishness that characterized capitalistic society."[51] The boys who attended ranch schools had been reared in and benefited from capitalist success. The assumption for many was that they would accept leadership roles to sustain family dynasties, and the goal was to ensure that they evolved into responsible, moral leaders who demonstrated character traits expected of their class.

Hunting trips at boys' ranch schools demonstrated a primitive aspect of masculine virtue based on restrained violence. Roosevelt was "attracted to a more violent masculinity" associated with "natural man," whose masculinity could be found in the American West. As Roosevelt saw it, "nature was brutal and primitive—a proving ground of manly prowess—as epitomized by conflict with bloodthirsty, lurking Indians."[52] From showdowns at the O.K. Corral to the Indian wars of the nineteenth century, the history of the West was violent. Even activities such as working with cattle added an element of masculine violence to boys' (and some girls') ranch school experience. Environmentalist Edward Abbey commented on the brutal nature of the range and livestock industry. "Anyone who's taken part in gathering, roping, branding, dehorning, castrating, ear notching . . . or winching a calf from its mother knows how mean and tough and brutal it can be."[53] The branding process as described by an Orme alumna affirmed the violence of branding. Student Suzy Royce wrote, "Foreman roped, Charlie cut ears and horns off, and Mr. Orme branded and vaccinated. . . . Jennie, Carol, Cinda, Jeb and Jolly all took turns painting the calves with bug medicine."[54] As an adult, Rosebrook described the branding process he participated in at the Orme School in an article for *Arizona Highways*. "After our lunch of frijoles and cornbread, we separate the mother cows from their calves, and branding begins. We move among the calves, flank them. . . . Holding them, one of us at each end, through dehorning, ear marking, castration for the males, vaccinations, and branding. The youngest of us carries the bucket and paints the wounds with black 'bug juice' to prevent infections."[55]

The practice of trapping at the Valley School in Wyoming was almost too gruesome for Philip Cummings to bear, as it was his assignment to make sure students visited their traps every day "to relieve suffering." Older boys who attended the Valley School trapped muskrat and mink, sometimes using the pelts to line their coats. In his journal, Cummings recognized a natural affinity for hunting among boys, while pointing out his opinion of the savagery of it all. The boys did not sell the furs or need them, "but he has that lust after the wild that seems a part of the adolescent nature of the normal boy . . . the boy's proving of cunning and superiority, his proof of power over animals, his vent to a cruel

"Swimming the Bear cubs. Some pets we caught." Domesticating wild animals as pets was a more humane means of conquering nature and demonstrated the ability to make the West a safe place to live. Los Alamos School, c. 1917–1920. Goldsberry Collection of open-air school photographs, Library of Congress Prints and Photographs Division, Washington, D.C.

strain which proves that man for all his spirituality can so easily slip to the portraying of an animal." Several months later he described accompanying a student to his traps. Much to his relief, it had been "three days that those steel instruments of torture have failed to furnish any carnal harvest."[56]

Although hunting was an accepted masculine practice, even G. Stanley Hall "stressed the masculinity of the 'hunting passion' . . . drove man to exterminate numerous animals . . . [to become] the lord of the animal creation."[57] Hunting in the West was an important tourist activity as early as the 1860s, when large numbers of wealthy sportsmen came west to hunt buffalo. "Americans took great pride in the lumbering beasts that roamed the plains, but they also loved to shoot them, most not realizing this would eventually destroy them." Even 1860s stagecoach passengers engaged in the "practice of shooting animals from the coach for amusement. Each passenger could kill dozens."[58] The train created a new version of hunting that slaughtered thousands of animals. According to a

December 1867 *Harper's* article, passenger trains slowed down to the speed of the herd. The passengers got out firearms and shot at animals from their open windows. This massacre left tons of rotting meat along the tracks, and killed an estimated six million buffaloes by 1875.[59] If nothing else, ranch school students at least learned the ethics of consuming the animals they shot rather than killing solely for sport. In 1923 the boys at the Evans School brought in about six hundred ducks "and on several occasions the school enjoyed duck dinners provided by this group of sportsmen."[60]

The idea of hunting as a strictly masculine enterprise becomes more evident when considering that none of the girls' ranch schools offered riflery or hunting as recreational activities, and even at the Orme School, where girls participated in almost every activity including branding, they were excluded from hunting trips. Charles Orme Sr. allowed the boys to bag their limit and some succeeded. Only the senior boys participated in a deer hunt led by Mort Orme. According to the student author, "they went hunting twice, both times on horseback, once in the mountains of Mayer and another time in the hills to the northeast of the ranch. Not a boy was disappointed in seeing bucks, but bringing them down was a different matter. On the hunts, Mort was the only hunter to bring in a buck, which was a four pointer." The student author concluded that "both hunting and shooting will always be a major sport here at the ranch."[61] At the Judson School, George Judson Jr. took the older boys on a number of hunting trips during the duck, dove, and quail seasons. According to yearbook author Barney Judson, "the Gila River, Brown's cattle ranch, and the Verde River proved to be excellent hunting grounds." On each trip the group shot enough game for their meals and took additional birds home for a school meal. Incidentally, Barney Judson loved fishing but was never enthusiastic about hunting.[62]

Some boys found they were more sensitive to the violence of hunting than they may have expected. Evans School avid hunter Lewis "Dip" Mowry came down with a case of "buck fever," which led to his prey's escape. Back at the school Dip claimed that his gun would not shoot far enough.[63] The seniors at the Los Alamos Ranch School considered themselves an elite group because they were trusted with the school's "high-powered rifles in the rugged wilderness." Boys were divided into groups of three and accompanied by an experienced teacher or "one of the native men who knew the country by heart and hunted every fall." Charles Pearce described the experience and his excitement for the adventure:

It was early morning, scarcely light, when the four of us saddled our horses, scabbarded our rifles, and set out for our assigned area. . . . If ever three boys felt tough and macho mean, Pete, Super, and I were those boys. With our rifles cradled under our arms, we were mountain men, lawmen, and outlaws, all rolled into one. We were mean hombres![64]

The group spotted a herd of deer and fired simultaneously. The adult leader of the group cried, "I got one!" and the group was "ecstatic that someone had made a kill, even if it was not one of us boys." They ran down to see where the deer was last seen and traced the animal by its trail of blood. Upon finding a doe, Charles explained, "suddenly the elation went out of us. What we saw on the ground at our feet, blood oozing from a hole in her chest, was a doe. She was still alive, but just barely. She looked at us with her soft eyes as though pleading, 'Please help me.' I don't know about the others, but I cried." The adult group leader put the doe out of her misery with a single shot. Charles described that he "felt as though the shot went through me!"[65]

Hunting trips made guns a necessity, and ranch school brochure after brochure shows photos of boys with rifles in cowboy attire. Marksmanship was a popular extracurricular activity at Green Fields School. Alumnus Duncan Taylor remembers that every Thursday was "Bring Your Gun to School Day."[66] Although Mr. Atchley organized two shooting teams, some of Green Fields' earliest students complained that there never seemed to be enough time for shooting. The tradition of riflery prevailed at Green Fields for more than thirty years, "disappearing apparently only with the advent of girls on campus and with the onset of the seventies."[67] Jeb Rosebrook remembered that in the 1930s and early 1940s Orme students were allowed to bring guns to school, mostly twenty-twos and rifles.[68] At the Palo Verde Ranch School, boys were "not permitted to have revolvers," but rifles were permitted.[69]

The presence of guns at school was a liability, and gun culture at the Judson School had serious consequences. David Lincoln, who attended the Judson School as an elementary-aged day student, recalled a dramatic experience with guns:

Many of the students had guns in their rooms and some would play with them. On one occasion I was studying in a room adjoining a student's bedroom and there were two students in the bedroom playing with guns. One

Inscription on back of photograph states, "Younger boys ready to go hunting with me. Notice red bandanas worn for safety." Los Alamos School, c. 1917–1920. Goldsberry Collection of open-air school photographs, Library of Congress Prints and Photographs Division, Washington, D.C.

went off and the bullet went through the wall and hit the ceiling above my head. The tragic part of the story is that some time later the same two students were again playing with guns and one of them, Sandy McDonald, was shot and killed.[70]

Judson alumnus Ormonde Parke also recalled the incident with great sadness and mentioned how it later affected Joe Haldiman, the boy who accidentally shot Sandy McDonald.[71] Apparently on April 25, 1939, Oakle Burton (Sandy) McDonald and classmate Joe Haldiman had been playing with what they thought to be unloaded guns from McDonald's gun collection when one went off. Sandy had a large collection of firearms and swords, many of them antiques that he kept with him at the school. George Judson and the school's nurse, Marjorie Carver, drove Sandy to the hospital. Shot above the heart, the eighteen-year-old Judson student died before he reached the hospital. Haldiman was exonerated from all charges the next day when the sheriff's office and coroner's jury declared

McDonald's death accidental.[72] The Valley Ranch school suffered a similar tragedy in 1934 when Wade Carpenter, a student, "accidentally shot and killed himself as he was handling a pistol in his cabin."[73]

Hunting was an important means for adolescent boys to demonstrate bravery and courage. Some schools, especially those for younger boys, had other
tests to demonstrate their worth as men-in-the-making. At the Arizona Desert
School, headmaster Matt Baird introduced the "Bareback Patrol," which revolved around mastery of cowboy skills. Membership on the Bareback Patrol
was the highest distinction in the School and included boys "who have in every
way shown themselves to be dependable and constructive members of the student body." Tests of worthiness included 150 miles of horseback riding, the ability to ride and jump bareback, the completion of 300 yards of trail, and
demonstrated knowledge and use of a compass. In addition, boys had to rope a
still object at twenty feet and a moving object from a horse. Proficiency in camping was demonstrated by the ability to cook on the trip, build a fire and boil
water in seven minutes, camp out five nights, and plan and manage an overnight
pack trip.[74] Similar to the ritual activity at summer camps, these tests served as
rites of passage "to foster children's sense of participating in a transformative
experience." In addition, mastering this new set of cultural references facilitated
a sense of shared community.[75]

A sillier spin-off of the "Bareback Patrol" was Matt Baird's "Brown Mule
Club." Baird had a particular fondness for Brown Mule chewing tobacco and,
according to alumni, had the ability to swallow it when anyone of importance
or a parent approached him. The qualifications for the Brown Mule Club were
simply to "sit on the top rail of a fence and chew for twenty minutes." Boys who
could do this without getting sick, made it into the club.[76] Spontaneous and
informal tests of bravery were constantly available to students who lived in the
desert Southwest. Arizona Desert School alumni remembered that snakes were
everywhere. One student told Matt Baird about a tarantula in the corner of his
room. Baird did nothing as he thought it was good for the boy to get used to the
idea because boys needed to learn not to be afraid of spiders.[77]

Chewing tobacco and smoking are examples of an inherent contradiction in
attempting to be authentically western at the same time as developing the character of boys. Horace Holden, the leading advocate for private school education
for young boys, believed smoking to be a more heinous offense than dishonesty
and lying.[78] In the Westerns, however, cowboys' sustenance consisted of

hardtack, boiled coffee, and cigarettes, and according to Tompkins's observation, "sometimes just the cigarette."[79] While the ideals of the myth of the West meshed well with character education, the specifics of cowboy culture often deterred character development. In his reflection of his experiences as a boy of seven who lived temporarily on his grandfather's ranch in the 1920s, Robert Athearn points out many of these contradictions in his prologue to *The Mythic West*. Although some would say that it was the ideal environment for a child to learn about traditional values, Athearn remembered being less than pleased that "nothing on the ranch belonged to the twentieth century." He described it as "the Old West of that time. Primitive, simple to an extreme, and isolated." They lived in the wilderness, "a place that easterners mistakenly envied as an unsullied land that Rousseau would have praised, a land that was pure, where the invigorating climate and clean moral atmosphere bred men, true Americans." Athearn witnessed the violence of breaking horses, picked up profanity from the ranch hands, and developed a smoking habit by the age of eight.[80]

Smoking was unhealthful and symbolic of lack of self-control. Furthermore, it was the epitome of flaming youth and the problems of modern America. In his advice manual for boys and parents published in 1932, Robert Badham warned that smoking was "no longer a manly habit since the girls and women have gone for it."[81] Valley Ranch school students were permitted to smoke with written permission from their parents, yet, according to Cummings, they all smoked. He was particularly shocked to find one sixteen-year-old who regularly smoked a pipe and a package of cigarettes a day.[82] Howard Heinz had his son Rust, "the party of the first part," sign a legal document on January 9, 1931, stating that he "hereby agrees that until he has passed his examination for college, or in any event not before he is twenty-one should he not pass his examination before then, he will not use tobacco in any form." As an inducement for compliance, "the party of the second part, father of the party of the first part" agreed to pay Rust $1,000. The document was signed by both parties and witnessed by Elizabeth Rust Heinz, mother of "the party of the first part."[83]

Captain Russell A. Fairgrieve, director of the Southern Arizona School for Boys, seemed particularly irritated with his students' penchant for smoking. By 1948 Fairgrieve instituted a policy whereby boys who had parental permission could smoke twice a day. He reminded students, however, that "perfection in one's ability to inhale is not going to do one single thing to help any of us in the worthwhile things for which we came here. No student's character will be made better by becoming a chain smoker. No student's health will be improved by smoking even one cigarette a week. No student's ability to pass a CEB exam will be improved at all." To be certain his argument was clear, he outlined the aims of the school and included an explanation of why smoking hindered those aims. Posing the question, "What are we trying to do at SASB?" Fairgrieve outlined the following:

A. We are trying to prepare boys (some with poor health) to do a better job later in life (Morally-Physically-Mentally).
B. We think that excessive smoking makes some of these things less likely to be possible.
C. We want to have a better polo, tennis, baseball and other teams as the years go by. We think to build stronger bodies we can do that.[84]

Ranch schools had to find ways to counterbalance the ideals of the cowboy with his lawlessness, bad habits, and raw behavior. Western novelist Wallace Stegner recollected from his experiences growing up on the northern plains that despite the rawness of the cowboys he knew, "they honored courage, competence, [and] self-reliance."[85] Teddy Roosevelt admired the American cowboy, and excused his often morally degraded and socially disreputable reputation by attributing his roughness to his pioneer role. "The cowboy," he wrote, illustrated "the theory of the survival of the fittest," on rugged American frontiers. Roosevelt went on to describe the cowboy as "brave, hospitable, hardy, and adventurous . . . he prepare[d] the way for civilization." Roosevelt assured readers that the cowboy of the past was the entrepreneur of the present. "There were many, even in the 'wildest and wooliest' period, who . . . kept their wits about them, saved their wages, and successfully became range-stockmen on their own account." This elevated the cowboy from the working class to the entrepreneurial class of ranch school students.[86]

Some of the men willing to step into the role of cowboy to authenticate the ranch school experience, however, were more like the nomadic, free-spirited nineteenth-century cowboys than the entrepreneurial types who settled on ranches of their own. Valley Ranch School's "hoss-wrangler" was "a scream of humor as well as a profuse fountain of profanity."[87] Evans School student Bob Heineman rode his horse from Mesa, Arizona, to Tucson with the school wrangler. The four-day journey included a two-night stop in Florence, where Henry

Wentworth, the wrangler, met up with several of his drinking buddies. On the third day of the trip, Heineman had a taste of white lightning when a stranger in Oracle Junction handed him a jug with what he thought was water. A friend of his conveyed that "Henry enjoyed this thoroughly but young Bob did not."[88] Through mentorship and advisement, boys learned to recognize that these were not the character traits that were expected of their class, even if they seemed authentic to the western experience. Robert J. Badham provided guidance on everything from choosing a school to behaving in a socially acceptable way once enrolled. On the subject of profanity, he declared that it was not manly, but "vulgar, repelling; and a sure mark of ill breeding." His own personal revelation resulted from his experience working in a coal mine owned by his father. Explaining that the "work was hard and the men with whom I was associated with were rough in every way," he had fallen "into habits of profanity, endeavoring to exhibit [his] manliness to their company." His father responded by inquiring as to whether Badham thought him to be manly and courageous. He then asked his son if he had heard his father use any such language, quietly pointing out "how useless and repulsive such words were, on the lips of an educated man."[89]

Profanity had no justification, but certain vices like drinking alcohol could be permissible, as long as men practiced moderation. Badham warned that giving into "any habit to the point of abuse" was failure, and this particular vice was not connected to one's social status. "Don't get the foolish idea that the man who drinks is a hardened sinner or weakling. Remember, while a 'drunk' is never respected anywhere; a sober man is respected everywhere." At a chapel service at the Valley Ranch School, headmaster Jarvie "spoke on the need to learn to be a 'gentleman drinker' now that prohibition was practically off." According to Philip Cummings, Jarvie did not approve of prohibition, but was disdainful of "men with uncontrolled appetites." Cummings thought this advice sound, since he understood that students would most likely drink when they went to college.[90]

Chapel services at the Arizona Desert School and Valley School were more secular than religious, and were an important means of counteracting some of the inherent contradictions in providing a rugged western experience and instilling character traits appropriate to students' class and gender. At least two schools, the Valley Ranch School and Arizona Desert School, offered Sunday chapel services. Headmasters, teachers, and guest speakers presented secular topics that often used current events to address character development and moral guidance. Cummings once spoke on World's Fairs and "their value to us, to the world, and toward business" in anticipation of the 1933 Century of Progress Exposition. Headmaster Jarvie addressed the idea of technocracy and "urged the boys who are the leaders of the morrow and who, by controlling wealth, will control lives, to beware the projects of improvement unless they tend to a future of progress for the race in other ways than materially." After reading Aldous Huxley's books on a mechanistic utopia, Henry Larom used his review to encourage his audience to ponder whether "we might now be wiser and learn to live for something besides money, when we considered the abysmal hell of those who, up to 1930, spoke only in terms of money and now had nothing at all to live for, for with all of their getting, they did not get understanding."[91] Chapel services reflected the preparatory school ideal of preparing students for life, not just college, which included mentorship from men who understood the needs of "the rich man's son."

Ranch school students' role models were the headmasters and teachers who followed in the tradition of Roosevelt, Wister, and Remington by remaking themselves in the pioneer spirit by traveling west to start ranch schools. These gentleman cowboys brought with them their noble Anglo-Saxon ancestry and Ivy League educations that protected them from the rougher and less civilized aspects of western life. Mesa Ranch School faculty member Major Lionel F. Brady epitomized the gentleman cowboy and the type of men Ranch Schools hired to oversee the character development of boys. He served in the Boer War, graduated from Cambridge with an interest in Greek and Latin classics, and earned his MA in geology and botany. His interests and expertise varied from mineralogy, desert lore, and living outdoors to billiards, photography, and tying a diamond hitch. John Davis Lodge remembered that he also sang in the local Episcopal choir.[92]

Educational philosophers identified mentoring by men of character as an important component of instilling masculine traits among boys. Ranch School masters were expected to be models of respectability, character, and masculinity. They were athletic, hardworking, and well traveled, and several served in the military. At the Palo Verde Ranch School, director James S. Hutchinson hired teachers for demonstrating "qualities of leadership among boys quite as much as for their scholastic attainment."[93] The Southern Arizona School highlighted this aspect in its brochure by stating, "When a boy comes to the

Southern Arizona School for Boys, he comes under the care and guidance of men who have been familiar with the problems of boys, in school and out, for many years."[94] Experts in the field further argued for mentoring rather than enforcement as the best avenue for character development. The Southern Arizona School made this explicit, stating that "true manliness and sportsmanship are qualities to be cultivated by expert guidance rather than by servile obedience to fixed rules."[95] Larry Larom carefully screened all instructors "for competence in academic fields and capability to coach or supervise boys in athletics." After he found his first headmaster to be more unruly than the boys, he desired that all future headmasters should be married and required them to sign a contract that forbade drinking.[96] Los Alamos Ranch School founder Ashley Pond hired A. J. Connell to run school operations. Connell had several years of experience working in the Forest Service, was a scoutmaster of the Santa Fe troop of Boy Scouts, and was "as enthusiastic an outdoor man as Pond and as interested in the well-being of boys."[97] Orme School alumnus Jeb Rosebrook believed Charles H. Orme Sr. to be "the strongest human being I had ever met. He had gone to Stanford, and been on the first crew team they had and won the national championship." Charlie Orme was a "big time football player" who played in the Rose Bowl for Stanford.[98] George Judson was an avid tennis player and played basketball in college. In a 1931 yearbook, a student author described Mr. Judson as "a real sport, and his ability as an athlete is appreciated by us all."[99] Captain Russell Fairgrieve, cofounder of the Southern Arizona School, served in World War I.

It was expected that these male role models adopt masculine traits of the rugged cowboy and the traditional conventions of marriage and family life. In many ways, these were contradictory. Although tourism brochures and American sentiment promoted the West as more open and less constrained by society than the more settled regions of the country, certain expectations for gender and sexuality remained intact. Prior to the shift from open grazing to settled ranching, cowboys lived outside of the mainstream, adopting alternative family structures and behavior that oftentimes mocked middle-class Victorian respectability. Bunking with other cowboys, engaging in temporary and long-term relationships with prostitutes, and even cross-dressing were common in all-male cowboy culture. The settled cowboy-rancher gave up "the masculine privileges of the margins" for the "class privileges of the respectable family rancher."[100] Matt Baird, headmaster at the Arizona Desert School, had constructed a masculine image for himself as an Oxford crew member who after moving to Arizona embraced several aspects of the roughness of cowboy culture. Baird was recently divorced when he arrived at the Arizona Desert School and hence was free of any female influence that might taint his masculine image. When Baird was accused of sexual impropriety with a student, the board promptly dismissed him.[101]

Male homosexuality was more visible in American cities in the interwar period and for many was an undesirable symptom of modern America. In the 1920s and 1930s Freudian psychology influenced how the profession thought about the development of sexual identity as less determined by biology and more so by cultural and social conditions. Some experts argued that psychosexual development occurred prior to adolescence and was directly impacted by the psychodynamics of the family environment.[102] Parents feared that gay men could influence boys to convert to a homosexual lifestyle. The all-male environment of preparatory schools might have attracted gay men looking for "familial intimacy with others of the same sex." For men who might not raise sons of their own, the preparatory school environment provided the chance to mentor boys they may otherwise have been denied. In their effort to promote a hypermasculine environment, and given the geographic distance that provided some degree of privacy and freedom from traditional societal taboos, ranch schools could provide a safe environment for homosexual men who did not violate explicit or implicit school policies.[103] Preparatory schools were intolerant of what they considered to be sexual deviance. In his advice manual, Robert Badham assured parents and students, under the heading "Perversion," that "perverted sexual relation between boys in boarding school is quite rare, fortunately, and detection in it entails prompt dismissal." This was the one act that was not covered by the code of "not telling" and the victim of "this vile habit is to be pitied and should be under the intelligent care of a good psychiatrist." As for the parents of "these unfortunates," he consoled that "these boys can be saved and often become the finest of men."[104]

Male-dominated cowboy culture was compatible with the interwar construct of boyhood and fraternal friendship, making it ideally suited to the character building of boys. The notion that adolescent boys wanted to date girls before they entered college did not emerge until World War II, according to sociologist Jeffery Dennis, who analyzed films, popular magazine articles, and yearbook entries to demonstrate that "teenage hetero-mania is an ideological construct."

In the interwar period, boys who did express an interest in girls were labeled effeminate or infantile. To like girls was to like feminine culture and risk ridicule as a sissy.[105] The term "sissy" emerged out of mid-nineteenth-century boy culture, but by the interwar period its meaning had evolved into a clinical term used by child psychologists to indicate gender deviation. "Real" boys participated in the escapades of boyhood and developed into men of character. By contrast, sissies or effeminate boys were deviants in the making. "The iconic sissy boy was a pale-faced neurasthenic aristocrat, with curly locks and immaculate dress" as compared to the "real" boy who was also Caucasian, but a "little scruffier and from less privileged origins."[106] Ranch school students, dressed in cowboy attire and constantly immersed in the dusty air of the Southwest, certainly had the opportunity to demonstrate an acceptable level of "scruffiness" more so than their traditionally clad eastern counterparts.

Ranch school yearbooks demonstrate evidence of gang culture among boys and an attachment to things masculine rather than to girls. A boy's companionship with his horse was celebrated and valued above all else. For example, the 1935 issue of Judson School's *El Conquistador* lists "the most notable horse and boy relationships at the school." In addition, each pupil was listed with state of origin and the name of his horse in the short student biographies. Howard Voth "fell in love at first sight with Winnie, his horse. He has been unfailing in his devotion to her, and has advanced from being practically a green-horn to a position of Mr. Judson's top cow hand." Each biography touts students' ability as sportsmen and horse enthusiasts. A few mention scholastic ability, humor, and weight gain, but none make any mention of interest in girls.[107] The traditionally all-male culture of cowboys, who were typically unmarried, was ideal for pre-collegiate boys. While cowboys remained in this stage of life, the married headmaster–gentleman cowboy provided the model of what boys would become. The cowboy ranchers hired by headmaster–gentleman cowboys served as a model for a developmental stage rather than a lifelong ambition.

Mature, successful adult men of character married, making wives an important accoutrement to the ideal that boys should aspire toward. The presence of wives, however, often conflicted with the desire to make boys into men through immersion in a hypermasculine environment. Overly possessive mothers who petted and spoiled boys produced effeminate men who weakened the nation. The Los Alamos Ranch School seemed particularly disdainful of the influence of women on the development of boys. In Charles Pearce's autobiographical account he mentioned specifically how the school's authorities insisted that women made boys soft. Charles and his friends had heard of women who baked wonderful cakes sold at a tearoom and asked the headmaster why the boys were never allowed to enjoy the sweet treats. The headmaster replied, "Boys your age should live in a man's world. Women are soft. They spoil boys. At L.A.R.S. there is no place for women." In their history of the school, Fermor S. and Peggy Pond Church confirmed that "in the beginning women were tolerated rather than welcomed into the school community."[108] However, wives and mothers were essential to the creation of a proper home environment and a ranch school's ability to shape boys' character. In their role as civilizers, they provided an important counterbalance to the roughness of the West, emphasizing the more cultivated traits of the gentleman cowboy.

CHAPTER 5

Ranch School Families

ALFRED STEARNS EMPHASIZED THE SANCTITY AND SUPREME IMPORTANCE of the home in building character and lamented the changes in modern American families that negatively impacted boys. "Yesterday's home was a home of moral standards and spiritual ideals," Stearns waxed nostalgically before providing a definition of a home as "not merely a building with a roof and walls in which the family resides, but rather an atmosphere, an influence, intangible but sacred and very real." "Parents sometimes reside in the modern homes on their way to and from the pressing duties of business and professional life and the alluring appeals of club and society," Stearns explained, "but the old atmosphere of self-sacrifice is lacking," leaving the younger generation to rule "pretty much as it wills."[1] Robert Danforth Cole's 1928 study on private schools reported that "substituting for or supplementing the home" was a significant aim of preparatory schools. Reference to a school's ability to provide a "homelike" environment appeared in 90 percent of brochures.[2] Boarding schools served students from broken homes as well as those suffering from general problems that experts warned resulted from inept parenting. Physicians, psychiatrists, educators, and social workers blamed neglectful and overprotective parents for hindering children's character development and often recommended environmental changes that included sending a child away to boarding school. Many children sent to ranch schools were geographically isolated from urban areas and, more importantly, their parents.

The idea that children were better off living with two-parent families with the mother dedicating herself to child rearing was uniformly applied to all social and economic classes. Attention focused on the habits and hardships of America's elite and working-class families more than the model middle-class family that had enough economic resources to live on one income but not enough to neglect or spoil their children. Private schools served America's wealthier families while charitable organizations and increasingly the government supported working-class families. Parental absenteeism seemed to plague all classes equally, but because of poverty some mothers had to work. In the case of more affluent families, parental absenteeism occurred because the father worked too much and mothers hired domestic servants to take care of children. Death, desertion, and divorce impacted all American families, but desertion tended to remain a problem of working-class families, and divorce was more prominent among America's elite. Despite the unique challenges as defined by each class, the solutions only differed slightly. In both cases, if the home situation could not be remedied, removal was the best option.

The film *Citizen Kane* (1941) subtly questioned the practice of removing a child from a family, even when it led to a child's future economic success. Charles Foster Kane's poverty-stricken parents come into some money, and it is the mother's decision to use the newly acquired funds to send her young son east to be educated and cared for by a banker who served as Kane's guardian. There was some insinuation that the father abused his family, which could have prompted the mother's sending Kane away rather than trying to use her new economic resources to improve the environment of the entire family. Throughout the film, Kane refers to banker Walter Parks Thatcher as his "guardian," demonstrating that he had no familial bond to the man charged with his upbringing. The audience has the sense that the loss of family contributed to Kane's inability to maintain meaningful relationships as an adult. This is exacerbated by the idea that at the end of life, his final word, "rosebud," may in fact be a nostalgic yearning for his days as a child spent with his mother and father in Colorado. The general thrust of the narrative leaves viewers to ponder whether or not it was best to remove Kane from his traditional home, problematic as it was.

In the Progressive Era through the early 1920s, abandoned children and those removed from their home resided in orphanages. By the 1930s, orphanages were falling out of favor because of their expense and the increasingly popular argument that children were best cared for in a family environment. Boarding homes began to replace orphanages because they offered "some assurance that children would be cared for in a family that did not need them merely for their labor." An agency paid foster parents a nominal board to cover some of the added expense. In 1923 only 10 percent of dependent children were in boarding houses, but by 1933, this increased to 27 percent. In cases of maternal absenteeism through death, divorce, or desertion, a father might choose to pay to board his children. In 1935, a widower in Connecticut paid $4.50 to have his two children live in a boarding home. At the same time, New Deal reforms promoted family security to keep two-parent households intact. Reformers in the 1930s hoped that the Social Security Act and other programs would drastically reduce poverty by providing support for families to care for their own children.[3] Thus the approach to ensuring that working-class children could be reared in a family environment was to re-form families first, and secondly, place them in boarding homes.

New Deal programs aimed at children and families heightened the sentiment of the agrarian self-sufficient family. "One of the sad things today is to see thousands of specialized workers," lamented M. L. Wilson at the 1934 National Conference of Parent Education, "who are almost helpless in doing anything for themselves." Harking back to earlier generations, "our great-grandparents of a hundred years ago did not have automobiles and wore homespun" but "had less to worry as to how they were going to get through the coming winter." He described poor coal-mining families "three or four generations removed from agriculture, who are almost as helpless as babes when it comes to doing anything besides mining coal." Wilson provided these examples in support of the New Deal subsistence homestead communities that were intended, among other goals, to keep families together in a sort of "family rehabilitation." Experts prescribed a new social order that could "retain those elements of the environment of rural life which are particularly valuable to the family" and combine this lifestyle with some industrial employment to supplement their income. Subsistence homestead communities were to provide modern services that families were used to and at the same time give them the land and skills to grow their own food and produce for themselves. In summary, Wilson proclaimed, "the movement for rural industrial communities and partial-subsistence homesteads adjacent to decentralized industry is the greatest potential contribution which the New Deal and contemporary civilization are making towards solving the problems of the industrial family in this country."[4]

Western ranch schools translated the ideals of settled ranch life and the sentiment of the self-sufficient agrarian family to maintain the tradition of the "family school" that began in the late nineteenth century. Husbands and wives operated ranch schools based largely on rural gendered divisions of labor, and incorporated scientific, modern practices of child rearing and home management at the same time as they harked back to America's agricultural past, before industrialization and immigration. The self-sufficient agrarian ranch family was as dominant a western motif as cowboys, miners, and explorers. "The true settlers of the West," according to Elliott West, "came as families" and the "modern companionate family flourished on the frontier." Because they were integral to family survival, pioneer children naturally developed independence and self-reliance.[5] Sherman Thacher asserted that the "life of the ranch is distinctly a family life."[6] The Homestead Act of 1862 fostered an image of the West as inhabited by middle-class agrarian families. In return for 160 acres of surveyed land on the public domain, homesteaders agreed to cultivate the land, improve it by constructing a house or a barn, and live on the claim for five years.[7] With the end of open-range cattle ranching after the winter of 1886–1887, cattlemen reduced herd size and began to accumulate private land in order to grow winter feed. According to Dee Garceau, "reduced herd size, private acreage, alfalfa crops, and the new emphasis on year-round care of herds made ranching more like farming. The family ranch replaced the trail drive."[8] This transition was extremely important for the formation of the idea that western ranch life was synonymous with middle-class family life. Like the ranch family, the ranch school family consisted of a married couple, usually with children, and "cowboys," or single men hired to perform ranch chores. These single working-class men perpetuated the image of the rugged, individualistic cowboy of the past; however, they maintained a respectable middle-class lifestyle under the influence of the headmaster and his wife. As wives and surrogate mothers, women transplanted culture and civilization to the frontier that was essential to maintaining social order. The headmaster's wife was a crucial counterbalance to the rawness of cowboys who served boys as adult companions.

The family approach to American boarding schools began with the first academies established in New England in the late eighteenth century. Students lived as boarders with families in the communities where the academies were located. Thus the "community served as an extension of the academy" and it was expected that it shared the same values as the school. Parents and educators assumed that the communities and families who took in boarding students protected children from any improper influence. By 1817, critics of the academy argued that "boys were left much to themselves as boarders and were making inappropriate use of their leisure time."[9]

After a trip to boarding schools in Germany and Hofwyl School in Switzerland, Boston Anthologists and educational leaders Joseph Green Cogswell and George Bancroft decided that an institutionalized family school–boarding system would sufficiently isolate youth from the degrading influences of the growing urban communities and would instill the moral values necessary for successful adulthood. Thus in 1823, the two idealists opened Round Hill School in rural Northampton, Massachusetts. They believed that their conception of a family model was the best method for "instilling virtue, intelligence, and happiness" among students. The boys lived under the same roof as teachers who exercised parental authority. There is little to suggest the presence of wives as surrogate mothers at the school. Bancroft did not marry his wife, Sarah Dwight, until 1827, so he was a bachelor for the first four years of the school's history. Round Hill closed within six years of its founding, partly because of a new preference among southerners for military academies, which sprung up everywhere in the South in the 1830s, '40s, and '50s.[10] The schools, including Muhlenberg's Flushing Institute, St. James in Maryland, and St. Mark's School in Massachusetts, accepted the Christian home as the best framework for the moral and cultural education of youth during the Victorian period.

The family boarding schools of the 1880s and 1890s were founded in reaction to the emergence of factory-like urban public schools and the lingering Victorian sentimentality toward childhood innocence and the virtues of the family. The Gilded Age nouveau riche perceived boarding schools as giving their children the best possible advantages and followed the long-standing tradition of sending children away to be educated. With the founding of Groton School in 1884, Endicott Peabody continued the family school tradition and emphatically believed that a homelike environment was needed to build character. Charles Francis Adams Jr., descendant of one of Boston's wealthiest families, equated the public school system with mechanical educational machines. He sent his sons to Groton, believing that it was difficult to build character in a factory. To schoolmasters, the intimate and moral family symbolized everything that the factory was not. "Faced with a choice between sending their children to public schools modeled on factories or to private schools modeled on families, many well-to-do parents made the obvious decision."[11]

Western ranch school owners and headmasters created homelike environments that continued the familial tradition as the organizing philosophy for boarding schools, meshed well with the ideal of a ranch life, and provided a respite for boys from their flawed families. With only twenty to forty students in any given year—with the exception of the Thacher School, which was double in size—owners, directors, headmasters, and headmistresses could get to know students on an individual basis but were unable to overindulge them by focusing too much attention on any one child, a persistent problem that threatened modern families. In the 1920s, the idea that a private boarding school provided a superior home environment reflected a national concern, supported by scientific research, over the stability of the modern American family. "There are many who feel that our home life has broken down," declared the author of a brochure from the Moran School in Washington. "The old-fashioned home is an institution of the past. . . . Where the home was once the center of family activities, now, under our highly socialized and industrial life, all members of the family above the cradle find that more and more activities draw them away from the home."[12] As families sought to isolate their children from urban evils by sending them away to boarding school, a nurturing and supportive family community was especially attractive to many early twentieth-century affluent parents, especially single parents whose families had been affected by death, divorce, or other absenteeism.

Based on his personal impression and conversations with other private school teachers, Cole wrote, "broken homes are one reason for attendance at private schools" and defined the causes as death, divorce, or a home with both parents working. His only statistical evidence came from the George School, "which in 1923 reported that in the case of 27.9 percent of 199 pupils, one or both parents were dead. A study of home life of the same school over a period of four years, showed that broken home life increased from 22 to 30 percent."[13] Divorce rates rose from one in every twenty-one marriages in 1880, to one in twelve by 1890, to one in seven by 1924 and contributed to a fear that American family life was crumbling.[14] Broken homes had dire consequences and contributed to the rise in juvenile delinquency. In a series of essays on character education published in 1930, one author lamented that "one of the most appalling facts in our social order is the prevalence of crime among young people." He cited "lack of parental interest and authority" as one of the three causes of juvenile delinquency. "The pressure of business, the call of society, and the ease with which the usual home interests are transferred to outside agencies have tremendously broken down the home influences." After providing several statistics showing a high percentages of juvenile delinquents who came from broken homes, the solution, he argued, was the "rehabilitation of these homes or the removal of children to a better environment."[15]

Death of a mother or father prompted some parents to send a school-aged child to a boarding school. Behaviorist John B. Watson, author of the influential *Psychological Care of the Infant and Child* (1928), shipped both of his sons off to boarding school after the death of their mother.[16] Ormonde Parke's father, a professor at the University of Arizona, had been a tennis partner of George Judson's before his untimely death during the Depression. At the funeral, Mr. Judson told Parke's widow that if she ever needed help with Ormonde to give him a call. Ormonde moved with his mother to Chandler, where she worked as a schoolteacher. Unfortunately, Ormonde had some disciplinary problems at the public school, leaving his mother with no other choice but to call upon George Judson for assistance. Judson enrolled Ormonde in his school and allowed Mrs. Parke to pay what she could. Ormonde's mother took a WPA job in Phoenix so that she could live and work near Judson School and occasionally see her son. In his interview, Ormonde expressed sincere gratitude for the Judsons, emphasizing his feeling that Mr. Judson was his surrogate father, and Barney, George Judson's youngest son, his surrogate brother. He described Mrs. Judson as a "very small gal—just a lovely person," who was "always very, very nice to me." Ormonde remembered with great pride how she told him once that he had "the nicest room of any little boy here."[17]

Parental absenteeism seemed to occur in working-class and wealthy families more than the middle-class ones. Families with means continued to hire domestic help to assist with the more mundane aspects of childcare, a practice that experts argued was equally as problematic as letting them wander the streets. In 1913, Holden was the director of the Lower School of Morristown School in New Jersey and wrote *Young Boys and Boarding School* to outline his reasons for establishing more private boarding schools for boys aged seven to fourteen. He articulated several common hazards of the upper-class home. "The mother may be an invalid, the father irregular, domestic misunderstandings may have occurred, parents may be dead, and—worse than all else—the boy may be left to the care of a nurse, and later to the companionship of a chauffeur, or allowed the freedom of the streets."[18] The highly sensationalized trial of eighteen-year-old

Richard Loeb and nineteen-year-old Nathan Leopold for the murder of Bobby Franks in 1924 demonstrated that youth from wealthy families could develop the same psychological disorders as any other children who grew up in broken homes. Defense attorney Clarence Darrow used psychiatrists and expert witnesses to "depict the crime as a reaction to loveless childhoods, sexual abuse by an overly controlling governess, feelings of physical inferiority, trauma over a mother's death, and pressures for extreme overachievement." Historian Steven Mintz argues that before the 1920s, juvenile delinquents were assumed to be subnormal in intelligence and uneducated. One juvenile court judge warned parents that the Leopold and Loeb case was "more than a story of murder" but in reality it was a "story of modern youth, of modern parents, of modern economic and social conditions, and of modern education."[19]

Whether or not a family experienced temporary difficulties due to death, divorce, or some other form of absenteeism was irrelevant to some private school educators, who advocated that the home should be avoided altogether. The interwar period ushered in an increased reliance on scientific experts for advice on child rearing that in many cases supported the idea that all children would be better off if they were separated from their parents. Reflecting a decline in birthrates, by the turn of the century, children had become "priceless" and parents needed to pay careful attention not only to their health, but their emotional and psychological development. The notion that mothers could use instinct to properly care for children began to decline in the late nineteenth century, and by the 1920s, the only competent mothers were those who sought out and followed expert advice. Physicians were particularly hostile to mothers and came up with detailed, foolproof instructions on how to bathe and feed infants that mothers were expected to follow without question. Motherhood became more scientific, professional, and indispensable on the one hand, but on the other, parents lost confidence in their ability to care for their own children and were often blamed for their children's faults, accidents, and even the high mortality rate. Child science flourished after World War I and focused on the development of "normal" children and ordinary problems as much as juvenile delinquency. In the process of the scientific study of children, parenting also became an object of study. The appropriate social and psychological development of adolescent sons focused on masculinity, which could be hindered by authoritarian or emotionally absent fathers and indulgent, overprotective, doting mothers.[20]

Child science was research-based for the purpose of devising scientific solutions to social problems. A 1928 study on the nature of character, conducted by Columbia University, investigated the effects of homelife on children's likelihood for deceit. The structure of the study as well as the results revealed concerns of parents, educators, teachers, and psychologists regarding the influence of families on children's character. The questions included in the study also revealed what authorities considered to be exemplary and nonexemplary parental behavior. In assessing the homelife of students, an experienced "school visitor" went to 150 representative homes to assess each family's economic situation; the intelligence, level of education, physical health, and church affiliation of both the father and the mother; mutual adjustment of parents; marital status; parental discipline; attitude of parents toward the child; and general atmosphere of the household.

Each factor was rated on a continuum and given a numeric score ranging from 0 to 100. Under the category "Home Life" one of the indicators of "handicap" was "Employment of mother." At the low end of a continuum was the statement "Working out by week. Sweatshop work at home. Occupation bad for children." In the middle of the range was "Work at home; children not involved. Occasional work out." A family would earn a score of 100 if the mother was "Not contributing to family support." In addition, children from public and private schools in urban, suburban, and village communities answered carefully contrived questions about their families. For example, students were asked to underline "usual" or "not usual" in response to several statements, including, "When the child kicked and screamed, the mother let her do whatever she wanted," "Each child in the family has a separate bed," and "The father made his children obey by hitting them over the head." Of the ten statements, only two had any sort of slightly positive connotation: "Sometimes the father reads stories to the children," and "The family took some of their friends to ride in an automobile."[21] These questions reflected a modern ideal of mothers who did not indulge their children, and companionate rather than authoritarian fathers. The results of the study supported the idea that home conditions, created by parents, were a significant factor in any propensity for deceit. The study concluded that "deceit is associated with such factors as parental discord, parental example, bad discipline, unsocial attitude toward children, impoverished type of community, and changing social or economic situation; and certain combinations of these 'handicaps' with personal handicaps tend to distinguish the group of most dishonest from the group of most honest children."[22]

Private school educators were among the new quasi experts who seemed to believe that no child's mental, moral, and physical development should be left in the hands of nonprofessional women. Historian Joseph Hawes suggests that experts themselves drove the perception of a crisis, motivated by a desire for intellectual power.[23] If it were up to Horace Holden, no boy of privilege over the age of seven would be reared at home because of the natural incompetence of parents.

The support of the parents is the corner-stone of success; yet in many instances—especially when the school is within a short distance of the home—the indulgent father or selfish mother attempts to thwart the influence of the school by continued efforts to secure privileges which are out of harmony with the regulation of the school. . . . I am personally of the opinion that the discipline of the home can never be as wholly effective as that of the boarding school. . . . The petting at home, the exaggeration of the slightest ailment into something serious, the home luxury and indulgence, all constitute to my mind, the most serious menace to the national character.[24]

In Holden's ideal world, boys would be reared in homes where fathers had time to devote to their sons' educational, moral, mental, and physical development, but since this was not the case, boarding schools were the next best thing. Furthermore, children of elite parents had unique challenges that were best dealt with by sending them to boarding school. He admitted that "the boarding-school may find quite as much missionary work to accomplish with the neglected children of the rich, as the city public school finds to do with the neglected children of the poor."[25] Other educators agreed that boarding school was one way of deterring the effects of wealth on the moral development of privileged children. In his 1940 address to the Association of Private School Teachers in New York, Dr. James McConaughy, president of Wesleyan, argued that "some of these boys (and girls) have tremendous privileges, yet they have great difficulty in becoming adjusted. Some parents are so loving that their children are weak and spineless, instead of being able to stand on their own feet."[26]

Removing children from their environment by sending them to boarding school seemed to many an ideal solution to counter the effects of maternal overprotection, peer pressure, and modern society. Writing for *Harper's* in 1926, Emily Newell Blair explained, "I was not satisfied that our home was the best place for her. Now I had a delightful home, pretty, neat, well run, and happy." However, "My husband was a busy man. His dinner hour varied from six to seven-thirty. He had insomnia and rose any time from seven to nine. He worked very hard. I confess that the home was run for his convenience." Blair believed that her daughter needed a structured regimen that she personally could not provide given that her attention was split between her husband and son, four years younger than her daughter. "I realized that then if ever my daughter must live a regular life with regular hours and must be made to feel that her studies were her business in life, just as the office was my husband's and my housekeeping was mine. She did not fit easily into any scheme. I could not lay down a regime and know it would be followed."[27]

In addition, her daughter "had reached the 'difficult' age when she knew better than I what she should do. She was socially inclined. There were 'beaux.' She yearned for high-heeled shoes and dresses in the extreme of style." Emily Blair began to place restrictions on her daughter, who rebelled. Before sending her daughter to boarding school, Blair described their relationship as one of "antagonism and dislike"; however, after her daughter went away to school and experienced homesickness, she had a renewed appreciation for her home and family. "Going away to school gave her back her home and her mother, not as workroom and mentor, but as haven and confidant." The women who worked at the school, as described by Blair, were the ideal role models and mentors for her daughter. "Grown women set the standard and determined the atmosphere, not girls." Boarding school life helped deter the negative impact of peer influence that mothers found difficult to control.[28]

Blair also sent her son to a boarding school and again reacted to her friends' concern about sending children away from home. In her response, she explained the problems of the modern home. She argued that by the time she sent him away at age fifteen, the "home has done its best for a boy" and after that "it often does its worst." If a home has done its duty, according to Blair,

it has given him his foundation of character, his ideals, his standards. It is now time for him to test them out. They are not tried out in the home. They may have been in the old-fashioned home where a large family was organized like a miniature social organism. But in a modern home, with two or perhaps three children of widely separated ages, it is very different. Such a home may be a nursery, a garden, but it cannot be a microcosm in which the social virtues may be developed or the ideals and standards having to do with social intercourse are tried out.

Furthermore, in the home the boy was "the center of everything; conversation, plans—all revolve around him, what he likes and what he wants come first." If a parent tried to deny a boy to put him in his place, "the boy knows that it is all forced for a purpose or he thinks it shows lack of sympathy on the part of parents, and this widens the gap of misunderstanding between him and them."[29]

Parents were clearly incapable of ensuring the future of American civilization by raising their own sons and sent their children to boarding schools under the care of experts dedicated to this important task. These headmaster experts of the interwar period met annually to discuss the problems of modern youth and usually came to the same solution—boarding school. During the administrators' discussion at the 1935 Annual Meeting of the Secondary Education Board on the topic of "Emotional Problems and Their Solutions," Herbert S. Carter, headmaster of the Harvey School in New York, argued that minor emotional disabilities could be solved by removing children from the home situation and getting them into a contemporary environment. Dr. Henry L. Bibby of Kingston, New York, who was formerly associated with St. Luke's Hospital, warned of the danger of guiding a child on an emotional basis. The schoolmaster must "bring the child constantly face to face with reality, to replace the ideal father or mother, in that he must himself exemplify and bring out in the child a completely unemotional standard of conduct." According to Dr. Bibby, "almost every parent, no matter how intelligent, is greatly in danger of handicapping a child by his own emotions and fostering dependence through unconscious projection of his own emotional attitudes." Because of sentimental attachments to their children, parents did not have the capacity to administer appropriate punishment or reward. Therefore, Dr. Bibby concluded, it was "important that a complete break in the highly emotional contacts with parents take place." Expert Dr. Percy G. Kammerer, provost of Avon Old Farms, added to the discussion by pointing out that "parents pass their own complexes on to their children," arguing that "the schoolmaster was the substitute for the father and must strive to represent to the child the ideally adjusted rational adult."[30]

Some educators believed that being an only child could hinder personal growth and character development. According to J. O. Engleman, superintendent of schools in Illinois, the "petted, spoiled only child . . . may be selfish and self-centered in the extreme. . . . He resents authority. He expects everybody to bend to his will. He is a social nonconformist."[31] Horace Holden also gave advice on how boys should spend their time away from school. He agreed that "boys who are sent to boarding schools at an early age, certainly should have some acquaintance with their families" and hoped "that the boy will have brothers and sisters and other companions his own age." The comradeship of a sister was of vital importance for the young boy in order to "reacquaint him with feminine ways, without leading him toward unnecessary temptations."[32] Whether they spoiled their children, neglected their children, or simply did not have enough children, parents ran the risk of endangering the character development of their offspring.

The attack on parents was particularly harsh when it came to mothers, especially when it came to the upbringing of sons. The ideal of Victorian moral motherhood prescribed that the maternal role was a lifelong occupation "incompatible with the demands of wage earning" and mothers needed to "bind their children (especially their boys) to home with 'silver cords' of love" to cultivate moral development. In the 1920s and 1930s, this traditional conception of motherhood competed with modernists' vision of mothers as simply females who went "through a certain biological experience." The antimaternalist arguments of the interwar period came from critics who believed the Victorian construction of motherhood was too sentimental and from a creation of "social scientists and experts who sought to extend their professional expertise." What had appeared as motherly self-sacrifice a generation earlier was viewed by modern critics as narcissistic, possessive, selfish, and manipulative. A widow, who declined to remarry in order to "devote herself fully to her children," was the exaltation of self-sacrifice in the nineteenth century. By the 1920s, the "growing skepticism of mother love" presented these women as pathogenic and selfish. Psychological experts and cultural commentators argued that a woman could not be a good mother outside of a sexually satisfying marriage because she would use mother love toward her sons to replace the sexual intimacy lacking in her own life. Modern mothers seemed unable to avoid smothering their children for a host of reasons, prompting experts to intervene for the sake of protecting boys.[33]

One of the more significant social problems throughout the first half of the twentieth century was maternal overprotection, especially when it prevented boys from becoming independent, self-reliant men of character. In the late 1930s, David M. Levy, MD, chief of staff of the New York Institute for Child Guidance, conducted a study of maternal overprotection and published the results in 1943. Based on twenty cases that he argued represented "pure" examples, those that had observable clinical manifestations, Levy suggested that the "maternal overprotective attitude is a very common one, very likely universal," and created three groups of expression: excessive contact, infantilization, and prevention of independent behavior. Of the twenty cases, nineteen were male, and since it was generally accepted that "the most potent of all influences on social behavior is derived from the primary social experience with the mother," she was largely to blame for rearing sons who were either too submissive or dominating. This was the result of allowing boys to sleep with mothers longer than was appropriate (sometimes into adolescence), lacking bedtime and mealtime routines, denying them freedom to develop friendships with other boys, interfering on their behalf at school, enforcing rigid discipline to do schoolwork at home to achieve academic success, and otherwise preventing "their growth in the direction of self-reliance." Lack of marital sexual compatibility, nonexistent social life outside of the home, affect hunger, thwarted ambitions, and even penis envy, according to experts, helped to explain maternal overprotection and mothers' need to dote on their male offspring.[34]

Levy found that mothers of dominating children were indulgent and mothers of submissive children were dominating. In the case of dominating children, some of the parents in the study were practically terrorized by their sons. A fifteen-year-old struck his mother and sister when his wishes were crossed, threw dishes during quarrels, and was "openly critical and disparaging of his parents." He was so tyrannical toward his mother "that on one occasion when he was visiting a relative, she moved to another residence, hoping to abandon him." Aggressive behavior resulted as an act of rebellion to overprotective mothers' denials of social contact or participation in sports. Boys who were the object of a mother's aggression were typically referred to the study by teachers or social workers because of "sissy" behavior. The consequences of overprotection were dire. Overprotected youths would become demanding, selfish, tyrannical adults who would respond to denials of wishes with impatience or outbursts of temper or assault. On the other hand, experts recognized that "bossy and demanding behavior might be modified into leadership and assertiveness" if treated. Treatment included psychotherapy for the mother, father, and child; educational therapy; and "environmental or manipulative therapy" to make the mother and child more independent of each other, which included sending a child to camp or boarding school.[35]

At least one ranch school teacher identified maternal overprotection as the source of boys' character deficiencies. Former master Harry L. Coderre's thesis, "Disciplinary Problem in the Western Ranch School," recognized at least two cases of hypochondria among ranch school students:

> P.L. and B.B., both fourteen, were confirmed hypochondriacs. Their backgrounds were amazingly similar. Both had been pampered and petted by their parents. This same treatment had different results, however. B.B. became commanding and over-bearing; P.L. developed into a shy, retiring youngster, literally afraid of his shadow. Both demanded continual attention and care. Both took advantage of the situation to invoke sympathies of certain of the more credulous and avoid school appointments and duties.[36]

Hypochondria was a clinically acknowledged symptom of maternal overprotection, resulting from mothers' attention to any signs of illness in their children. Furthermore, mothers of weak or frail children with physical ailments tended to develop heightened overprotective tendencies. The parents' pampering and petting caused one to be dominant and the other submissive—the two expected outcomes of overprotection through parental indulgence and dominance respectively. Because so many ranch school students suffered from respiratory ailments and sinus trouble with expectations that the warm dry climate would alleviate such illnesses, cases of hypochondria must have plagued several masters. Coderre described another student as a classic example of infantilization. "J.T." was thirteen years old, and "up to the age of twelve" had "never dressed himself, had not brushed his teeth, or combed his hair." All of this had been done by a governess and left him "completely helpless." To make matters worse, in "acknowledging their own failure," the parents "demanded that his progress in school be equal to that of boys his own age . . . who were years ahead of him in maturity."[37] Boys suffering from hypochondria and infantilization not only benefited from going away to boarding school; ranch schools with the emphasis on re-creating the "Old West" had the ability to teach self-reliance and help boys overcome adversity.

Recognizing the modern problems of child rearing and especially the tendency for maternal overprotection or other "spoiling" among wealthy households, some ranch schools did their best to prevent mothers from further ruining sons. According to former faculty member Fermor Church, the Los Alamos Ranch School was purposefully located in a remote area of New Mexico because of a "conviction that boys become men more easily when separated from over-solicitous mothers." The Churches justified their child-rearing philosophy by emphasizing the southwestern heritage of the "Pueblo Indians, whose settlements on the mesas go back to pre-Columbian times" and who "still take their young boys at a certain age and segregate them in the kivas away *from* women to receive their indoctrination into manhood." Their son Theodore wrote that "in the beginning women were tolerated rather than welcomed into the school community because wives were known to have a distracting habit of becoming mothers."[38] Sherman Thacher had to contend with maternal meddling as parents came to live in Ojai, California, to be closer to their sons while they attended his school. A typical notice in the local paper began "Mrs.—, will make her home in the valley for several years. Her son attends Thacher School." Unable to relocate herself, one eastern mother "sent her son under the protection of a nurse who remained in Ojai as a proxy nuisance." On one of his occasional outbursts, Thacher asserted that he had "no fundamental objections to mothers.... It is only when Mother, like Mary's lamb, follows him to school that Teacher is annoyed."[39]

Emily Blair, the mother who wrote about sending her son and daughter to boarding school, explained that "modern homes could not produce artificially what the old-fashioned home produced naturally—the discipline that comes from many people acting and reacting on one another." Blair astutely understood the complexities of the modern family. Because couples had fewer children, they could expect to have a more intimate relationship with them than had their forebears. On the other hand, such intimacy lessened parental authority and could lead to overprotection or spoiling. Many parents who could afford to send their children to boarding schools hired servants who permitted parents, mothers especially, more time to devote to their children and risk smothering them, or gave them more time to spend outside of the home, thus neglecting them. Even during the Depression, David Wilhelm's family employed a cook and two maids.[40] The constructed family environment of ranch schools had the advantage of producing an atmosphere much like "the old-fashioned home" because many children, near the same age, lived in one community. The size of ranch schools allowed the headmaster and headmistress an appropriate degree of familiarity to provide comfort and support to the students in their care. Because the care of boys was their livelihood, the relationship was more professional than could ever be achieved at home.

Ranch school owners and headmasters well understood their obligation to provide the benefits of a nuclear family for students who came from broken homes, or "normal" homes with parents who had the best intentions but could not help but be too intimate or intrusive to properly cultivate successful, independent, self-reliant men. Because so many ranch school students suffered from health problems, the smaller student-to-faculty ratio ensured that ranch schools could be both nurturing and rugged as boys transformed from delicate children to robust leaders. At the Fresnal Ranch School, for example, "the life of the school is an intimate one and is made as much like a home as possible."[41] In 1927, Mrs. Arthur Woods and her husband financed and opened the Arizona Desert School "in order that there might be a place in the dry, bracing climate of the Arizona desert where young and delicate boys could live a healthy outdoor ranch life, and at the same time receive expert physical care and sound teaching amid friendly, homelike surroundings." The brochure further assured that the smaller size of the school allowed for "individual care and understanding" under "watchful guidance in the general development of his mind and character which he could ordinarily find only at home."[42] One year later, the Arizona Home School, a ranch school for boys under the age of fourteen, opened in Tucson. Wealthy parents of eastern children who wished to place their sons in the warm, dry atmosphere of Arizona planned and financed the school. Accordingly, only a small number of students were to be admitted to the school in order to maintain "a homelike atmosphere rather than a school-like one."[43] The Judsons' efforts to create a family environment at their school were noticed by their students. In the 1935 yearbook, a student author proclaimed, "Mr. and Mrs. Judson have been father and mother to us all for the last seven months. They have watched our diets, attended our minor ills, rewarded our efforts, and occasionally, have punished our misdemeanors."[44]

Much of the architecture reflected the effort to offer a homelike environment, with modern sanitary amenities and health-promoting, sun-filled, ventilated rooms. Many western ranch schools chose to build suites, where students occupied a single room or had one roommate, rather than large institutional

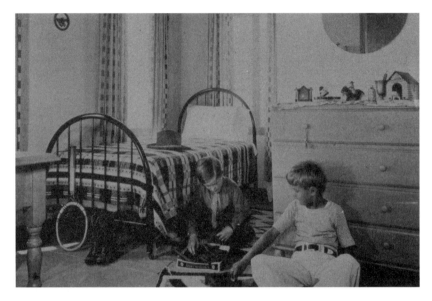

This image from a promotional brochure for the Judson School showcases the home-like interiors of boys' rooms. Notice the cowboy boots by the bed, cowboy hat on the bed, and the cowboy figurine on the dresser. These props seem strategically situated in the photo to indicate that although the rooms were comfortable, the school was still "western." Courtesy of David C. Lincoln, Phoenix.

dormitories where many students slept in barrack-like rooms. "In order to strengthen the homelike atmosphere" of the Arizona Desert School, the building was planned "as a private house rather than an institution." Each boy had his own room with a bathroom provided for every three to four students. Dormitories at the Judson School contained a classroom, a master's room, and five private boy's rooms designed so that sunlight reached every room. Bathrooms were touted as "modern and sanitary," and a pumping plant furnished an "abundance of exceptionally pure water from a depth of more than two hundred feet."[45]

Attention to water sources and sanitation reflected a modern scientific approach to protecting children from disease. By the early twentieth century, physicians and scientists had widely disseminated research confirming that germs spread in crowded areas. In addition to nineteenth-century contentions that children's health could be protected through nutrition, cleanliness, and clean air, the bacteriology revolution added increased emphasis on fighting germs. The routines of scientific motherhood required copious amounts of water for bathing, drinking, and cleaning that was oftentimes unavailable in rural areas. This reassurance from the Judson School that clean water was available in the desert Southwest was an important selling point for parents who understood modern practices of health and hygiene. Most schools also publicized the availability of homogenized milk fortified with vitamin D and fresh citrus, reflecting early twentieth-century discoveries and treatment for nutritional-deficiency diseases like rickets and scurvy. In doing so, they assured parents that their schools were not only "homelike" but scientific and modern.[46] In promoting the health benefits of Arizona, one physician proclaimed that the state was "the natural home of the orange, lemon, date, pomegranate, apricot, peach, and of almost every other fruit and vegetable."[47]

Headmasters, teachers, and students gathered in common rooms for evening activities that facilitated a model of the ideal middle-class Victorian and early twentieth-century families. At the Judson School, "upon entering the spacious, sunny dining room, the homelike atmosphere" was readily apparent. "The living room is a pleasant gathering place for the school family" and contained a piano, radio, and Victrola that made "evenings pass quickly."[48] Sherman Thacher relished his after-supper evening readings when, for forty minutes each day, he became the patriarch of a large family. "In addition to digestive advantages," it was highly educational, as he introduced boys to Odysseus, the Trojan Horse, Dickens, and Shakespeare, often in dialect. It was also an opportunity for Thacher's mother, faculty wives, and later his daughters to participate in school activities and foster a sense of a family community he so desired for his school. According to his biographer, "in the twilight his voice was accompanied by the 'click' of knitting needles and the occasional squeaking of a chair under a squirming boy."[49] The main school-wide social gathering at the Arizona Desert School consisted of sunset services held every Sunday at an open-air chapel built by boys and faculty. Services were not necessarily of a religious nature and speakers included members of the clergy, school faculty, local community leaders, and faculty from the University of Arizona.[50]

The small enrollment at ranch schools made it convenient for owners to run their schools as a family operation but may have created difficulty in implementing disciplinary matters, since headmasters became personally known to students. At larger schools, masters and mistresses served as intermediaries between headmasters and owners. Harry Coderre, a former master at one of the Arizona ranch schools, asserted that in attempting to offer a different system of training, ranch schools "had the temerity to dispense with the tradition of formality at the eastern schools." The ranch school headmaster dealt with all infractions of rules in a rather subjective manner, since "the headmaster is guided by his own opinion of a student," which could work to the advantage, as well as the disadvantage, of the student. "Because the headmaster is so close to the student body," Coderre contended, it was a "common move for the students to appeal all decisions of the masters to the headmaster," effectively diminishing masters' disciplinary authority.[51]

Traditional gender roles dictated the division of labor for the management and daily responsibilities of ranch school operations and contributed to an ideal of middle-class expectations for the home environment. The nature of running a ranch, however, often enabled husbands and wives to labor as equal partners, much like America's preindustrial, agricultural families. In his seminal work on dude ranches, Lawrence Borne found that "both as guests and as managers or owners, women were consistently active in the operation of dude ranches."[52] Ranch school wives supervised domestic staff and performed household chores while husbands supervised ranch operations, faculty, and the instruction of pupils. With the introduction of science and psychology into American homes during the interwar period, the status of all mothers was somewhat elevated. Women who served in the domestic operation of ranch schools were truly professional mothers, whose labor was essential to their family's economic livelihood. In the absence of wives, ranch school owners hired women to assume these responsibilities. Los Alamos Ranch School hired Miss Genevieve Ranger to serve as both matron and nurse. She lived in a small cottage that also functioned as the infirmary and guesthouse for visiting parents. As matron, Ranger oversaw the general housekeeping, "which meant coping with temperamental cooks and elusive Indian or Spanish-American houseboys, as well as planning menus both wholesome and abundant." Ranger also contributed to creating a domesticated atmosphere by keeping "black pottery bowls filled with local wild flowers."[53] In order to fulfill their primary aim of character development by making men out of boys, women's involvement with teenaged boys was limited, but they often assisted in the care of younger boys. At the Fresnal Ranch School, for example, a brochure assured prospective parents that "each boy receives the very closest attention from the masters and directors—both in class and during the day, and younger boys are given special care by the headmaster's wife."[54]

The housemother, usually the wife of the headmaster or co-owner, played an integral role in creating the homelike atmosphere in addition to managing domestic work. According to Holden, the housemother "must have the general supervision of domestic affairs and give her personal attention to the care and comfort of boys. In the matter of selection, she is of no less importance than the masters." Mature, older women were preferable to "inexperienced young girls, just from college or normal school," who were "unwilling and unable to deal with the vital, bodily side of life."[55] In other words, Holden wanted women with experience as mothers. It seems Judson students also recognized this need for maternal instinct and wisdom. According to one student author, Laura Judson was "ideally suited" to her position as headmistress because "she gives the place an atmosphere of comfort and attends to our needs with the sure knowledge of boys acquired in raising her two sons."[56] Before he married, Sherman Thacher's mother, Madam Thacher, "mended their manners" but refused to mend boys' clothing, "knowing that if she once weakened, she would never have any peace." To keep boys clothed and presentable, Thacher hired a local woman one day a week. In addition, he hired local Chinese men for most domestic tasks, including cooking and cleaning.[57] At ranch schools especially, women's role as "civilizers" was a significant counterbalance to the masculine culture of cowboys.

An important responsibility of women at private schools was the cultivation of manners. Cole ranked the category "Manners and General Culture" just above "Substitute or Supplement for the Home" in importance for meeting the aims of private school education for boys. Cole found that enforcement of table etiquette, dances, lectures, and exams on the subject of manners and social custom were the primary means of instilling "manners and general culture." Headmasters' wives' role in instilling the qualities necessary for social poise was mentioned by forty-two schools.[58] The introduction of manners and culture was largely the responsibility of the home, although reformers did advocate that some instruction should be part of all school curricula. Data collectors for Columbia University's study on children's likelihood for deceit developed an indicator of children's knowledge of manners and culture and found that "children who have better manners, who are better acquainted with art and music and the influences that indicate culture and refinement, and whose parents treat them decently are less deceptive than others who do not show these refinements." In the assessment of students' knowledge of manners, they were asked to answer true or false to a series of statements, including "Food may be carried to the mouth with either a fork or knife," "A waiter, in passing a dish, offers it at your right hand," "One should give attention to another who is talking to him whether he is interested or not," and "The wearing of much jewelry marks a girl as a person of poor taste." The authors of the study stated that they included an assessment of manners because this information "might afford a key to refinement of a sort that would be symptomatic of careful family training."[59] Because boarding schools served as both the family and the school, it was expected that graduates would obtain manners appropriate to their class while away at school.

Although nothing indicates that ranch school students took tests on the topic of etiquette, most ate in a family setting where manners were enforced, attended social functions, and were expected to act like gentlemen. For example, school attire at the Fresnal Ranch School consisted of western wear with the exception of the requirement that boys dressed for dinner. Dances and social functions were usually orchestrated by faculty wives or mothers of students. In the 1940–1941 edition of the *Gopher World*, written and produced by Judson students, a page is dedicated to "Items of a Social Nature." In November 1940, Mr. and Mrs. Judson hosted a formal Friday evening party for Judson School boys and girls from the Jokake School. According to the student author, "dinner was served in the dining room, and later dancing was enjoyed in the spacious living room of the Judson's home. A Phoenix orchestra played popular dance numbers until the closing hour of midnight." Younger boys attended birthday parties in honor of their classmates hosted by their own families. Mrs. H. Edward Manville gave a party in honor of her grandson, Folke Bernadotte. Judson boys had a "sumptuous luncheon at the Manville home" before going to the "Biltmore corral where cowboys entertained with roping, singing, and games."[60] Evening meal rituals further served as a means of instilling a sense of family and community at western ranch schools, and at the same time enforced dining etiquette. Mr. and Mrs. Judson always sat together in the dining room, ate with the students family style, and enforced appropriate table manners. Ormonde Parke remembered that "you sat up straight and you couldn't bring your face down to the food . . . you didn't speak until spoken to."[61]

The celebration of holidays and birthdays at ranch schools further demonstrated women's significant role in the instruction of social customs and in creating a homelike atmosphere for the students who attended ranch schools. For example, at the Orme School, "Aunt Minna" made "angel food cake for every student to serve on their birthday and placed dimes in front of each piece for good luck."[62] Many ranch school students did not go home over holiday vacations, which required ranch school owners to plan activities for students, many times opening up their own homes to "holiday orphans." The Ormes hosted dinners for students on Thanksgiving and Christmas. At the Judson School in 1940, the Judsons hosted a Christmas Eve dinner party "followed by a visit from St. Nick and the opening of gifts around a beautifully decorated tree (a spruce from the forest near Prescott, Arizona)."[63] Because holiday preparations typically fell under the purview of wives and mothers, this too became an important responsibility of ranch school women.

Although the tasks were different for men and women, married couples functioned as equal partners, which was clearly apparent in the relationship between most ranch school husbands and wives. George A. Harper and Captain Russell B. Fairgrieve established the Southern Arizona School for Boys (SASB) in 1930. Upon its opening, Harper served as headmaster and Fairgrieve as the business superintendent. The founders' wives were also employed at SASB. Mrs. Mabel Baker Fairgrieve was the school secretary and Mrs. Mary E. Harper "held the significant position of housemother."[64] According to an SASB brochure, "the housemother's interest, particularly with the younger boys, is an invaluable asset."[65] By 1940, both couples still held positions at the school, with Fairgrieve now serving as director, his wife Mabel as the housemother, and Mary Harper in the position of "Boys' Advisor." The Fairgrieves relocated to Tucson from Columbus, Ohio, with daughter Beverly in 1926, and Captain Fairgrieve remained the director of the school until his retirement sometime in the 1960s. In its 1940–1941 brochure under the heading "An Ideal Ranch School," the author described the atmosphere of the school as a big family whose interests and responsibilities were shared by each member of the group.[66]

Most other Arizona ranch schools were similarly run by husband-and-wife teams who strove to create a family atmosphere at their schools. George Howard Atchley and his wife, Rubie Hammarstrom Atchley, cofounded Green Fields School in 1933. Rubie was born in San Francisco in 1891, graduated with a degree in history from the University of Oregon in 1912, and taught at the Franklin

High School in Portland, where she met her future husband. For a brief period prior to her marriage, Rubie accompanied her younger sister Grace to New York and launched her career in private education by securing a teaching position at St. Mary's School in Peekskill. Upon their marriage, the newlyweds moved to Tucson, where George assumed a position in the Tucson City Engineer's Office. The couple lived in Tucson for approximately three years before George accepted a management position at Jones and Laughlin Steel, requiring the couple to move to Aliquippa, Pennsylvania. While in Pennsylvania, Rubie taught at the Sewickly Academy in Pittsburgh, where she made important contacts that later facilitated her recruitment efforts for Green Fields.[67]

After ten years of failing health, George was ready to return to the dry climate of the Southwest. Rubie's dream and vision led to the couple's decision to start an academically sound school in a rural environment. Initially, the school's aim was to prepare younger boys for admittance to prestigious eastern preparatory schools like St. Paul's Academy and Exeter. In this partnership, Rubie taught all of the classes and recruited students from her connections with the upper-class families in Pittsburgh. When enrollment increased, requiring additional teaching staff, Rubie hired and supervised faculty. George took care of building construction and maintenance, instructed students in riflery, took care of discipline, and worked on the alfalfa farm that gave the school its name— Green Fields. The school's historian and author described George Atchley as "a kind of distant but kindly paterfamilias, well-loved and respected, but known well only to a few; yet his later messages" to the boys "attest that he knew and cared for them all."[68]

The Atchleys provided their young students with a home away from home. Students bunked with the directors in the main house at least until the late 1940s and early '50s. Sometime prior to 1940, several small houses with private baths, each accommodating two boys, appeared on the campus. Meals were formal and were presided over by Mr. Atchley. Many students remembered playing with "Pittsburgh Smog," the Atchley family's pet dog, and there were strict orders never to sit in the chair that belonged to Mrs. Atchley's white Persian. Other family pets included Petunia the burro, peafowls, rabbits, and assorted lizards and horned toads. When the student population rose to twenty-four in 1936, the Atchleys hired Frederick Baltzell as the school's first employed teacher. Baltzell had a BA in English and a BS from Ohio State University and earned a salary of $26 a month plus board.[69] Although the Atchleys had no children, the family's legacy continued after George's and Rubie's deaths. Upon George Atchley's death in 1942, Baltzell, who had advanced to the position of assistant director, was appointed codirector with Rubie Atchley. Her sister, Grace, arrived in 1947 to take over Rubie's teaching responsibilities so that she could devote her full attention to the administration of the school. A dedicated leader, Rubie continued to run the school until her death in 1950. Rubie Atchley left the school to her sister, Grace Hammarstrom, and her brother, Captain Lloyd Hammarstrom. Capably assisted by Baltzell, Grace carried on her sister's legacy and vision for Green Fields until her retirement in 1962.[70]

The Orme family ran the Orme School for two generations. Both generations of Ormes created the ideal western family experience for students and used traditional gender roles to divide the tasks of running a school and ranch. Upon the insistence of the owners, students referred to the Ormes as "Aunt Minna" and "Uncle Chick." Minna served as the housemother for the children of the school, and to the students' good fortune, she was also a great amateur astronomer and botanist who took every opportunity to share her experience with Orme School children.[71] According to one student, "Aunt Minna is like a mother to all of us. She sews on buttons for us, takes care of us when we are sick, and adds a cheerful atmosphere to the whole ranch which wouldn't be the same without her." She described Uncle Chick as "the jack of all trades on the ranch" who "does such things as putting up telephone lines, fixing light and power difficulties and fuses. He also teaches welding." Alumni Jeb John Rosebrook described Charles Orme Sr. as a "true Jeffersonian man." He was an educator, a state senator for sixteen years, and a rancher who embodied middle-class ingenuity and self-reliance when he decided to attend welding school in order to save himself the trip of going into Phoenix every time a piece of ranch equipment broke.

Of the Ormes' three children, Charlie Orme Jr. took over the school and ranch, assuming the responsibility of headmaster in 1945 upon his graduation from Stanford. That same year, he married Mimi Royce. According to one Orme student, Charlie "has probably more work than any other two people on the ranch. He not only does office work, but also has an agricultural class. Charlie has won the confidence of every student so that if he has to make a disciplinary move it is soon forgotten." The student described Mimi, Charlie's wife, as "a teacher, mother, and a big sister all combined. Many times if there are a few minutes between dinner and study hall, she may be seen surrounded by girls getting the latest styles."[72] Charlie's younger brother, Mort, and his wife Lynn also worked at the Orme School and ranch. In the late 1940s, Mort was in charge of the shop activities, planting, and irrigation. Lynn helped with the house activities in Minna's absence and taught home economics.[73]

The Judson family further illustrated ranch school owners' efforts and strategies to create a family atmosphere at their boarding schools as well as the gendered division of labor. George and Laura Judson cofounded and co-owned the school, dividing daily tasks equally based on early twentieth-century gender norms. Ormonde Parke remembered that Mrs. Judson supervised the cleaning women, the nurse, and the cook and his wife. If students chose to attend Christian religious services, Laura accompanied them to the Episcopal Church. The Judsons' daughter-in-law, Gloria, believed that Laura was "especially nice to the boys who didn't really fit in. And of course Barney [her son] would have to be because it was the family's living." According to the students' yearbook, Mrs. Judson was "always nice to us, and in many ways has been a mother to each boy. She always has a cheery smile and a welcome 'Good Morning.'"[74] George could then function as the disciplinarian. His preferred form of punishment was to send students to bed and make them stay there during the afternoon activities. One of George's other responsibilities was to go to market to purchase food.

As the patriarch of the Judson School family, George Judson also represented the ideal of the self-made man, demonstrating how the American West still served as a place of great opportunity for anyone willing to work hard and make something of themselves. Judson was born in Michigan and put himself through Kalamazoo College, where he earned his bachelor of science degree. During his summers, he worked for Madame Heard, who introduced Judson to her son, Dwight Heard, a prominent man in the developing city of Phoenix, whose legacy includes the world-renowned Heard Museum. Dwight met George and "thought he was an up and coming young man with a lot to offer" and suggested that George move to Phoenix. Judson moved to Phoenix in 1911 after his college graduation and was employed as principal of the Osborn School. In a short time he became the superintendent of the Osborn School District while earning a second bachelor's degree and later a master of arts from the University of Arizona. In 1928 Judson built and directed the Judson School for Boys with his wife Laura.

The couple had the rare ability to work as equal business partners while maintaining a strong marriage. After selling the Judson School to J. Blake Field and Henry Wick, George taught at Williams Air Force Base before purchasing the Arizona Desert School in 1948. During the summer of that year, Laura stayed at the school in Tucson while George traveled in an effort to recruit students. In a series of letters that Laura wrote to George that summer, it was apparent she had complete authority for budgeting, purchasing, and contracting the equipment and services necessary to open the school for the fall semester. Her letters were filled with sentiments as well as progress updates and expenditures. In one letter to George, she wrote, "Just remember I think of you whatever I am up to and will be inspired by thinking of our month or two together in the east" and signed it, "Fond love, Laura." Yet in a hurried letter she wrote that "we have 16 boys' rooms ready," and informed him of a $182.00 bill for mattresses that could be paid in October since she purchased them from "your old friend Jenkins mattress factory."[75]

Irma Dew Larom of Cody was one of the few ranch school wives who was a western native. Before marrying Larry Larom in 1920 she was a teacher at the Sunlight School at Painter, Wyoming, and a librarian in Cody. According to Larom's biographer, "neither Irma nor members of her family had the social and economic status to be considered" as guests at Valley Ranch. He speculated that Larom, determined to make his living in Wyoming, "may have become convinced that no upper-class eastern debutante could adjust to the isolation, rough comforts, and responsibilities of Valley Ranch." While it seemed a good thing for boys to be cut off from urban pleasures, few upper-class women from the East wanted to live permanently isolated from the lifestyle they had become accustomed to, and Larom had already suffered one broken engagement. In a letter Larom wrote to his business partner in 1923, he acknowledged the challenges of hosting strangers and caring for the boys who attended the school. Their marriage lasted fifty-three years.[76]

Other marriages were not as successful and demonstrated what experts warned was becoming of modern American families. The Jokake School for Girls, founded by Barbara and George Ashforth in 1932, was located on the property of the Jokake Inn, owned and operated by Barbara's parents, Sylvia Gates Evans and Robert T. Evans. George came from a New York family that was involved in real estate and met Barbara when he was a guest at the Inn. When asked how she and her husband came up with the idea to start a ranch school, Barbara replied "it was my father's idea really." Apparently Robert Evans was concerned that the young couple was not doing much of anything and expressed his preference that they "get going and do something." Although it was Barbara's family with historic and economic connections to the property that held both the Inn and the school, her name is mysteriously absent from Jokake School's promotional brochures and yearbooks. Barbara explained that "I didn't teach anything. I didn't have the degrees to be a teacher." George Ashforth graduated from Yale and served as the school's director. Barbara ran the housekeeping, supervised the chefs, supplied the food, and did the bookkeeping. Barbara and George Ashforth divorced sometime prior to 1941. Despite Barbara's departure, George continued to run the school for a short period of time before the school closed.[77]

The headmaster of the Arizona Desert School, Matt Baird, was recently divorced when he came out to Tucson to lead the school. In the absence of a headmistress, Mrs. Woods, founder of the school and president of the Board of Directors, served as the school's long-distance matriarch. She and her husband maintained a residence in New York City where the Arizona Desert School had an eastern office. When it came time for students to travel to Tucson for the start of the school year, Mrs. Woods was charged with organizing the trip and rounding up Arizona Desert School–bound boys at Grand Central Station. Matt Baird, however, was truly the heart of the school. Alumni remembered him as very charismatic, a "macho type of crew man" who "activated" the school, and at least three claimed that their mothers were in love with him.[78] Very few if any of the masters at the Arizona Desert School were married, which left the maternal responsibility to students' mothers, whose involvement was sporadic because of distance.

The idea of a prep school as a family community was not exclusive to ranch schools, but it meshed well with a mythic ideal of middle-class ranches. Whether students were from broken homes or suffering from parental neglect or maternal overprotection, experts recommended boarding school as a means to behavioral modifications through "environmental manipulation." The end result was that many students received much more personalized attention, yet this may have contributed to school disciplinary problems. Nuclear families ran these schools much like a family business, and often grown children worked at the schools, taking over a ranch school upon the retirement or death of their parents. As the result, the schools represented the ideal of the self-sufficient family that was especially celebrated during the Depression. Women and men had equally important roles in the management of the schools and in accomplishing the daily tasks necessary to sustain all aspects of ranch school operations. Much like the ideal of the ranching family who raised cattle and corn, this western tradition was appropriately and necessarily adopted by ranch school entrepreneurs. Creating this sense of community that embraced middle-class family values was an important attribute of western ranch schools, especially during the 1920s and 1930s when modern society seemed to have a negative impact on American families.

CONCLUSION

We have a heavy stake in this younger generation so soon to take our places
on life's great stage. We are all building for the future. Our task will never be
completed as we wish to have them. Others must carry on our work and
carry it to the higher levels our vision has pictured for it. And these others
are the youth of the present day.

—*Alfred E. Stearns, 1923*

STEARNS CONVEYED HIS AND PREVIOUS GENERATIONS' ANXIETY ABOUT
the future as expressed through a concern for youth. The post–World War I era
realized that the world had changed, and many were unsure about the direction
it was headed. Private school headmasters like Stearns took an antimodern approach to curing society's ills by harking back to a time before urbanization,
materialism, extreme wealth, broken homes, and progessive education had so
greatly challenged the character of youth. "In the new and somewhat changed
conditions under which youth is forced to fight its upward way we are a bit
perplexed as to the part we should play," he confided to his readers. "The old
standards do not seem to fit. The old rules will not always hold. Many of the
most helpful agencies of former days have been swept away. We need help; and
we turn eagerly to any who by experience or position seem likely to offer any
helpful clue to the solution of our baffling problem." In place of church and
home, he believed that private school leaders provided parents with the expert
guidance they so desperately needed in order to preserve family legacies and
ensure the moral future of America.[1]

By the time Stearns wrote *The Challenge of Youth* in 1923, he had served as principal of Phillips Andover for twenty years. In his book he described the degrading influence of materialism, movies, and literature, and the social condition of the times with its "lack of the old and tested moral standards; the increasing disrespect of the law; the undermining of the home; the flippancy with which many of the sacred things of life are discussed and treated; all-night dances for children in their early teens"; and the list continued. Throughout the account parents were the common link to each of these challenges and emerged as the true problem. Parents permitted their children to see movies that appealed to "the weakest in human nature," chose not to emphasize religion in the home, and refused to discipline their children. "Yesterday's home was a home of moral standards and spiritual ideals," lamented Stearns. Parents ruled supreme to children's benefit, and discipline was "freely administered when the occasion required." In his years dealing with "modern parents of varying types," Stearns concluded he was "more and more impressed with the inherent value that exists in youth. The wonder is that youth has done so well, facing so often a handicap."[2]

Private school headmasters' constant critique of parents echoed state and federal government anxiety of Native American, Mexican, and Mexican American families. Referring to its high foreign-born population, a report by the Arizona State Board of Education noted the predominance of children born to unwed mothers, concluding that "home influence as an educative and controlling factor is therefore weak and a tendency exists toward transiency, social instability and unsatisfactory home conditions."[3] In both cases, the underlying principle was that educational institutions, teachers, and trained professionals could produce better American citizens than could natural parents. The primary aim of private preparatory and government-run Native American boarding schools was to remove children from their homes in order to prepare them for their role as American citizens, according to their race, class, and gender. An important secondary outcome explicit in Native American boarding schools was the ability to impact parents through their children. Upon returning to their communities, it was intended that Native American children would introduce American culture to their Indian homes by teaching parents what they had learned at school.

Private school educators sought similar authority, and parents often received a lecture in character development when they dared question any disciplinary actions of a headmaster. There are significant and obvious exceptions, however. Parents often collaborated with headmasters and shared their goals. If they did not approve of the cultural values that were being instilled in their children, the parents who elected to send their sons to boarding school could take them out. Since private schools depended on revenue from tuition, headmasters had to be careful not to offend too many parents. Native American parents were forced to give up authority for rearing their children while they were at boarding school and had few options for protesting how a school operated other than removing their children altogether. Since Native American boarding schools were government-funded, there was little financial repercussion in such cases.

The proliferation of ranch schools in the interwar period reflected the significant impact of neonatives who relocated to the Southwest. The emigration of families from the Great Lakes region and Atlantic Seaboard was directly related to the growth of tourism and the advice of medical professionals who advocated a warm, dry climate as a curative for a host of respiratory and other ailments. A 1925 report from the Arizona State Board of Education noted how the state's cosmopolitan population positively impacted public education. Three-fourths of Arizona's population was from other states, ranking it forty-fifth among states in terms of its low proportion of native-born citizens. This was not a cause of concern but a great benefit, the report explained. Because of its diverse population, the state "shows no cramping of influence of established traditions, no marked social distributions," and its "people represent the hardy pioneer stock, active, vigorous natures who left established environments to develop new areas." Freedom of thought and a willingness to experiment unburdened by "binding traditions" further characterized the potential benefits of the public school system. Whereas in other areas of the country public schools had to "win their way slowly and with difficulty," Arizona was "settled by people where this fight has already been won, people who have fought and won, people who are familiar with the well-established school systems, and who bring with them an already created demand for good education."[4] Similar remarks could be made about ranch schools. The vast distance from the Atlantic Seaboard and Great Lakes region freed them to improve upon the established preparatory schools by using the region's cultural geography to instill character. The neonatives who established and taught at ranch schools had experience with traditional preparatory schools that they brought with them in the form of credentials and an acceptance of a standard curriculum designed to get students admitted to college, but beyond that, they used the local natural and cultural resources to infuse the values they believed only an immersive experience in the West could provide. While it is true that ranch schools were experimental and less hindered by tradition than their eastern counterparts, their establishment threw into question one of the fundamental aspects of the West that they promoted. The existence of the most expensive private schools in the nation contradicted the notion that fewer class distinctions existed in the American West.

Although distinctly American in its emphasis on the West and its landscape, cultural attributes, and mythic past, the legacy of travel as a rite of passage for manhood has historic ties to the tradition of the Grand Tour of the English nobility. The purpose of the eighteenth-century Grand Tour was to prepare Britain's youth for their role as gentleman leaders and was an essential part of their liberal education. Staple destinations included Rome and Paris, where young men collected artwork and artifacts for their country estates and town houses as a demonstration that they completed this educational and transformative experience. By going to Rome, adolescents would appreciate republican civic virtue, much like ranch school students were expected to pick up the character traits of American pioneers. Enlightenment came from the opportunity to survey one's nation from a distance. This "perspective on otherness" promoted national identity and could "polish" British youth, but critics also feared that instead of "consolidating cultural hegemony of the upper classes," the unstructured, unsupervised experience would leave some in a weakened state, unable to control baser instincts. Travel is disorienting and "by removing individuals from their native soil, incorporates a corresponding removal of the 'rules' which govern their behaviour."[5] Some youths returned a little too polished and had evolved into a state of "unmanly foppery."[6] In reviving the idea of travel as essential to gentlemanly education, ranch schools improved upon the Grand Tour by providing structure and purpose in the form of a preparatory school. They promoted specific masculine traits, rather than leaving it up to a boy's own ability to select the appropriate male role models, and guarded boys' interactions with others who could potentially disrupt the development of character.

Tourism for youth, elite male youth in particular, had different aims than tourism for adults and middle-class-family travel in interwar America. Travel for men-in-the-making had to be enriching, educational, and transformative rather than solely for leisure. Youth traveling alone were not "tourists" but "students." Ranch school students were not sightseers, but in essence became western for seven to eight months out of the year. In her analysis of the children's cottage at the Breakers in Newport, Rhode Island, Abigail Van Slyk argues that the nature of play for children of the elite involved actual doing, rather than playing. While their activity "was akin to the play of middle-class children whose pretend work was often enhanced by toys that were minature versions of tools their parents used," the Vanderbilt children's cottage had a working stove for their daughter Gertrude to cook "an edible meal on a real range."[7] Boys at ranch schools did not play Indian like their middle-class counterparts as part of scouting programs, but stepped into the role of pioneer, gentleman cowboy, and rancher. They used real guns and rode live horses. Since they could not enact activities of Native Americans in a beneficial way, they became amateur archaeologists who dug up artifacts. As collectors of Indian relics, they learned an important cultural practice of the adult world they were expected to inhabit.

Ranch schools were greatly affected by the all-encompassing social and economic changes ushered in by World War II. Across the nation, private school curricula changed to reflect the increased need for students to excel in science, engineering, and technology to assist with the war effort. Veteran private school commentator Porter Sargent noted a "rush to the military school" by nervous parents "advised by friends in the Army or public school men to get their boys into military schools in the hope that they might receive preferred treatment when taken into the armed forces."[8] Mrs. James Conley of West Virginia told a friend that her oldest son was accepted at Williams College, but instead chose a military college "so he wouldn't be called now."[9]

As ranch school teachers, nurses, and cowboys temporarily left their posts to join the war effort, headmasters across the nation expressed concern over their ability to keep their schools in operaton as they faced the "loss by the draft of many of their young unmarried teachers so much needed for dormitory duty." One of the larger preparatory schools reported losing one-quarter of its faculty. Some headmasters had been drafted, including Ashforth of Jokake School for Girls.[10] Judson School students dedicated their final issue of the 1942 *Gopher World* to resident nurse Jeanne Bartlett, who left the school for a tour of duty in the Army Medical Corps.[11] Charlie Orme was granted an agriculture deferment, while cowboy Bruce McDonald took a brief hiatus from the Orme Ranch to serve in the Army.[12] By the end of the war, most ranch schools had closed. The main campus of the Evans School in Mesa closed in 1936. During World War II, it housed Italian prisoners of war transported from California to work on projects for the Salt River Water Users' Association. The Tucson branch continued until the war forced its closing.[13] Both Hacienda del Sol and the Jokake School for Girls closed during the war.

Throughout their history, independent schools have always been at financial risk. Few had endowments, so they relied (and many still rely) solely on tuition and donations from alumni. The wartime economy combined with a decline in financial health during the Depression forced private schools to reexamine their management strategies. Porter Sargent partly blamed lower enrollments of the 1930s and early 1940s on declining birth rates. "As a result of the last war," he argued,

> the birth rate in this country has decreased. And immigration has gradually been choked off. So the crop of children for the schools has shown a marked falling off. . . . By 1940 there were a million less children in the country than there were in 1920. And as the number continues to fall, schools close and teachers lose their jobs. Our educational system cannot operate without a supply of raw material.[14]

For schools that relied solely on tuition from maximum enrollments, this situation exacerbated financial problems.

Practical financial realities pushed several privately owned preparatory schools to transition into not-for-profit corporations governed by boards of trustees. Even as early as the 1920s, prominent eastern schools, including Hill, Spence, Choate, and Riverdale, abandoned private ownership. Schools that delayed the changeover were placed at an enormous financial disadvantage because "hardly anyone would make substantial gifts to institutions run by an individual or family . . . By World War II the standard governance structure of most private schools was an incorporated nonprofit board of trustees who appointed a head, made general policy, and raised money."[15]

After World War II, the Ormes invested their savings in building improvements and added the college preparatory program. In 1960, when the school separated from the family ranching operations, it received nonprofit status and began to operate under a board of trustees. This made it possible for the school to receive tax-deductible gifts. Faced with similar financial pressure, Fred Baltzell presented his concern to a group of parents who convinced him of the advantages of reorganizing Green Fields as a nonprofit corporation. In 1964, the first Green Fields Board of Trustees convened. Baltzell entered into a contract with the board as headmaster, at a salary that was more than he had previously paid himself. The board leased the twelve acres of school and ranch property from Baltzell with a ten-year option to purchase twenty acres and the school buildings from him.[16] That same year, Captain Russell Fairgrieve sold the Southern Arizona School for Boys, which became a nonprofit organization.

Larger economic trends in the post–World War II era brought about some of this decline. Dramatic changes transformed the tourism industry when middle-class Americans, eager to spend their wartime savings, began traveling in record numbers. Many of these travelers found their way to Arizona.[17] Travel, no longer the domain of the upper class, had a profound effect on Arizona's dude ranches. Middle-class guests stayed for days rather than weeks. Arizona's dude ranchers adjusted to their new clientele; in 1948, there were 153 guest ranches in operation across the state.[18] Ranch schools, however, could not adjust as easily. They depended on the elite nature of western travel and the extended visit. Prior to World War II, none had endowments and all relied on the hefty tuition fees paid by parents.

Changes in western masculinity may have also affected the marketability of ranch schools. Prior to World War II, Theodore Roosevelt was the most recognized spokesperson for western masculinity. In the 1950s, a new western hero emerged who became the ideal masculine icon by way of his numerous western films. John Wayne, whose movies provided an escape for the millions of postwar male breadwinners and devoted dads, was the new symbolic western male. Wayne represented a "vanishing symbol of individualism in an age of togetherness and conformity."[19] Striking differences separated Theodore Roosevelt and John Wayne as role models for promoting a western education for boys. Roosevelt, a real, living example of an aristocrat-turned-masculine by his western experience, went on to have a very successful political career. He was of the same economic class and geographic background as the boys who were potential ranch school students and overcame many of the same obstacles eastern boys would need to overcome to achieve similar aspirations.

The western men Wayne portrayed, on the other hand, were already masculine, independent, rough. Furthermore, most of his characters were of working-class background and did not have the professional expectations of the boys destined for preparatory school. While this new western male hero provided an escape for millions of men and boys from their postwar prescribed masculine roles, he was not someone that prep school boys could easily emulate. The closest comparison to the ideal masculine persona that upper-middle- and upper-class boys could aspire toward in the postwar era was John F. Kennedy, who overcame the burden of his aristocratic image through his heroism during World War II. Kennedy did not need the West to create his masculine image, and Arizona's preparatory schools could no longer depend on a masculine western approach to recruit students.

Several ranch schools went co-ed long before eastern preparatory schools even considered admitting girls. Nationally, in 1950 about three-quarters of prep school students were enrolled in single-sex institutions.[20] The sudden decline of the single-sex tradition in the late 1960s was the result of many external forces that schools could not easily control. The social unrest of the 1960s provoked agonizing changes within independent education. In addition to dress code reforms, more relaxed classroom environments, and the lessening or elimination of required religious observances, one especially strong student desire was co-education. Of these demands, the "abandonment of single-sex environments was a major concession that schools (and colleges) could defend on educational and economic grounds. It could be portrayed positively instead of as abject surrender to the mob."[21]

Although student opinion was important, the bottom line was that by admitting girls, private schools basically doubled their applicant pools and tuition-paying students. Green Fields School went co-ed in 1966, six years after the school changed from a boarding school to a day school. George Judson, finding his retirement from Judson School unsuitable, assumed leadership of the Arizona Desert School in 1948 and initiated a merger of this well-established school with the two-year-old Silver Spur school. Judson continued as the president of the board of trustees, and C. V. Hughes, the headmaster of Silver Spur, became the headmaster of this newly consolidated school that continued to be known as the Arizona Desert School. According to a newspaper description of the event, the new school offered a "complete and recreational program for boarding students from sixth grade through high school." A limited number of girls were accepted as day students in the lower grades.[22] Judson's planned retirement in July 1950 was preceded by his death in June. Louise Krueger, founder of the Walt Whitman school in New York City, assumed directorship of the school and opened the campus to girls, broadening the curriculum to include music, sculpture, painting, and additional courses to prepare students for the college entrance exams. During her three years of leadership, admissions increased dramatically from six to eighty-nine.[23] Krueger was replaced in 1953 by Princeton graduate William O. Morgan Jr. from the Peddie School. Unfortunately, accumulated debts and low enrollment were blamed for the Arizona Desert School's demise in 1953. Its financial problems were exacerbated when Morgan killed a man while allegedly driving under the influence of alcohol, which led to a $75,000 damage suit against the school.[24]

Many other changes took place in the postwar era. Those private schools that persisted succeeded by adapting school policies and a curriculum to attract broader audiences. In addition to opening their doors to girls, they expanded their curriculum to include a broader age range, deemphasized ranching, and sought out a more diverse student clientele. This trend was not unique to Arizona ranch schools. By the mid-1960s, the U.S. commissioner of education argued that prep students would be "culturally deprived" unless their schools contained significant numbers of the urban disadvantaged. Later another liberal critic claimed that too much consensus around school purpose and values denied students the skills they would need for "managing conflicts" in the "complex organizations" of a "culturally diverse society."[25]

According to Arthur Powell, the rise of diversity in preparatory schools is best traced through several distinct changes in student body composition since World War II. Independent schools first attempted to diversify economically while attracting more able students through meritocratic strategies. Serious attention to financial aid started in most schools during the Depression, when they began to experiment on a large scale with tuition reductions or discounts. Their original intention was not to change the kinds of students enrolled but to assist familiar constituencies who had suffered economic losses during the Depression.[26] In the 1960s, preparatory schools added gender and ethnic diversity to their student bodies. The Orme School began to diversify its student population in the 1960s by offering a competitive scholarship program. By the 1970s, African American, American Indian, and Hispanic students attended Orme School. Most of the Indian students came from the Hopi community in northern Arizona.[27]

The decision to drop "ranch" from many titles and deemphasize the myth of the West was in part a national trend. The postwar revolution of rising college expectations filled preferred colleges and permitted them to become much more choosy or meritocratic in admissions. The switch from the College Board Examination to the SAT as an entrance requirement actually had a democratizing effect. Any student could do well on the SAT tests, whereas exemplary performance on the College Board essay exams depended largely on having attended a preparatory school with a curriculum designed specifically with the essay exams in mind. The result was reflected in the proportion of Harvard freshmen who were admitted from private schools: "percentages plummeted at Harvard—from 57 percent of freshmen in 1941 to 32 percent in 1980."[28]

As college admissions became more particular, the academic quality of a school mattered more to parents than a unique identity. They cared less that their sons and daughters reaped the benefits gained from living in the West and more about SAT scores, Advanced Placement participation rates, National Merit winners, a school's reputation for placing students in prestigious colleges, and its ability to provide an environment conducive to improving the performance of the average college-bound student. The Fenster Ranch School, opened in 1944, switched its emphasis from improving the health of its students to preparing them for college. Sometime during the 1960s, the word "Ranch" was dropped from the school's title to more accurately reflect its aims. In 1973, the Fenster School took over the Southern Arizona School's old adobe buildings at the mouth of Sabino Canyon after a fire and the loss of accreditation forced the Southern Arizona School to close in 1972.[29] Horses disappeared from the campus of Green Fields in 1961. Its students' waning interest in the Old West was further illustrated by the lack of entries in Tucson Rodeo parades—only two in 1965 and 1966. Boys who participated rode their own horses and others participated on bicycles.[30] Fenster, Judson, Orme, and Green Fields deemphasized their "westernness" and evolved into well-known preparatory schools. In 1986, Green Fields Country Day School could advertise that it had received exemplary recognition by the U.S. Department of Education.[31] The Orme School is unique because its growth period occurred after World War II by continuing to market its Old West appeal.

As many of the earlier ranch schools either closed their doors or adapted to meet the needs of a changing market, a new private school opened that retained many ranch school traditions but had a clearly different vision of what the West had to offer. Hamilton Warren opened the Verde Valley School in 1948 for "the express purpose of training students for world citizenship responsibilities at the same time they prepare for college."[32] A graduate of the Evans Ranch School with Harvard degrees in anthropology and business administration, Warren conceived the idea for the Verde Valley School during World War II. Upon seeing "the utter futility of war as a means of settling international problems and recognizing the frequent inability of diplomacy to do much better," Warren believed that the solution lay in cultivating a citizenry that has "tolerance and understanding for the rights and view of others, based upon a firm foundation of conviction of what is good and right."[33] Immediately after the war, Warren and his wife traveled across the country looking for an appropriate location for the school they had in mind. They chose the red rock country of Sedona. Warren's choice reflected the lingering ideal of the West as a symbol for all that was good and unspoiled in America. The landscape, climate, people, and proximity to Indian reservations and Mexico provided the tools Warren needed to achieve his vision.

Although the Verde Valley School practically eliminated ranching from its curriculum, traces of the ranch experience remained. Horse riding was still an important activity and students took short trips to see a cattle roundup.[34] On the other hand, the word "cowboy" is largely absent from existing brochures and newsletters. The school did not have an on-site professional rancher, nor did it host its own rodeo. Instead of collecting prehistoric Indian artifacts as a recreational activity, students took one year of study in anthropology and were offered a course in "pottery analysis." The Verde Valley School emphasized interaction with diverse cultures rather than treating them as props in a mythic version of the Old West. Nevertheless, the Verde Valley School continued to subtly incorporate the mythic West into its promotional material. The cover of the school's 1952–1953 brochure depicted students on horseback against the backdrop of Sedona's well-known red rock spires. Other photos showed interior space similar to earlier ranch schools. Stone fireplaces and Navajo rugs contributed to the stereotypical southwestern ambiance, while exteriors adhered to the standard Old Spanish Mission style of architecture. Finally, the brochure captured students studying outdoors, a ranch school marketing tradition too valuable to omit.

One of the Verde Valley School's strategies for instilling intercultural sensitivity was participation in two extended field trips every year. On a twenty-two-day annual field trip to Mexico, students lived with Mexican families; became familiar with Mexican arts, crafts, and industries; and listened to American consular officials talk about international trade, immigration, emigration, and other international issues.[35] Study projects included Mexican public health institutions, Mexican prisons, and ancient sites. During the school's eight-day trip into Navajo country, students stayed with Indian families, with Indian service workers, in missions, and at reservation schools.[36] Students mingled with Navajo people, witnessed night ceremonial dances, and listened to Navajo officials and United States Civil Service employees. One school year, some of the female students "accompanied public health nurses to various parts of the reservation. They saw field clinics in action and with the nurses they visited sick Navahos in their hogans."[37] Students experienced the same sort of activities on the Hopi Reservation.[38]

Other remaining postwar schools adopted similar cultural programs, previously absent from ranch school curricula. This important change ended cultural isolation that predominated earlier in the century. At Green Fields, the only indication of interaction with Native peoples prior to World War II was that George Atchley hired an assistant named Pancho to teach him the art of adobe making. Decades later, under the leadership of assistant headmaster Paul Cleaver, students participated in a "Hands Across the Border" program, competed with soccer teams who visited from Mexico, and took spring trips into Mexico.[39] Social movements of the 1960s ended cultural isolation, and as a result, students in Arizona benefited from the state's cultural diversity.

Arizona private schools also diversified their communities by looking toward a global market rather than relying on the East for tuition-paying students. By admitting students from global communities, the schools would offer American students the positive experience of contact with cultures from around the world. Recruiting students from other countries also provided a practical advantage to schools. The students who traveled from foreign countries to attend American boarding schools typically came from the same economic classes as American students who attended private schools. This preserved homogeneous communities and saved money by reducing the number of scholarships needed to recruit a diverse student population.

Attracting students and faculty from across the globe was essential to Hamilton Warren's vision for the purpose of Verde Valley School. Warren believed that diversity of national and ethnic backgrounds of staff and students in and of itself contributed to the goals of national and international understanding that would foster global citizenship. A ten-year summary report prepared by visiting education scholar Dr. Franklin Patterson explicitly pointed out the international character of Verde Valley's faculty and student body. In the fall of 1958, students and faculty claimed backgrounds from China, Germany, Iran, Pakistan, Czechoslovakia, Belgium, Argentina, Spain, Canada, Italy, Venezuela, Guatemala, Egypt, England, Mexico, Hungary, and Switzerland. In addition, the student group included "one Negro, two Laguna Indians, one Navajo Indian, and several Asians."[40] In a reflection written for *Arizona Highways* in 1966 about the founding of Verde Valley based on the principles of international, intercultural, and interracial understanding, the author stated, "today this concept is popular, it's 'in.' But in the school's early years it was considered by many to be so far out as to be practically radical."[41]

Twenty-first-century visitors to the Orme School and Fenster School will notice flags from a host of foreign countries prominently displayed in communal buildings. A 1964 Tucson newspaper article titled "'Far Away Places' Send Students To Fenster Ranch" proclaimed that students from Kuwait, Indonesia, the Philippines, and other foreign countries would attend Fenster School during the ensuing school year.[42] In yearbooks from Judson School in the postwar era, some pages are dedicated to the international variety of the students who attended the school. Students from Brazil, Colombia, Japan, and Mexico attended Judson during the 1954–1955 academic year. In 1967, students representing Brazil, Canada, Costa Rica, Mexico, France, Netherlands Antilles, Nigeria, Peru, Philippines, Saudi Arabia, and South Africa participated in Judson's Student United Nations, a school-sponsored student group with the purpose of helping "students to become better acquainted with the various customs and traditions of the different areas represented" as well as helping "students gain a better and clearer insight into the world problems of today."[43]

Although the idealistic ranch schools of the pre–World War II era exist only in the memory of alumni, a smattering of material culture, the visual imagery of photographs, a few published histories, and a small number of school buildings that remain, their legacy continues in the cultural and economic contributions of the people who migrated to the Southwest to create and experience these remarkable institutions of learning. Many alumni stayed to form a new generation of neonatives who shaped the postwar West. Hamilton Warren's return to Arizona to found the Verde Valley School is a significant example of the impact graduates have had in determining the cultural, social, and economic landscape of the postwar Southwest. His belief that cultural geography could impact students' social awareness to make them better citizens may very well have been the result of his experience at the Evans School. Arizona Desert School alumnus John Donaldson made ranching his career and was inducted into the Cowboy Hall of Fame for the restoration of ranch land in Tucson.

Green Fields, Fenster, and Orme School are the only private schools in 2013 still in existence that have their origins as western ranch schools. These historic institutions have at times demonstrated their interest in the history of their schools and have used it for celebratory, promotional, and development purposes. In 1983, Green Fields headmaster Phineas Anderson commissioned Suzanne Tumblin Gary to write a history of the school in honor of its fiftieth anniversary. Newspaper journalists announced the publication of the book and wrote brief commemorative historical accounts of the school in the *Arizona Daily Star* and the *Tucson Citizen*. In a recent informational brochure, Fenster School published historical photographs and included a brief history of the school. The narrative incorporated nostalgic images of the Old West by describing George and Kitty Fenster as "exhibiting the spirit of true pioneers" who "packed up their family and belongings and trekked west from New York City."[44]

The Orme School retains several of its original buildings, and as of 2015 it has hosted several reunions and other social events to keep its alumni engaged in the activities of the school. Its 2002 edition of the *Orme School Bulletin* published updates on alumni, its annual fund report, and articles and historic photographs that celebrated the school's history. Alumni, parents, and friends of Orme who made a provision for the school in their estate plans were included in "The Heritage Club."[45]

The rise and decline of Arizona's ranch schools closely parallels the history of the twentieth-century West. Ranch schools, much like western dude ranches, offered a western lifestyle that combined outdoor activities with natural landscape and a warm winter climate that appealed to wealthy easterners. That easterners not only invested money in Arizona ranch schools, but entrusted the intellectual, physical, and character development of their children to these institutions, suggests that the ideal of the mythic West was very much alive in the American mind. The ranch school experience promised a healthful environment and important life experiences that parents believed were the best opportunities they could offer their children. Ranch schools that succeeded in the post–World War II era did so by broadening their markets to include diverse audiences. In 2000, the Wick family's decision to close Judson School, in existence since 1928, epitomized the most recent chapter in Arizona's history. Judson's owners found that the land the school occupied was too valuable to warrant its continued use as a school and sold it to housing developers. The need to solicit easterners and their investments to Arizona by promoting an idyllic rural image of the West gave way to urban residential and commercial growth that occurred after World War II and has continued ever since.

NOTES

INTRODUCTION

1. Collection of H. J. Heinz Company, MSS #57, Box 5, Folder 16, Thomas and Katherine Detre Library and Archives, Senator John Heinz History Center, Pittsburgh, PA.

2. Robert C. Alberts, MS 0037 Series II, Box 3, Folder 2, Thomas and Katherine Detre Library and Archives, Senator John Heinz History Center, Pittsburgh, PA, contains the phrenological analysis; Address, Howard Heinz Memorial Service, 1941, Box 1, Folder 1, H. J. Heinz Co. collection, MSS #57, Thomas and Katherine Detre Library and Archives, Senator John Heinz History Center, Pittsburgh, PA.

3. Collection of H. J. Heinz Company, MSS #57, Box 5, Folder 16, Thomas and Katherine Detre Library and Archives, Senator John Heinz History Center, Pittsburgh, PA.

4. Alan Dawley, "The Abortive Rule of Big Money," in *Ruling America: A History of Wealth and Power in a Democracy*, ed. Steve Fraser and Gary Gerstle (Cambridge, MA: Harvard University Press, 2005).

5. E. Digby Baltzell, *Philadelphia Gentlemen: The Making of A National Upper Class* (Glencoe, IL: Free Press, 1958), quoted in James McLachlan, *American Boarding Schools: A Historical Study* (New York: Charles Scribner's Sons, 1970), 8. Baltzell argued that sixteen schools "serve the sociological function of differentiating the upper classes from the rest of the population." They were Phillips Academy, Phillips Exeter Academy, Episcopal High School, Hill School, St. Paul's School, St. Mark's School, Lawrenceville, Groton, Woodbury Forest, Taft, Hotchkiss, Choate, St. George's, Middlesex, Deerfield, and Kent.

6. *A Handbook of Private Schools for American Boys and Girls*, ed. Porter Sargent (Boston, MA: Porter Sargent Publishers, Inc., 1928), 785.

7. "San Luis Ranch School: An Open Air School for Girls," brochure, Colorado Springs, 1939, Arizona Historical Society, Tucson; *A Handbook of Private Schools for Boys and Girls*, ed. Porter Sargent (Boston, MA: Porter Sargent Publishers, Inc., 1931–1932), 578.

8. Kent Baxter, *The Modern Age: Turn-of-the-Century American Culture and the Invention of Adolescence* (Tuscaloosa: University of Alabama Press, 2008), 3, 8, 19, 24, 36.

9. Joseph M. Hawes, *Children Between the Wars: American Childhood 1920–1940* (New York: Twayne Publishers, an Imprint of Simon & Schuster Macmillan, 1997), 1–2, 7–9. Hawes defined the two most important trends in the history of childhood and youth in the interwar period as the rise of "experts" and peer groups.

10. "A Ranch School in Arizona for Younger Boys," brochure, Tucson, 1932, private collection of David C. Wilhelm, Denver, CO.

11. Lynn Dumenil, *The Modern Temper: American Culture and Society in the 1920s* (New York: Hill and Wang, 1995), 146. Dumenil argues that in the 1920s, intellectual ideas put forth by Sigmund Freud, John. B. Watson and other behaviorists, Albert Einstein, and Charles Darwin gave the public new ways of understanding the world. Peter Stearns, *Anxious Parents: A History of Modern Childrearing in America* (New York: New York University Press, 2003), 65–67.

12. Robert Danforth Cole, *Private Secondary Education for Boys in the United States* (Philadelphia, PA: Westbrook, 1928), 1.

13. B. Edward McClellan, *Moral Education in America: Schools and the Shaping of Character from Colonial Times to the Present* (New York and London: Teachers College, Columbia University, 1999), 48.

14. David I. Macleod, *Building Character in the American Boy: The Boy Scouts, YMCA, and Their Forerunners* (Madison: University of Wisconsin Press, 1983), xii, 3, 130, 173–74, 221, 227. Macleod notes that some private schools sponsored Boy Scout troops in 1921. Scouting was able to "reach upward from the middle class more easily than downward."

15. Leslie Paris, *Children's Nature: The Rise of the American Summer Camp* (New York: New York University Press, 2008), 8–9.

16. Bill Osgerby, *Playboys in Paradise: Masculinity, Youth and Leisure-Style in Modern America* (Oxford and New York: Berg, 2001), 3, 9.

17. Hal Rothman, *Devil's Bargains: Tourism in the Twentieth-Century American West* (Lawrence: University Press of Kansas, 1998). In the introduction, Rothman explores the historical origins of an experience economy.

18. Elliott West, *Growing Up with the Country: Childhood on the Far Western Frontier* (Albuquerque: University of New Mexico Press, 1989), xi, 247–49.

19. McClellan, chapter 4.

20. Hawes, 11. Hawes argues that American life was a three-way struggle between modernizers, traditionalists, and young people.

21. David C. Wilhelm, *Cowboy Ace: The Life Adventures of David Wilhelm, An Autobiography* (Parker, CO: Thornton, 2010), 53.

22. Philip H. Cummings, unpublished 1932–1933 Valley Ranch journal, used with permission, Jan. 15, 1933.

23. "The Rodeo," Evans School, 1923, Arizona Historical Society, Tucson.

CHAPTER 1

1. "Arizona Ranch Schools," *Arizona Highways* 15, no. 9, Sept. 1939.

2. Sybil Ellinwood, "East Meets West in the Field of Education," *Journal of Arizona History* (*JAH*) 15, no. 3 (Autumn 1974): 270.

3. Robert Danforth Cole, *Private Secondary Education for Boys in the United States* (Philadelphia, PA: Westbrook, 1928), 37, appendix a.

4. Ellinwood, "East Meets West," 276, 285; "Wealthy Easterners Underwrite School," newspaper article, Sept. 24, 1928, Tucson Schools, Arizona Historical Society (AHS); Judson School for Boys brochure, n.d., Arizona Collection (AC), Arizona State University Libraries (ASUL).

5. Nancy Isenberg, *Fallen Founder: The Life of Aaron Burr* (New York: Viking, 2007).

6. Frederic Cople Jaher, *The Urban Establishment: Upper Strata in Boston, New York, Charleston, Chicago, and Los Angeles* (Urbana: University of Illinois Press, 1982), 11.

7. Ibid., 23; J. Jackson to H. Jackson, Nov. 20, 1793, in Jaher, *The Urban Establishment*, 39.

8. Amos Lawrence to A. A. Lawrence, Jan. 6, 1883, Amos Lawrence Papers, in Jaher, *The Urban Establishment*, 80.

9. J. S. Mill, *Principles of Political Economy*, 1929, quoted in Ronald Chester, *Inheritance, Wealth, and Society* (Bloomington: Indiana University Press, 1982), 27, 28.

10. Brownson, "The Descent of Property," *Boston Quarterly Review* (1840), 493, quoted in Chester, *Inheritance, Wealth, and Society*, 33, 50.

11. Chester, *Inheritance, Wealth, and Society*, 4, 59–60, 51, 73.

12. David Nasaw, "Gilded Age Gospels," in *Ruling America: A History of Wealth and Power in a Democracy*, ed. Steve Fraser and Gary Gerstle (Cambridge, MA: Harvard University Press, 2005), 125.

13. Chester, *Inheritance, Wealth, and Society*, 60.

14. G. P. Watkins, *The Growth of Large Fortunes* (1907), 160–63, quoted in Chester, *Inheritance, Wealth, and Society*, 61.

15. Chester, *Inheritance, Wealth, and Society*, 61–62.

16. Andrew Carnegie, "Wealth," *North American Review* 316 (June 1889): 653–64, reprinted in *The American 1890s: A Cultural Reader*, ed. Susan Harris Smith and Melanie Dawson (Durham, NC: Duke University Press, 2000), 29.

17. James McLachlan, *American Boarding Schools: A Historical Study* (New York: Charles Scribner's Sons, 1970), 270.

18. McLachlan, 243, as based on his researching of letters from Roosevelt to Endicott Peabody archived in the Houghton Library, Harvard University, and *The Letters of Theodore Roosevelt*, ed. Elting E. Morison et al., 8 vols. (Cambridge, MA: Harvard University Press, 1951), 62, 75–76, 80, 91, 107–8, quoted in Edward N. Saveth, "Education of an Elite," *History of Education Quarterly* 28, no. 3 (Autumn 1988): 372; Jaher, *The Urban Establishment*, 99.

19. Memo from Mr. H. J. Heinz to his brother, Feb. 17, 1915, Robert C. Alberts, MS 0037, Series II, Box 3, Folder 3, Thomas and Katherine Detre Library and Archives, Senator John Heinz History Center.

20. Article in the *Pittsburgh Sun Telegraph*, Jan. 22, 1939, Robert C. Alberts, MS 0037, Series II, Box 3, Folder 2, Thomas and Katherine Detre Library and Archives, Senator John Heinz History Center.

21. Emerson Hough, "Owners of America VIII: The Swifts," *Cosmopolitan Magazine*, Mar. 1902, 399–407.

22. Paul A. Gusmorino III, "Main Causes of the Great Depression," *Gusmorino World*, May 13, 1996, http://www.gusmorino.com/pag3/greatdepression/index.html. Accessed Aug. 29, 2008. This portion of Gusmorino's essay cites Robert S. McElvaine, *The Great Depression: America 1929–1941* (New York: Times Books, 1981).

23. Daniel Horowitz, *The Morality of Spending: Attitudes toward the Consumer Society in America, 1875–1940* (Baltimore, MD: Johns Hopkins University Press, 1985), xviii, 30, 162–63.

24. Ibid., 37–39, 73–74, 109–10, 113, 120, 135.

25. Rebecca Jo Plant, *Mom: The Transformation of Motherhood in Modern America* (Chicago, IL: University of Chicago Press, 2010), 10, 33.

26. Julia Grant, "A 'Real Boy' and not a Sissy: Gender, Childhood, and Masculinity, 1890–1940," *Journal of Social History* 37, no. 4 (Summer 2004). Grant argues that during the early decades of the twentieth century, "little boys—once thought to be exempt from the demands of masculinity—were recast as men in the making, placing their behaviors, characteristics, and temperaments under a microscope for manifestations of gender deviations" (830).

27. Dennis Clayton Troth, ed., *Selected Readings in Character Education* (Boston, MA: Beacon, 1930), 53.

28. Secondary Education Board Annual Report, 1940, 82–83, National Association of Independent Schools (NAIS) Archive, Washington, D.C.

29. Holden, 135, 138.

30. Philip H. Cummings, unpublished 1932–1933 Valley Ranch journal, used with permission, Oct. 15–19, 30, 1932.

31. LeRoy McKim Makepeace, *Sherman Thacher and His School* (New Haven, CT: Yale University Press, 1941), 158–59. The author drew from official correspondence, minutes, catalogues, scrapbooks, personal letters, and school publications. Quotes from primary sources are not cited. I have indicated when the

quote is from Makepeace and otherwise include original quotes from his research in quotation marks.

32. Albert W. Atwood, "The Rich Man's Son," *Saturday Evening Post*, Nov. 10, 1928.
33. Irvin S. Cobb, "The Generation that Comes Next," *Saturday Evening Post*, Sept. 17, 1921.
34. Booth Tarkington, *The Magnificent Ambersons* (New York: Doubleday, 1918), 21–22, 26, 28, 37.
35. Ibid., 16, 221–22.
36. Ibid., 80, 252–53.
37. Ibid., 143.
38. Ibid., 242, 104–5, 259.
39. Ibid., 387, 433, 472, 475.
40. Pearl Buck, *Sons* (New York: John Day, 1932), 14, 24, 58, 61.
41. Ibid., 109, 72, 106.
42. Ibid., 211.
43. Ibid., 222, 366.
44. Ibid., 369, 376, 465.
45. Edgar Rice Burroughs, *Tarzan of the Apes* (New York: A. L. Burt Company, 1914), 59, 80–81.
46. Ibid., 112.
47. John F. Kasson, *Houdini, Tarzan, and The Perfect Man: The White Male Body and The Challenge of Modernity in America* (New York: Hill and Wang, 2001), 160, 164, 170, 174.
48. *A Fight to the Finish*, directed by Reaves Eason (1925).
49. *The Adventurous Soul*, directed by Gene Carroll (1927).
50. *Girl Crazy*, directed by Norman Taurog and Busby Berkeley (1943).
51. G. Edward White, *The Eastern Establishment and the Western Experience* (New Haven, CT, and London: Yale University Press, 1968), 6–7.
52. Emily Post, *By Motor to the Golden Gate*, ed. Jane Lancaster (Jefferson, NC: McFarland, 2004), 241.
53. George B. Price, *Gaining Health in the West (Colorado, New Mexico, Arizona)* (New York: B. W. Huebsch, 1907), 69, 94.
54. Jane Tompkins, *West of Everything: The Inner Life of Westerns* (New York: Oxford University Press, 1992), 11, 13–14, 84.
55. Article clipping, Dec. 13, 1934, Robert C. Alberts, MS 0037, Series II, Box 3, Folder 2; Article clipping, H. J. Heinz Co. collection, MSS #57.
56. Engleman, J. O., *Moral Education in School and Home* (Chicago, IL; New York; and Boston, MA: Benj. H. Sanborn, 1920), 185–87.
57. Horace Holden, *Young Boys and Boarding School* (Boston, MA: Gorham, 1913), 147.
58. Peter N. Stearns, *Anxious Parents: A History of Modern Childrearing in America* (New York: New York University Press, 2003), 137–39.

59. Fresnal Ranch School brochure, n.d., Tucson Schools, Fresnal Ranch School, AHS.

60. *Gopher World*, 1942, Judson School, private collection of Gloria Judson, Phoenix, AZ.

61. *Rattler*, 1931, Judson School, vol. 2, 24, private collection of Gloria Judson, Phoenix, AZ.

62. David C. Wilhelm, *Cowboy Ace: The Life Adventures of David Wilhelm, An Autobiography* (Parker, CO: Thornton, 2010), 60. In 2000, Wilhelm and fellow alumnus John Donaldson found the remains of the chapel, which was still identifiable. To locate it, go to the Pima Canon trailhead marker and walk through the brush about 300 to 400 yards slightly west of north or about 345 degrees from the trailhead marker.

63. Charles S. Pearce, *Los Alamos Before the Bomb and Other Stories* (New York: Vantage, 1987), 34.

64. Marguerite S. Shaffer, *See America First: Tourism and National Identity, 1880–1940* (Washington, D.C.: Smithsonian Institution Press, 2001), 2–5, 34, 308–9.

65. Ibid., 263–65.

66. Robert Kilmarx, interview by author, Barrington, RI, Sep. 2003. Tape recording.

67. Cummings, May 29, 1933.

68. Collection of H. J. Heinz Co., MSS #57, Thomas and Katherine Detre Library and Archives, Senator John Heinz History Center, Pittsburgh, PA.

69. Newspaper article, Dec. 12, 1970, Tucson Schools, Arizona Desert School, AHS.

70. "Desert School Will Entertain," Dec. 22, 1934, Tucson Schools, Arizona Desert School, AHS.

71. Abigail Van Slyck, "The Spatial Practices of Privilege," *Journal of the Society of Architectural Historians* 70, no. 2 (June 2011): 214.

72. Cole, *Private Secondary Education for Boys in the United States*, 128.

73. Arthur Powell, *Lessons from Privilege: The American Prep School Tradition* (Cambridge, MA: Harvard University Press, 1996), 44–46.

74. Palo Verde Ranch School brochure, n.d., Mesa Southwest Museum (MSM).

75. Edmund Morris, *The Rise of Theodore Roosevelt* (1979; reprint, New York: Modern Library, 2001), 68, 78.

76. Nicholas Roosevelt, Photo Album 1909–1910, AHS.

77. Fermor S. Church and Peggy Pond Church, *When Los Alamos was a Ranch School* (Los Alamos, NM: Los Alamos Historical Society, 1998), 1, 149.

78. Jean Dunn Porter, interview by author, Tucson, Feb. 17, 2002. Tape recording.

79. Merrick Pratt, "Annual Dinner Dance," *The Ocotillo*, 1938, private collection of David C. Lincoln.

80. Sven Beckert, "Merchants and Manufacturers in the Antebellum North," in *Ruling America: A History of Wealth and Power in a Democracy* (Cambridge, MA: Harvard University Press, 2005), 98–99.

81. Church and Church, *When Los Alamos was a Ranch School*, iii.

82. Jean Porter interview.

83. Ormond Parke interview.

84. Hal K. Rothman, *Devil's Bargains: Tourism in the Twentieth-Century American West* (Lawrence: University Press of Kansas, 1998), 10–11.

85. "Arizona Attracts Many Notables," *Arizona Highways*, Jan. 1945, 9–14.

86. Names and geographic origins cross-referenced in Jokake yearbooks, 1937 and 1939, Arizona Collection (AC), Arizona State University Libraries (ASUL), Tempe, and *The Ocotillo*, Judson School for Boys yearbook, 1938, private collection of David C. Lincoln. Lincoln identified Judy Upton from a list of Jokake students as the sister of his friends, Steve and Dave Upton.

87. This was suggested by Gloria Judson, interview by author, Phoenix, Feb. 2002. Tape recording.

88. Robert Porter, interview by author, Tucson, Feb. 2002. Tape recording.

89. Sophie Burden Collection, brochure, n.d., and "Dude Ranch Offers School For Children," *Miami Herald*, Dec. 30, c. 1951, Box 30, DCWM, Wickenburg, Arizona.

90. "We Go to School Out-of-doors," Old Pueblo School brochure, n.d., Arizona Historical Society (AHS), Tucson.

91. *Rattler*, 1931, Judson School, vol. 2, 12–19, private collection of Gloria Judson, Phoenix, AZ.

92. "Arizona Attracts Many Notables," 9–10.

93. Raymond Moley, *The American Century of John C. Lincoln* (New York: Hawthorne, 1965), 106–8.

94. The Lincolns continued to have ties to the old Judson School for Girls. In 1936, with Jack Stewart, John Lincoln planned and built Camelback Inn. The old Judson School for Girls was transformed into El Chorro Lodge and became very popular among the Camelback Inn guests, who would go there to have drinks before their dinner at the inn. David C. Lincoln, interview by author, tape recording, Phoenix, Feb. 15, 2002.

95. Moley, *The American Century*, 108

96. Judson Certificates of Shares, collection of Gloria Judson, Phoenix, AZ; Judson School brochures, c. mid-1930s, collection of David C. Lincoln, Phoenix, AZ.

97. Gerald D. Nash, *The American West in the Twentieth Century: A Short History of an Urban Oasis* (Englewood Cliffs, NJ: Prentice-Hall, 1973), 90.

98. G. Wesley Johnson Jr., "Directing Elites: Catalysts for Social Change," in *Phoenix in the Twentieth Century: Essays in Community History*, ed. G. Wesley Johnson Jr. (Norman: University of Oklahoma Press, 1993), 21.

99. Jokake School yearbook, 1939, Arizona Collection (AC), Arizona State University Libraries (ASUL), Tempe.

100. Church and Church, *When Los Alamos was a Ranch School*, 17, 18.

101. "Wealthy Easterners Underwrite School," newspaper article, Sept. 24, 1928, Tucson Schools, Arizona Desert School, AHS.
102. "Boys' School Has Twenty-Four Pupils Enrolled This Year," *Tucson Citizen*, Dec. 10, 1932, Tucson Schools, Arizona Desert School, AHS.
103. *Rattler*, 1931, Judson School, vol. 2, 12–19, private collection of Gloria Judson, Phoenix, AZ.
104. Kel M. Fox, "Of Dudes and Cows: The Foxboro Story," *JAH* 32, no. 4 (Winter 1991): 413.
105. Russell B. Fairgrieve, "A Memorandum Regarding Summer Plans," June 12, 1933. Tucson Schools, Southern Arizona School, AHS.

CHAPTER 2

1. "A Ranch School in Arizona for Younger Boys," brochure, Tucson, AZ, 1932, private collection of David C. Wilhelm, Denver, CO.
2. Robert Danforth Cole, *Private Secondary Education for Boys in the United States* (Philadelphia, PA: Westbrook, 1928), 79–81. "Preparation for College" ranked second in Cole's 1928 snapshot of private education for boys, with 81 percent of brochures indicating this as an aim of the school.
3. Palo Verde Ranch School, brochure, n.d., Mesa Southwest Museum (MSM).
4. "Arizona Desert School Has Ideal Setting in Foothills," *Arizona Daily Star*, Feb. 22, 1935, Tucson Schools, Arizona Desert School, AHS.
5. Lawrence Cremin, *The Transformation of the School: Progressivism in American Education 1876–1957* (New York: Vintage, 1964), x, 22, 85, 241. Cremin quoted a description of an invitation sent to Charles W. Eliot to serve as the organization's first honorary president.
6. Ibid., 109, 118, 183, 122, 123.
7. Cremin cites John and Evelyn Dewey's *Schools of To-Morrow*, 153, published in 1915, as an invaluable snapshot of progressive education to that date. Cremin, *The Transformation of the School*, 181, 213, 217–19.
8. Ibid., 245, 249–50, 276–77, 279.
9. Ibid., 281, 283, 278–79, 291–94. Cremin cites the Porter School, a one-teacher public institution in Missouri, as a "quintessential example of progressive education in a one-room country school." Marie Turner Harvey transformed curriculum content by centering it on the everyday life of the community. The standard work in the three Rs was achieved through activities like gardening, cooking, and animal husbandry that were documented by students in notebooks, reading bulletins of the Department of Agriculture, and using "arithmetic on the problems of farm accounts."
10. Ibid., 306–7.
11. Powell, *Lessons from Privilege*, 67.

12. Fresnal Ranch School, brochure, n.d., AHS.
13. David Wick, interview by author, Scottsdale, AZ, Dec. 2002. Tape recording.
14. Bonnie Henry, "From An Old Adobe," *Arizona Daily Star*, May 1989, Tucson Schools, Southern Arizona School, Arizona Historical Society (AHS).
15. "Hacienda del Sol Located in Foothills of Catalinas," *Arizona Daily Star*, Feb. 1930, Tucson Schools, Hacienda del Sol, AHS.
16. Fermor S. Church and Peggy Pond Church, *When Los Alamos was a Ranch School* (Los Alamos, NM: Los Alamos Historical Society, 1998), 4, 21, 23.
17. http://www.lanl.gov/worldview/welcome/history.html; Los Alamos National Laboratory In Memoriam Archive, http://www.lanl.gov/collaboration/fellows/_assets/in-memoriam/colgate_vita.pdf.
18. Louise Dunham Goldsberry, "The Open-Air School and Out-Door Education," 1921, 5, 23, Library of Congress Prints and Photographs Division.
19. Avis Tarrant Burke, "Open Air Schools," *Bulletin of the Extension Division, Indiana University*, vol. vii, no. 7. Bloomington, Mar. 1922, 12.
20. Sherman Kingsley and F. B. Dresslar, "Open-air Schools," Bureau of Education Bulletin, no. 23, Department of the Interior, Washington, D.C. Government Printing Office, 1917, 7.
21. B. S. Warren, *Open Air Schools for the Prevention and Cure of Tuberculosis Among Children*, Public Health Bulletin, no. 58, Treasury Department, United States Public Health Service, Washington, D.C. Government Printing Office, October 1912, 5.
22. Kingsley and Dresslar, "Open-air Schools," 33, 35, 52, 175; Burke, "Open Air Schools," 9, 26.
23. Warren, *Open Air Schools*, 13.
24. Warren, *Open Air Schools*, 14. Kingsley and Dresslar, "Open-air Schools," 7, 30, 176.
25. Cremin, *The Transformation of the School*, 278.
26. Palo Verde Ranch School brochure, n.d., MSM, Mesa, AZ.
27. Arizona Sunshine School brochure, n.d., AC, ASUL.
28. Ibid., 167.
29. Palo Verde Ranch School brochure, n.d., MSM, Mesa, AZ.
30. Suzanne Tumblin Gary, *Green Fields Country Day School: The First Fifty Years, 1933–1983* (Tucson, AZ: Green Fields Country Day School, 1983), 6, 7.
31. Judson School for Boys brochure, n.d., AC, ASUL.
32. "A Summary of Interesting Events at Judson School," *Gopher World*, 1940–1941, 21, collection of Gloria Judson, Phoenix, AZ.
33. Arizona Desert School brochure, c. 1953, Tucson Schools, AHS.
34. Letter in the private collection of Gloria Judson written to Patty D. Judson, who was the sister-in-law of Gloria and Barney Judson. This letter originated from The Greenbrier and Cottages, White Sulphur Springs, West Virginia, where Patty's family lived. The name of the boy referred to in the letter was Ted

Conley, and the writer was relaying a conversation they had with his mother, Mrs. James Conley from Charleston, WV.

35. http://www.lanl.gov/worldview/welcome/history.html.

36. Palo Verde Ranch School brochure, n.d., MSM.

37. Alfred E. Stearns, *The Challenge of Youth* (Boston, MA: W. A. Wilde, 1923), 128–33.

38. W. Hudson Kensel, *Dude Ranching in Yellowstone Country: Larry Larom and Valley Ranch, 1915–1969* (Norman, OK: Arthur H. Clark Company, 2010), 128; Pearce, *Los Alamos Before the Bomb*, 40.

39. Philip H. Cummings, Valley Ranch journal, 1932–1933, used with permission, Dec. 7, 1932.

40. Fresnal Ranch School brochure, n.d., Tucson Schools, AHS.

41. Cremin, *The Transformation of the School*, 44–45.

42. Endicott Peabody, "Academic Influence," in Alfred E. Stearns et al., *The Education of the Modern Boy* (Boston, MA: Small, Maynard, 1925), 115–20.

43. Arthur G. Powell, *Lessons from Privilege: The American Prep School Tradition* (Cambridge, MA: Harvard University Press, 1996), 124–26, 131.

44. Emily Newell Blair, "Why I Sent My Children Away to School," *Harper's Monthly Magazine*, Mar. 1926, 428–30.

45. Alfred E. Stearns, "Introduction," in Stearns et al., *The Education of the Modern Boy*, xix, xxiv–xxvi.

46. W. L. W. Fields, "Entrance Requirements," in Stearns et al., *The Education of the Modern Boy*, 209.

47. Secondary Education Board Annual Report, 1925, 3, National Association of Independent Schools (NAIS) archive, Washington, D.C.

48. Secondary Education Board Annual Report, 1926, 9, NAIS archive, Washington, D.C.

49. Palo Verde Ranch School Brochure, n.d., Mesa Southwest Museum (MSM), Mesa, AZ; "Boys' School Has Twenty-Four Pupils Enrolled This Year," *Tucson Citizen*, Dec. 10, 1932.

50. "School Is Set in Green Field," *Arizona Daily Star*, Feb. 20, 1937, Tucson Schools, Green Field, AHS; Suzanne Tumblin Gary, *Green Fields Country Day School: The First Fifty Years, 1933–1983* (Tucson, AZ: Green Fields Country Day School, 1983), 12.

51. Secondary Education Board Annual Report, 1931, 15, NAIS archive, Washington, D.C.

52. Secondary Education Board Annual Report, 1932, 20; 1938, 31, NAIS archive, Washington, D.C.

53. Harry L. Coderre, "Disciplinary Problems in the Western Ranch School," master's thesis, Massachusetts State College, Amherst, 1942, 15.

54. Sylvia Jukes Morris, *Edith Kermit Roosevelt: Portrait of a First Lady* (New York: Modern Library, 1980), 367.

55. Collection of H. J. Heinz Company, MSS #57, Box 5, Folder 16, Thomas and Katherine Detre Library and Archives, Senator John Heinz History Center, Pittsburgh, PA. Several letters in this collection indicate that H. J. Heinz II, "Jack," had trouble with his knees, which required a hospital stay while he attended Choate. In letters to his parents from the Evans School, he often assured them that his knees were fine.

56. Brian Cook, *Frank Boyden of Deerfield, The Vision and Politics of an Educational Idealist* (Lanham, MD: Madison Books, 1994), 25, 60–61.

57. Powell, *Lessons from Privilege*, 85.

58. Cole, *Private Secondary Education*, 197.

59. Lynn Dumenil, *The Modern Temper: American Culture and Society in the 1920s* (New York: Hill and Wang, 1995), 214, 261. According to Dumenil, the American Jewish community was divided between the German-born Jews who had arrived earlier and the more recent immigrant eastern European Jews. The "Yiddish-speaking, Orthodox, working-class Eastern European Jews were contemptuous of the German Jews' sensitivity to the Gentile world and condemned both their Reform Judaism and their eliteness." German Jews were alarmed at the "foreignness" of the eastern Europeans and did not like how Protestant Americans saw all Jews in terms of these newcomers. Dumenil states, "German Jews embarked on charitable activities and Americanization programs, both from a sense of communal responsibility and from anxiety about anti-Semitism." Listing for the Block family in Irving Cutler, *The Jews of Chicago: From Shtetl to Suburb* (Urbana and Chicago: University of Illinois Press, 1996), 18; Helen Block from this Chicago family attended Hacienda del Sol from 1931 to 1932 according to the *Sun God* yearbook and "Society Girls 'Go Native' at School," *Arizona Daily Star*, Apr. 2, 1933, Hacienda del Sol School Ephemera File, AHS; Jean Porter, interviewed on February 17, 2002, who attended the school as a freshman, recalled that her roommate, Joanne Fox, was Jewish; Ormonde Parke, Judson alumnus interviewed in February 2002, recalled that his roommate was Jewish and that there were other Jewish students at Judson when he attended the school in the 1930s.

60. Philip H. Cummings, unpublished 1932–1933 Valley Ranch journal, used with permission, Sept. 28, 1932, Oct. 17, 1932, Jan. 19, 1933.

61. Coderre, "Disciplinary Problems," 8, 14, 22–23.

62. "A Summary of Interesting Events at Judson School," *Gopher World*, 1940–1941, 7, collection of Gloria Judson, Phoenix, AZ.

63. Ellinwood, "East Meets West," 274–75.

64. Don Rodriguez, "School is 50—and Much has Changed," *Tucson Citizen*, Feb. 18, 1983, Tucson Schools, Green Fields, AHS.

65. Southern Arizona School for Boys Brochure, n.d., SPL.

66. Charles S. Pearce, *Los Alamos Before the Bomb and Other Stories* (New York: Vantage, 1987), 41.

67. Letter from William Percy Sharpe to George Judson, June 15, 1948, Saint Louis, collection of Gloria Judson, Phoenix, AZ.
68. "Arizona Ranch Schools," *Arizona Highways* 15, no. 9, Sept. 1939, 2.
69. Cole, *Private Secondary Education*, 145–46.
70. Ellinwood, "East Meets West," 271.
71. Ibid., 273, 277.
72. Gary, *Green Fields Country Day School*, 13.
73. Judson School brochure, n.d., Private Schools, Scottsdale Public Library (SPL) Vertical File; "Judson Boys' School Sold to Educators," newspaper article, n.d., collection of Gloria Judson; "Two Ranch Schools for Boys Will Consolidate February 26," newspaper clipping, n.d., collection of Gloria Judson.
74. *El Conquistador,* Judson School yearbook, 1935, 4–6, collection of Gloria Judson, Phoenix, AZ.
75. Judson School for Boys brochure, n.d., collection of Gloria Judson, Phoenix, AZ.
76. LeRoy McKim Makepeace, *Sherman Thacher and His School* (New Haven, CT: Yale University Press, 1941), 44–46, 70–76, 164. The author drew from official correspondence, minutes, catalogues, scrapbooks, personal letters, and school publications. Quotes from primary sources are not cited. I have indicated when the quote is from Makepeace and otherwise include original quotes from his research in quotation marks.
77. Ibid., 78–79, 84, 94, 99, 144–49.
78. Ibid., 112, 158.
79. Southern Arizona School for Boys brochure, 1940–1941, Arizona Collection (AC), Arizona State University Libraries (ASUL), Tempe.
80. Laura Judson to George Judson, Sept. 15, 1948, private collection of Gloria Judson, Phoenix, AZ.
81. John Dewey, *Democracy and Education: An Introduction to the Philosophy of Education* (New York: MacMillan, 1916), 247–48.
82. Brian Cook, *Frank Boyden of Deerfield, The Vision and Politics of an Educational Idealist* (Lanham, MD: Madison Books, 1994), 26. Boyden's biographer argues that because Boyden accepted students who were dismissed from other schools and gave them another chance, Deerfield got away from the English public school model and was more democratic, and therefore, was more "American."
83. Cummings, Feb. 26, 1933.
84. Marguerite S. Shaffer, *See America First: Tourism and National Identity, 1880–1940* (Washington, D.C.: Smithsonian Institution Press, 2001), 4. Shaffer argues that "the emergence of the United States as a modern urban-industrial nation-state" launched the search for American identity and what she terms "national tourism." *See America First*, 2–3.
85. Charles C. Moore, "San Francisco and the Exposition: The Relation of the City to the Nation as Regards the World's Fair," *Sunset*, Feb. 1912, 198, quoted in Shaffer, *See America First*, 33.

86. Bruce Barton, quoted in Cook, *Frank Boyden of Deerfield*, 86–87.
87. Michael C. Batinski, *Pastkeepers in a Small Place: Five Centuries in Deerfield, Massachusetts* (Amherst: University of Massachusetts Press, 2004), 164–96. Batinski cites George Sheldon from his addresses to the Pocumtuck Valley Memorial Association; George Sheldon, Old Home Week, Scrapbooks, PVMA.
88. Makepeace, *Sherman Thacher and His School*, 87.

CHAPTER 3

1. Frederick Jackson Turner declared in 1893 that the frontier had closed and explained to the American public that access to the frontier and the ability to remake oneself in this sparsely settled region had defined American character. I use the term "Old West" to refer to Turner's idea of a pre-1890 West. Frederick Jackson Turner, "The Problem of the West," *Atlantic Monthly* 78 (Sept. 1896), reprinted in *The American 1890s: A Cultural Reader*, ed. Susan Harris Smith and Melanie Dawson (Durham, NC: Duke University Press, 2000), 396–407. Jane Tompkins, *West of Everything: The Inner Life of Westerns* (New York: Oxford University Press, 1992), 93.
2. Fresnal Ranch School brochure, n.d., Tucson Schools, Arizona Historical Society (AHS), Tucson.
3. *Gopher World*, May 1940, Judson School for Boys, Collection of Gloria Judson, Phoenix, AZ.
4. Lawrence Borne, *Dude Ranching: A Complete History* (Albuquerque: University of New Mexico Press, 1983), 17.
5. Hal K. Rothman, *Devil's Bargains: Tourism in the Twentieth-Century American West* (Lawrence: University Press of Kansas, 1998), 14.
6. Robert G. Athearn, *The Mythic West in Twentieth-Century America* (Lawrence: University Press of Kansas, 1986), 155. David W. Teague, *The Southwest in American Literature and Art: The Rise of a Desert Aesthetic* (Tucson: University of Arizona Press, 1997), 93. Teague explained that the *Atlantic, Harper's*, and *Scribner's*—and a few cheaper magazines such as *McClure's* in particular—were considered "polite, refined, intellectually rigorous, and exclusive." Throughout the monograph he describes in detail how various authors shaped the desert aesthetic of the Southwest. Mark Pry, *The Town on the Hassayampa: A History of Wickenburg, AZ* (Wickenburg, AZ: Desert Caballeros Western Museum, 1997), 97, explains that Arizona in particular was perceived as unspoiled because it had "experienced much less development than other states, offering travelers a chance to rediscover 'untamed nature' and the primitive, rustic conditions of the frontier." Marguerite S. Shaffer, *See America First: Tourism and National Identity, 1880–1940* (Washington, D.C.: Smithsonian Institution Press, 2001), 234–35, 259. In researching touring narratives of the Progressive Era and interwar period, Shaffer noted expressions of anxiety about the status of American society and a

tendency toward a celebrated "nostalgic image of America that referred back to a nineteenth-century society of small towns, middle landscapes, and face-to-face interaction."

7. Emily Post, *By Motor to the Golden Gate*, ed. Jane Lancaster (Jefferson, NC: McFarland, 2004), 96, 104.

8. John C. Tibbetts, "'Arizona Jim': The Westerns of Douglas Fairbanks, Sr." *Journal of Popular Film and Television* 39, no. 2 (2011), 48.

9. Patricia Nelson Limerick, *Something in the Soil: Legacies and Reckonings in the New West* (New York and London: W. W. Norton, 2000), 23, 25.

10. Quarter-Circle V-Bar Ranch Summer Camp brochure, n.d., Arizona Collection (AC), Arizona State University Libraries (ASUL), Tempe.

11. Joy S. Kasson, *Buffalo Bill's Wild West: Celebrity, Memory, and Popular History* (New York: Hill and Wang, 2000), 161–62, 177. Kasson argues that "the Wild West's great achievement—giving audiences excitement and adventure in a safe, secure context—was made possible largely through the contribution of the American Indian performers." Wrobel also asserts that in order to demonstrate that the American West was safe, settled, and cultured, promoters emphasized that it was "closing" yet not "closed" (Promised Lands: Promotion, Memory, and the Creation of the American West [Lawrence: University Press of Kansas, 2002], 26).

12. Wrobel, *Promised Lands*, 2–3.

13. Philip H. Cummings, unpublished 1932–1933 Valley Ranch journal, used with permission, Oct. 20, 1932.

14. *Arizona Health Resorts*, Atchison, Topeka, and Santa Fe Railway Company Passenger Department (Chicago, IL: Henry O. Shepard Co. Printers, November 1902), 15.

15. Ibid., 17–19.

16. "A Ranch School in Arizona for Younger Boys," 1932, private collection of David C. Wilhelm, Denver, CO.

17. Arizona Sunshine School brochure, n.d., AC, ASUL.

18. Southern Arizona School for Boys brochure, n.d., AHS.

19. Wrobel, *Promised Lands*, 25, 39. Wrobel found that "education [was] featured prominently in promotional works on the West."

20. Shaffer, *See America First*, 4, 119–23, 293.

21. "Arizona Ranch Schools," *Arizona Highways* 15, no. 9, Sept. 1939, 2.

22. Southern Pacific Railroad, "Guest Ranches Along the Southern Pacific Lines," 1934, 1938, and 1951, University of Arizona Special Collections, Tucson.

23. Alex Jay Kimmelman, "Luring the Tourist to Tucson: Civic Promotion During the 1920s," *Journal of Arizona History* 28, no. 2 (1987), 135, 137–39. The advertisement Kimmelman cited was printed in the *Outlook*, Nov. 21, 1923, Classifieds Section.

24. Fermor S. Church and Peggy Pond Church, *When Los Alamos was a Ranch School* (Los Alamos, NM: Los Alamos Historical Society, 1998), 11.

25. Teague, *The Southwest in American Literature and Art*. Teague describes how Josiah Gregg, "the quintessential self-made American" who explored the plains and deserts of New Mexico in the 1830s and 1840s, asserted that a formative tour would be healthful and a proving ground for young men. Teague argues that Washington Irving also saw the desert as a "stumbling block to the advancement of civilization," but it "held potential as a kind of proving ground for young Americans" (25–27). Anne F. Hyde, *An American Vision: Far Western Landscape and National Culture, 1820–1920* (New York and London: New York University Press, 1990), 13, 148. Borne, *Dude Ranching*, 27. Rothman, *Devil's Bargains*, 114–15, 141.

26. Rothman, *Devil's Bargains*, 132–33; Borne, *Dude Ranching*, 27–28.

27. Borne, *Dude Ranching*, 27–28, 35–37; Rothman, *Devil's Bargains*, 134.

28. Borne, *Dude Ranching*, 55, 58–59.

29. Suzanne Tumbin Gary, *Green Fields Country Day School: The First Fifty Years, 1933–1983* (Tucson, AZ: Green Fields Country Day School, 1983), 6.

30. Emory Harrison, "Maricopa County Education," *Works Progress Administration, Arizona Writers Project Manuscript*, 15–16, History and Archives Division, Arizona Department of Library, Archives, and Public Records (ADLAPR), Phoenix.

31. *Rattler*, 1931, Judson School, vol. 2, private collection of Gloria Judson, Phoenix, AZ.

32. Cross-continental motoring was not widespread until 1915, when several travelers set out to make it to the Panama-Pacific International Exposition by automobile. Newspaper proprietor William Randolph Hearst awarded seventy-nine silver medals to those who reached the Exposition by automobile, according to Jane Lancaster; see Emily Post, 3.

33. Charles S. Pearce, *Los Alamos Before the Bomb and Other Stories* (New York: Vantage Press, 1987), 3–4.

34. Jane Lancaster summarizes this observation in her introduction to Post, *By Motor to the Golden Gate*, 8. Collection of H. J. Heinz Company, MSS #57, Box 5, Folder 16, John Henry Heinz to his parents, Evans School, Tucson, Thomas and Katherine Detre Library and Archives, Senator John Heinz History Center, Pittsburgh, PA.

35. John Donaldson, Howard Bremond, David C. Wilhelm, Alexander Woods, interview by author, Tucson, AZ, 2006, tape recording.

36. Wrobel, *Promised Lands*, 97–99, 104–5, 240. In an endnote, Wrobel argues that the Old Pioneers' point of emphasis was that it was impossible to "know and understand the West" unless they had traversed it prior to the Pullman car era (240).

37. Rothman, *Devil's Bargains*, 127–28. The decision to engage in dude ranching was often precipitated by a lack of resources for agricultural production, and distance from commercial centers, extractive industries, and railroads. In the case of the

dude ranches in Jackson Hole, the remoteness provided more than "symbolic distance" that "was essential to the conceptualization of dude ranching."

38. Donaldson, Bremond, Wilhelm, and Woods interview, Tucson, AZ.
39. Tompkins, *West of Everything*, 74.
40. Earl Pomeroy, *In Search of the Golden West: The Tourist in Western America* (1957; reprint, Lincoln: University of Nebraska Press, 1990), 159–60. Anne F. Hyde also makes this point in *An American Vision*; see Shaffer, *See America First*, 32–39.
41. Porter Sargent, "The World We Come Into," in *A Handbook of Private Schools For American Boys and Girls*, ed. Porter Sargent (Boston, MA: Porter Sargent, 1940), 36.
42. Teague, *The Southwest in American Literature and Art*, 112–14, 117–18.
43. Southern Arizona School for Boys brochure, 1941–1942, Tucson Schools, AHS.
44. Palo Verde Ranch School brochure, n.d., Mesa Southwest Museum (MSM), Mesa, AZ.
45. Jokake School for Girls, 1939 yearbook, AC, ASUL.
46. Ted Simmons, "Mighty Monarch of the Desert Succumbs," *Gopher World*, Judson School for Boys, Phoenix, AZ, May 1940, collection of Gloria Judson, Phoenix, AZ.
47. Shaffer, *See America First*, introduction, chapters 1, 4.
48. "Arizona Ranch Schools," *Arizona Highways* 15, no. 9, Sept. 1939, 4.
49. Foxboro Ranches brochure.
50. Quarter-Circle B-Bar Ranch School brochure, n.d., AC, ASUL.
51. Fresnal Ranch School brochure, n.d., Tucson Schools, Fresnal Ranch School, AHS.
52. At the Los Alamos Ranch School, boys wore Boy Scout uniforms that consisted of flannel shorts with long underwear underneath them in the winter, and they wore leather chaps when out on all-day horseback-riding trips. Dakota Stetsons and bright bandannas worn around the neck completed the Los Alamos students' ensemble. When hired to run the school, A. J. Connell adopted the Boy Scout organization plan for the school. See Church and Church, *When Los Alamos was a Ranch School*, 12, 22.
53. Wrobel, *Promised Lands*, 1. He argues that these sentiments were reflected in two genres of writing: promotional literature and pioneer reminiscences.
54. Shaffer, *See America First*, 38–39.
55. Jack Van Ryder, illustrated map of Foxboro in Foxboro Ranches brochure, n.d., AC, ASUL.
56. Palo Verde Ranch School brochure, MSM.
57. Southern Arizona School for Boys brochure, AHS.
58. Hyde, *An American Vision*, 158, 212.
59. Judson School for Boys brochure, n.d., private collection of Gloria Judson, Phoenix, AZ.
60. Judson School for Boys brochure, AC, ASUL.

61. Hacienda del Sol brochure, n.d., Tucson Schools, Hacienda del Sol, AHS.

62. Southern Arizona School for Boys brochure, 1941–1942.

63. Church and Church, *When Los Alamos was a Ranch School*, 35. In 1973 several oral history interviews of former students were conducted at a Los Alamos Ranch School reunion. Excerpts are included in Church and Church, *When Los Alamos was A Ranch School*. It appears that after World War II, ranch schools took greater measures to involve professionals in these excavations. In 1959, for example, several Orme students excavated a Yavapai Indian cave under the direction of Orme science teacher Robert Schley and Museum of Northern Arizona archaeologist David Breternitz.

64. Don Everitt, "Excavations at the Sabino Canyon Ruins, 1937–1950," *Old Pueblo Archaeology* (Dec. 1996). The experience of conducting archaeological fieldwork as part of their ranch school curriculum must have had an impact on boys like Alexander Patterson, who after retirement took up archaeology as a hobby in New Mexico, and Garman Harbottle, who went to the California Institute of Technology and became an international authority on carbon dating. According to Everitt, Harbottle attributed his interest in archaeology to the shovel work on Pit #1 at Southern Arizona School. As of 1996, Harbottle was conducting research at Brookhaven National Laboratory with other archaeologists on origins and dates of turquoise artifacts.

65. "Souer Plans Ranch School in Mountains," *Benson News*, Feb. 1927, University of Arizona Special Collections, Tucson.

66. Shaffer, *See America First*, 181–82, 189–96.

67. Philip J. Deloria, *Playing Indian* (New Haven, CT: Yale University Press, 1998), 7, chapter 4, 96–97, 101–5, 110, 115. There is no indication that children at ranch schools played Indian. In addition to its decline before the heyday of most western ranch schools, geographic proximity to living Native American cultures made Indian play and its American character lessons improbable. It was one thing for northeastern and midwestern men's and boys' clubs to play Indian, but quite another for children to participate in such pageantry with real southwestern Indian people in close proximity.

68. "Capital City Sojourn: The Pierre Journal of Philip H. Cummings," ed. Patricia A. Billingsley, *South Dakota History* 39, no. 2 (Summer 2009), 117–18, 121–22, 124.

69. Hyde, *An American Vision*, 140–44, 191, 203, 229–36.

70. Sylvia Byrnes, *Jokake Inn: One of the Earliest Desert Resorts* (n.p., n.d.), 12–14.

71. Ibid., 14.

72. Pearce, *Los Alamos Before the Bomb*, 26–27.

73. David C. Wilhelm, *Cowboy Ace: The Life Adventures of David Wilhelm, An Autobiography* (Parker, CO: Thornton, 2010), 67.

74. Richard Slatta, *Cowboys of the Americas* (New Haven, CT: Yale University Press, 1990). Slatta explains the many distinctions between vaqueros, gauchos, and Anglo-American cowboys. Gauchos' "beloved serape" seemed indestructible and

curious to American cowboys, 41–42. He describes the Spanish and Mexican origin of the rodeo on 68, 128, 130, and 147.

75. Wilhelm, *Cowboy Ace*, 66–67.

76. Church and Church, *When Los Alamos was A Ranch School*, 3, 65–66, 21.

77. *Rattler*, 1931, Judson School, vol. 2, 35, private collection of Gloria Judson, Phoenix, AZ; and *El Conquistador*, Judson School, 1935, private collection of Gloria Judson, Phoenix, AZ.

78. Palo Verde Ranch School brochure, MSM.

79. Byrnes, *Jokake Inn*, 4–5.

80. Larry May, *The Big Tomorrow: Hollywood and the Politics of the American Way* (Chicago, IL: University of Chicago Press, 2000), 19, 46–47. May included an interior photograph of Rogers's ranch, courtesy of the Will Rogers Memorial Commission of Oklahoma.

81. Pomeroy, *In Search of the Golden West*, 45.

82. Hyde, *An American Vision*, 295.

83. Gerald D. Nash, *The American West in the Twentieth Century: A Short History of an Urban Oasis* (Englewood Cliffs, NJ: Prentice-Hall, 1973), 60.

84. "A Ranch School in Arizona for Younger Boys," brochure, 1932, private collection of David C. Wilhelm, Denver, CO.

85. Bonnie Henry, "Alfalfa's Gone: Green Fields Still Making Hay," *Tucson Daily Star*, Dec. 7, 1988, Tucson Schools, Green Fields, AHS.

86. "Boys' School to Open at Canyon Site," *Tucson Citizen*, Sept. 21, 1930, Tucson Schools, Southern Arizona School, AHS. Bonnie Henry, "Prepping in Desert: School Was Born Because of WWI Vet's Cough," *Arizona Daily Star*, May 3, 1989, Tucson Schools, Southern Arizona School, AHS.

87. Rothman, *Devil's Bargains*, 72–73.

88. The Valley Ranches, Valley, WY, booklet, 1940. American Heritage Center, Laramie, WY.

89. "Orme School Community—A Different Way of Learning," *Arizonan*, May 15, 1969, AC, ASUL.

90. Dee Garceau, "Nomads, Bunkies, Cross-Dressers, and Family Men: Cowboy Identity and the Gendering of Ranch Work," in *Across the Great Divide: Cultures of Manhood in the American West*, ed. Matthew Basso, Laura McCall, and Dee Garceau (New York and London: Routledge, 2001), 150–53.

91. Judson School for Boys brochure, n.d., AC, ASUL.

92. Nash, *The American West*, 27, 98.

93. Bill Barrow, "The Southern Arizona School for Boys," *The Saguaro* (Dec. 1986), 4, AHS.

94. The Valley Ranches, Valley, WY, booklet, 1940. American Heritage Center, Laramie, WY.

95. Foxboro Ranches brochure, n.d., AC, ASUL.

96. Fresnal Ranch School brochure, n.d., Tucson Schools, Fresnal Ranch School, Arizona Historical Society (AHS), Tucson.
97. "A Ranch School in Arizona for Younger Boys," 1932, private collection of David C. Wilhelm, Denver, CO; Wilhelm, *Cowboy Ace*, 58.
98. Sybil Ellinwood, "East Meets West in the Field of Education," *Journal of Arizona History (JAH)* 15, no. 3 (Autumn 1974): 270, 285–86. "The Rodeo, 1923, Evans School," 16, AHS.
99. http://www.lanl.gov/worldview/history.html; Church and Church, *When Los Alamos was A Ranch School*, 4–9.
100. Church and Church, *When Los Alamos was A Ranch School*, 10.
101. Sherman Bloomer, "The Quarter V Bar Ranch," *Orme School Yearbook, 1939–1940*, Orme School Archives (OSA), Mayer, AZ.
102. Susan Adams Samuelson, "The Orme School on the Quarter Circle V Bar Ranch," *JAH* 25, no. 4 (Winter 1984): 406.
103. Ellinwood, "East Meets West," 274.
104. Barbara Ferris, interview by author, Paradise Valley, AZ, Dec. 29, 2002, tape recording.
105. Jean Dunn Porter, interview by author, Tucson, AZ, Feb. 17, 2002, tape recording.
106. Diane Frazier, "Cowboy of Yesterday," *Orme School Yearbook, 1939–1940*, OSA.
107. Quarter-Circle V-Bar Ranch Summer Camp brochure, AC, ASUL.
108. Tompkins, *West of Everything*, 89, 93.
109. *A Handbook of Private Schools For American Boys and Girls*, ed. Porter Sargent (Boston, MA: Porter Sargent, 1940), 861. Sargent lists fourteen schools under the category "Schools with Stables." Of the fourteen, four were ranch schools and seven were located in the West. Sixteen schools offered polo. In the 1934–1935 edition, twelve schools are listed as having stables and thirty-five as offering horseback riding. Of those thirty-five, seventeen were located in the West and nine were ranch schools. Ranch schools were more likely to pay the additional expense to include a photo in Sargent's *Handbook*, and all depicted horses and western landscape scenes.
110. LeRoy McKim Makepeace, *Sherman Thacher and His School* (New Haven, CT: Yale University Press, 1941), 88; H. J. Heinz Co. collection, MSS #57, Thomas and Katherine Detre Library and Archives, Senator John Heinz History Center, Pittsburgh, PA.
111. Foxboro Ranches brochure, AC, ASUL.
112. "We Go To School Out-of-Doors," Old Pueblo School brochure, n.d., Old Pueblo, AHS.
113. Pearce, *Los Alamos Before the Bomb*, 43.
114. Judson School for Boys brochure, AC, ASUL.
115. Palo Verde Ranch School, MSM.

116. David Glassberg, *American Historical Pageantry: The Uses of Tradition in the Early Twentieth Century* (Chapel Hill: University of North Carolina Press, 1990), 1, 5, 87, 268–69; Pomeroy, *In Search of the Golden West*, 178.

117. Kel M. Fox, "Of Dudes and Cows: The Foxboro Story," *JAH* 32, no. 4 (Winter 1991): 416–17.

118. "250 Tucsonans See Rodeo At Arizona Desert School," *Arizona Daily Star*, Jan. 21, 1934, Tucson Schools, Arizona Desert School, AHS. Jokake School for Girls 1939 yearbook, AC, ASUL.

119. Jokake School for Girls 1939 yearbook, AC, ASUL.

120. *Cactus Needle* 4, no. 3 (Mar. 1923), Tuscon, AZ, AHS.

121. "Boys' School in Catalinas Has a Charming Site," *Arizona Daily Star*, Feb. 22, 1935, Tucson Schools, Southern Arizona School for Boys, AHS.

122. Ellinwood, "East Meets West," 287.

123. Cummings, Valley Ranch journal, Feb. 3, 1933, Mar. 12, 1933.

124. Wilhelm, *Cowboy Ace*, 63–66.

125. Michael A. Amundson, "'These Men Play Real Polo': An Elite Sport in the 'Cowboy State,' 1890–1930," *Montana The Magazine of Western History* 59, no. 1, Spring 2009, 3–5, 7, 11. All quotes are Amundson's. Amundson cites Owen Wister; see "How They Taught Me Polo," *Harper's Weekly*, 1895.

126. Alex Jay Kimmelman, "Luring the Tourist to Tucson: Civic Promotion During the 1920s," *Journal of Arizona History* 28, no. 2 (1987): 139–40.

127. Bianca Premo, "Recreating Identity: Recreation on the Arizona-Sonora Border, 1880–1930," *Studies in Latin American Popular Culture* 16 (1997): 10.

128. Edward N. Saveth, "Education of an Elite," *History of Education Quarterly* 28, no. 3 (Autumn 1988): 375.

129. Nick Thimmesch and William O. Johnson, *Robert Kennedy at 40* (New York: W. W. Norton, 1965), 28, quoted in Saveth, "Education of an Elite," 375.

130. Fresnal Ranch School brochure, AHS.

131. Wilhelm, *Cowboy Ace*, 74.

CHAPTER 4

1. Susan Lee Johnson, "'A Memory Sweet to Soldiers': The Significance of Gender," in *A New Significance: Re-envisioning the History of the American West*, ed. Clyde A. Milner (New York: Oxford University Press, 1996), 255.

2. A Summary of Interesting Events at Judson School," *Gopher World*, 1940–1941, 21, private collection of Gloria Judson, Phoenix, AZ.

3. Alfred E. Stearns, *The Challenge of Youth* (Boston, MA: W. A. Wilde, 1923), 68, 77–78.

4. Robert Danforth Cole, *Private Secondary Education for Boys in the United States* (Philadelphia, PA: Westbrook, 1928), 79–81; William J. Hutchins, *Children's Code of Morals for Elementary Schools* (Washington, D.C.: Character Education Institution, 1917), quoted in B. Edward McClellan, *Moral Education in America:*

Schools and the Shaping of Character from Colonial Times to the Present (New York and London: Teachers College, Columbia University, 1999).

5. George A. Judson, "Editorial," *Ocotillo*, Judson School yearbook, 1938, private collection of David C. Lincoln, Paradise Valley, AZ.

6. Kristin L. Hoganson, *Fighting for American Manhood: How Gender Politics Provoked the Spanish-American and Philippine-American Wars* (New Haven, CT: Yale University Press, 1998), 3, 10, 32, 37, 65, 118, 180.

7. Michael Kimmel, *Manhood in America: A Cultural History* (New York: Free Press, 1996), 136, 192; Peter G. Filene, *Him/Her/Self: Gender Identities in Modern America*, 3rd edition (Baltimore, MD: Johns Hopkins University Press, 1998), 105, 148–49.

8. Gail Bederman, *Manliness and Civilization: A Cultural History of Gender and Race in the United States, 1880–1917* (Chicago, IL: University of Chicago Press, 1995), 176.

9. Ibid., 43, 91–92.

10. Theodore Roosevelt to G. Stanley Hall, Nov. 29, 1899, quoted in Bederman, *Manliness and Civilization*, 100–101 (emphasis in original). Lester F. Goodchild, "G. Stanley Hall and an American Social Darwinist Pedagogy: His Progressive Educational Ideas on Gender and Race," *History of Education Quarterly* 52 (Feb. 2012).

11. Frederick Jackson Turner, *The Frontier in American History* (New York: Henry Holt, 1950), 3.

12. Frederick Jackson Turner, "The Problem of the West," in Turner, *Frontier in American History*, 205.

13. Bederman, *Manliness and Civilization*, 219, 221.

14. Ibid., 226.

15. Foxboro Ranches Brochure, n.d., AC, ASUL.

16. Robert Athearn, *The Mythic West in Twentieth-Century America* (Lawrence: University Press of Kansas, 1986), 74–75, 224, 228, 231.

17. Turner, *Frontier in American History*, 4, 30.

18. Jane Tompkins, *West of Everything. The Inner Life of Westerns* (New York: Oxford University Press, 1992), 145.

19. Larry May, *Screening Out the Past: The Birth of Mass Culture and the Motion Picture Industry* (Chicago, IL: University of Chicago Press, 1980), 101–2.

20. Scott Simon, *The Invention of the Western Film: A Cultural History of the Genre's First Half-Century* (Cambridge, UK: Cambridge University Press, 2003), 122–29.

21. J. O. Engleman, *Moral Education in School and Home* (Chicago, IL; New York; and Boston, MA: Benj. H. Sanborn, 1920), 79.

22. Patricia Nelson Limerick, *Something in the Soil: Legacies and Reckonings in the New West* (New York and London: W. W. Norton, 2000), introduction and part 1.

23. David M. Wrobel, *Promised Lands: Promotion, Memory, and the Creation of the American West* (Lawrence: University Press of Kansas, 2002), 95–112, 124, 129–30.

Wrobel quotes Meeker's *The Busy Life of Eighty-five Years* (Washington, D.C.: n.p., 1916) and Elisha Brooks, *A Pioneer Mother of California* (San Francisco, CA: Harr Wagner Publishers, 1922), introduction.

24. This biographical discussion of Roosevelt's career as assemblyman draws primarily on Edmund Morris, *The Rise of Theodore Roosevelt* (New York: Ballantine, 1979), 159-202, 227-70, quoted in Bederman, *Manliness and Civilization*, 170-71.

25. Bederman, *Manliness and Civilization*, 170.

26. Fresnal Ranch School brochure, n.d., Tucson Schools, Arizona Historical Society (AHS), Tucson.

27. *Gopher World*, May 1940, Judson School for Boys, collection of Gloria Judson, Phoenix, AZ.

28. H. David Evans, "Twenty-five Years of the Evans School," *Rodeo*, 1927, 51-63, quoted in Sybil Ellinwood, "East Meets West in the Field of Education," *Journal of Arizona History* (JAH) 15, no. 3 (Autumn 1974): 269; Ellinwood, "East Meets West," 276.

29. Palo Verde Ranch School brochure, n.d., Mesa Southwest Museum (MSM), Mesa, AZ.

30. Ibid.

31. Ellinwood, "East Meets West," 278.

32. Kent Baxter, *The Modern Age: Turn-of-the-Century American Culture and the Invention of Adolescence* (Tuscaloosa: University of Alabama Press, 2008), 130-31.

33. Sherman Kingsley and F. B. Dresslar, "Open-air Schools," Bureau of Education Bulletin, no. 23, Department of the Interior, Washington, D.C. Government Printing Office, 1917, 224.

34. Leslie Paris, *Children's Nature: The Rise of the American Summer Camp* (New York: New York University Press, 2008), 124.

35. Judson School for Boys brochure, n.d., AC, ASUL; Southern Arizona School for Boys brochure, n.d.

36. Southern Arizona School for Boys brochure, n.d., AHS; Southern Arizona School for Boys brochure, 1941-1942, AC, ASUL.

37. John F. Kasson, *Houdini, Tarzan, and the Perfect Man: The White Male Body and The Challenge of Modernity in America* (New York: Hill and Wang, 2001), 30-32.

38. *El Conquistador*, Judson School yearbook, 1935, private collection of Gloria Judson, Phoenix, AZ.

39. Fresnal Ranch School brochure, n.d., Tucson Schools, Fresnal Ranch School, AHS.

40. Ibid.

41. John A. Garraty, *Henry Cabot Lodge: A Biography* (New York: Alfred A. Knopf, 1953), 193; Hoganson demonstrates (76, 143, 147-50) that Lodge, Roosevelt, and

Albert J. Beveridge led the cohort of politicians who felt this generational struggle and adamantly supported war and imperialism.
42. H. David Evans, "Evans School in the Making," *Rodeo*, Apr. 1920, quoted in Ellinwood, "East Meets West," 276.
43. Rodman E. Griscom Jr., interview with Sybil Ellinwood, quoted in Ellinwood, "East Meets West," 287.
44. Nicholas Roosevelt, photo album, AHS.
45. "The Rodeo, 1923, Evans School," 13, AHS.
46. *El Conquistador*, Judson School yearbook, 1935, private collection of Gloria Judson, Phoenix, AZ.
47. Philip H. Cummings, unpublished 1932–1933 Valley Ranch journal, used with permission, Oct. 16, 1932; *Cactus Needle* 4, no. 3, Mar. 1923, 10, Arizona Historical Society, Tucson.
48. David C. Wilhelm, *Cowboy Ace: The Life Adventures of David Wilhelm, An Autobiography* (Parker, CO: Thornton, 2010), 65.
49. Collection of H. J. Heinz Company, MSS #57, Box 5, Folder 16, Thomas and Katherine Detre Library and Archives, Senator John Heinz History Center, Pittsburgh, PA.
50. Charles S. Pearce, *Los Alamos Before the Bomb and Other Stories* (New York: Vantage Press, 1987), 27–28.
51. Baxter, *The Modern Age*, 94, 101.
52. Bederman, *Manliness and Civilization*, 172–74.
53. Edward Abbey is quoted in Karen R. Merrill, "Domesticated Bliss: Ranchers and Their Animals," in *Across the Great Divide: Cultures of Manhood in the American West*, ed. Matthew Basso, Laura McCall, and Dee Garceau (New York and London: Routledge, 2001), 169.
54. Orme School yearbook, 1945–1946, private collection of Jeb John Rosebrook, Scottsdale, AZ.
55. Jeb J. Rosebrook, "The Spring and Fall Cattle Drives at Orme School Provided Kids with Memories for a Lifetime," *Arizona Highways* (Aug. 1999): 49.
56. Cummings, Valley Ranch journal, Nov. 14, 1932, Jan. 27, 1933.
57. Bederman, *Manliness and Civilization*, 115.
58. Anne F. Hyde, *An American Vision: Far Western Landscape and National Culture, 1820–1920* (New York and London: New York University Press, 1990), 73–74.
59. Ibid., 132. The article she cites was published in *Harper's* in Dec. 1867.
60. "The Rodeo, 1923, Evans School," 13, AHS.
61. Johnny Wiester, "Hunting and Shooting," Orme School Year Book, 1951–1952.
62. Barney Judson, "Camping," *Ocotillo*, Judson School yearbook, 1938, private collection of David C. Lincoln. Barney's distaste for hunting was described by Gloria Judson in an interview conducted by the author, 2002.
63. "The Rodeo, 1923, Evans School," 12, AHS.

64. Pearce, *Los Alamos Before the Bomb*, 37.
65. Ibid., 37–38.
66. Bonnie Henry, "Alfalfa's Gone; Green Fields Still Making Hay," *Arizona Daily Star*, Dec. 7, 1988, Tucson Schools, Green Fields, AHS.
67. Suzanne Tumblin Gary, *Green Fields Country Day School: The First Fifty Years, 1933–1983* (Tucson, AZ: Green Fields Country Day School, 1983), 10.
68. Jeb John Rosebrook, interview by author, Scottsdale, AZ, Feb. 2002, tape recording.
69. Palo Verde Ranch School brochure, n.d., MSM.
70. David C. Lincoln, Judson School Alumni Questionnaire, prepared by author, May 2000.
71. Ormonde Parke, interview by author, Phoenix, Feb. 16, 2002.
72. "Youthful Student is Killed By 'Unloaded Gun' Discharge," *Arizona Republic*, Apr. 25, 1939; "Inquest Held In Gun Death," *Arizona Republic*, Apr. 26, 1939, 4.
73. W. Hudson Kensel, *Dude Ranching in Yellowstone Country: Larry Larom and Valley Ranch, 1915–1969* (Norman, OK: Arthur H. Clark Company, 2010), 160.
74. *Arizona Desert School Handbook*, 2–4, ASKB, Nicholas Brown, Arizona Desert School, Providence, RI.
75. Paris, *Children's Nature*, 98.
76. Wilhelm, *Cowboy Ace*, 61.
77. John Donaldson, Howard Bremond, David C. Wilhelm, Alexander Woods, interview by author, Tucson, AZ, 2006, tape recording.
78. Horace Holden, *Young Boys and Boarding School* (Boston, MA: Gorham, 1913), 175.
79. Tompkins, *West of Everything*, 84.
80. Athearn, *The Mythic West*, 4–7.
81. Robert J. Badham, *Preparatory School Manual for Boys and Parents: A Handbook for the Use of Parents and the Guidance of School Boys* (Philadelphia, PA: Robert J. Badham, 1932), 36.
82. Cummings, Valley Ranch journal, Oct. 26, 1932.
83. Robert C. Alberts, MS 0037 Series II, Box 3, Folder 3, Thomas and Katherine Detre Library and Archives, Senator John Heinz History Center, Pittsburgh, PA.
84. Russell Fairgrieve, "Meeting of Students Who Have Smoking Permission," Oct. 21, 1948. This is either an outline for a speech or possibly a memo. Southern Arizona School Ephemera files, Fenster School, Tucson.
85. Robert V. Hine and John Mack Faragher, "Open Range," in *The American West: A New Interpretive History* (New Haven, CT: Yale University Press, 2000), 314.
86. Dee Garceau, "Nomads, Bunkies, Cross-Dressers, and Family Men," in *Across the Great Divide: Cultures of Manhood in the American West*, ed. Matthew Basso, Laura McCall, and Dee Garceau (New York and London: Routledge, 2001), 163. Garceau extracted these quotes from Roosevelt from William Savage, *Cowboy Life: Reconstructing an American Myth* (Niwot: University Press of Colorado, 1993), 171–72, 175.

87. Cummings, Valley Ranch journal, Sept. 28, 1932.
88. Ellinwood, "East Meets West," 286.
89. Badham, *Preparatory School Manual*, 27–29.
90. Ibid., 29; Cummings, Valley Ranch journal, 243.
91. Cummings, Valley Ranch journal, 155, 165, 205.
92. Ellinwood, "East Meets West," 273–74.
93. Palo Verde Ranch School brochure, n.d., MSM.
94. Southern Arizona School for Boys brochure, n.d., AHS.
95. Ibid.
96. Kensel, *Dude Ranching in Yellowstone Country*, 155–56.
97. Church and Church, *When Los Alamos was A Ranch School*, 5.
98. Rosebrook interview.
99. *Rattler*, 1931, Judson School, vol. 2, 8, private collection of Gloria Judson, Phoenix, AZ.
100. Dee Garceau, "Nomads, Bunkies, Cross-Dressers, and Family Men," 154–65.
101. Wilhelm, *Cowboy Ace*, 61.
102. Julia Grant, "A 'Real Boy' and Not a Sissy: Gender, Childhood, and Masculinity, 1890–1940," *Journal of Social History* 37, no. 4 (Summer 2004): 836–37.
103. Paris, *Children's Nature*, 153. Paris articulates these reasons for her speculation that summer camps were attractive work environments for some gay men and lesbians.
104. Badham, *Preparatory School Manual*, 31.
105. Jeffrey P. Dennis, *We Boys Together: Teenagers in Love Before Girl-Craziness* (Nashville, TN: Vanderbilt University Press, 2007), ix, 1, 3.
106. Grant, "A 'Real Boy,'" 829–32. Grant argues that boys who exemplified the psychological ideal were called "real" or "regular" boys in contrast to the sissy.
107. *El Conquistador*, Judson School, 1935, private collection of Gloria Judson, Phoenix, AZ.
108. Rebecca Jo Plant, *Mom: The Transformation of Motherhood in Modern America* (Chicago, IL: University of Chicago Press, 2010), 46; Pearce, *Los Alamos Before the Bomb*, 15; Church and Church, *When Los Alamos was a Ranch School*, 2.

CHAPTER 5

1. Alfred E. Stearns, *The Challenge of Youth* (Boston, MA: W. A. Wilde, 1923), 31–32.
2. Robert Danforth Cole, *Private Secondary Education for Boys in the United States* (Philadelphia, PA: Westbrook, 1928), 80, 85.
3. Catherine E. Rymph, "From 'Economic Want' to 'Family Pathology': Foster Family Care, the New Deal, and the Emergence of a Public Child Welfare System," *Journal of Policy History* 24, no. 1 (2012): 9–11, 20.
4. M. L. Wilson, "How New Deal Agencies are Affecting Family Life," *Journal of Home Economics* (May 1935): 274–78.

5. Elliott West, *Growing Up with the Country: Childhood on the Far Western Frontier* (Albuquerque: University of New Mexico Press, 1989), xi, 124, 176.

6. LeRoy McKim Makepeace, *Sherman Thacher and His School* (New Haven, CT: Yale University Press, 1941), 76.

7. Robert V. Hine and John Mack Faragher, "The Safety Valve," in *The American West: A New Interpretive History* (New Haven, CT: Yale University Press, 2000), 330–34.

8. Dee Garceau. "Nomads, Bunkies, Cross-Dressers, and Family Men," in *Across the Great Divide: Cultures of Manhood in the American West*, ed. Matthew Basso, Laura McCall, and Dee Garceau (New York: Routledge, 2001), 150.

9. James McLachlan, *American Boarding Schools: A Historical Study* (New York: Charles Scribner's Sons, 1970), 47.

10. Ibid., 87–88, 99, 101.

11. Ibid., 256–57.

12. Cole, *Private Secondary Education*, 85.

13. Ibid., 143, 238.

14. Lynn Dumenil, *The Modern Temper: American Culture and Society in the 1920s* (New York: Hill and Wang, 1995), 130.

15. *Selected Readings in Character Education*, ed. Dennis Clayton Troth (Boston, MA: Beacon, 1930), 50–52.

16. Ann Hulbert, *Raising America: Experts, Parents, and a Century of Advice About Children* (New York: Alfred A. Knopf, 2003), 152.

17. Ormonde Parke, interview by author, Phoenix, AZ, Feb. 16, 2002.

18. Horace Holden, *Young Boys and Boarding School* (Boston, MA: Gorham Press, 1913), 18–19.

19. Steven Mintz, *Huck's Raft: A History of American Childhood* (Cambridge, MA: Belknap Press of Harvard University Press, 2004), 213–14. Mintz found the statement by Judge Ben Lindsay quoted in Paula S. Fass, *Kidnapped: Child Abduction in America* (New York: Oxford University Press, 1997), 67.

20. Rima Apple, *Perfect Motherhood: Science and Childrearing in America* (New Brunswick, NJ: Rutgers University Press, 2006), 2, 6–9, 36–39, 55–58; Mintz, *Huck's Raft*, 186–91, 219, 222–23; Shari L. Thurer, *The Myths of Motherhood: How Culture Reinvents the Good Mother* (Boston, MA: Houghton Mifflin, 1994), 225–26, 240; Peter N. Stearns, *Anxious Parents: A History of Modern Childrearing in America* (New York: New York University Press, 2003), 19–20, 37–38, 40–42. For more on child science, see Joseph M. Hawes, *Children Between the Wars: American Childhood 1920–1940* (New York: Twayne Publishers, an Imprint of Simon & Schuster Macmillan, 1997), xiii, 66–73.

21. Character Education Inquiry, Teachers College, Columbia University. *Studies in the Nature of Character*, vol. 1: Studies in Deceit (New York: Macmillan, 1928), 200, 204–5, 306.

22. Ibid., 306, 408–9.
23. Hawes, *Children Between the Wars*, 7–9.
24. Holden, *Young Boys and Boarding School*, 26–27.
25. Ibid., 22.
26. Secondary Education Board Annual Report, 1940, 83, National Association of Independent Schools (NAIS) Archive, Washington, D.C.
27. Emily Newell Blair, "Why I Sent My Children Away to School," *Harper's Monthly Magazine*, Mar. 1926, 430–31.
28. Ibid., 431.
29. Ibid., 434.
30. "Administrators' Section," Secondary Education Board Annual Report, 1936, 61–65, NAIS Archives, Washington, D.C.
31. J. O. Engleman, *Moral Education in School and Home* (Chicago, IL; New York; and Boston, MA: Benj. H. Sanborn, 1920), 57–58.
32. Holden, *Young Boys and Boarding School*, 192.
33. Rebecca Jo Plant, *Mom: The Transformation of Motherhood in Modern America* (Chicago, IL: University of Chicago Press, 2010), 2–8, 6. Plant explores "how the ideology of moral motherhood came to be largely discredited in favor of a more narrow, psychological and biological conception of the maternal role."
34. David M. Levy, *Maternal Overprotection* (New York: W. W. Norton, 1966), 37, 3, 15, 39, 71, 147, 151, 163; Mintz, *Huck's Raft*, 220, 223.
35. Levy, *Maternal Overprotection*, 163, 176, 200.
36. Harry L. Coderre, "Disciplinary Problems in the Western Ranch School," master's thesis, Massachusetts State College, Amherst, 1942, 21.
37. Ibid., 24.
38. Fermor S. Church and Peggy Pond Church, *When Los Alamos was a Ranch School* (Los Alamos, NM: Los Alamos Historical Society, 1998), 2–4.
39. Makepeace, *Sherman Thacher and His School*, 116.
40. David C. Wilhelm, *Cowboy Ace: The Life Adventures of David Wilhelm, An Autobiography* (Parker, CO: Thornton, 2010), 52.
41. Fresnal Ranch School brochure, n.d., Tucson Schools, Arizona Historical Society (AHS), Tucson.
42. "A Ranch School in Arizona for Younger Boys," brochure, Tucson, AZ, 1932, private collection of David C. Wilhelm, Denver, CO.
43. "Wealthy Easterners Underwrite School," unidentified newspaper clipping, Sept. 24, 1928, and "School's Walls Rising Rapidly," Sept. 30, 1928, both in Tucson Schools, Arizona Desert School, AHS.
44. *El Conquistador*, Judson School yearbook, 1935, 3, private collection of Gloria Judson, Phoenix, AZ.
45. "Judson School for Boys," brochure, c. 1933, private collection of Gloria Judson, Phoenix, AZ.

46. Apple, *Perfect Motherhood*, 6–7, 16, 91.
47. *Arizona Health Resorts*, Atchison, Topeka, and Santa Fe Railway Company Passenger Department (Chicago, IL: Henry O. Shepard Co. Printers, November 1902).
48. "Judson School for Boys," brochure c. 1933, private collection of Gloria Judson, Phoenix, AZ.
49. Makepeace, *Sherman Thacher and His School*, 87.
50. "A Ranch School in Arizona for Younger Boys," brochure, Tucson, AZ, 1932, private collection of David C. Wilhelm, Denver, CO.
51. Coderre, Disciplinary Problems," 8, 14, 22–23.
52. Lawrence Borne, *Dude Ranching: A Complete History* (Albuquerque: University of New Mexico Press, 1983), 6–7.
53. Church and Church, *When Los Alamos was a Ranch School*, 2–3. Peggy Pond was the daughter of the school's founder, Ashley Pond. In this account, there is no mention of Peggy's mother, the wife of Ashley Pond. It seems that Miss Ranger was hired to serve in this capacity.
54. Fresnal Ranch School brochure, n.d., AHS.
55. Holden, *Young Boys and Boarding School*, 147, 130.
56. *El Conquistador*, Judson School yearbook, 1935, 3, collection of Gloria Judson, Phoenix, AZ
57. Makepeace, *Sherman Thacher and His School*, 77, 81.
58. Cole, *Private Secondary Education*, 115–16.
59. Character Education Inquiry, Teachers College, Columbia University, *Studies in the Nature of Character*, vol. 1: Studies in Deceit (New York: Macmillan, 1928), 198, 409, and Book Two, 290.
60. "A Summary of Interesting Events at Judson School," *Gopher World*, 1940–1941, private collection of Gloria Judson, Phoenix, AZ.
61. Parke interview; Judson interview.
62. Rosebrook interview.
63. "A Summary of Interesting Events at Judson School," *Gopher World*, 1940–1941.
64. "School for Boys Has Ideal Location in Sabino Canyon," unidentified newspaper article, Sept. 20, 1931, Tucson Schools, Southern Arizona School for Boys, AHS.
65. Southern Arizona School for Boys brochure, n.d., AHS.
66. Southern Arizona School for Boys brochure, 1940–1941, Arizona Collection (AC), Arizona State University Libraries (ASUL), Tempe.
67. Suzanne Tumblin Gary. *Green Fields Country Day School: The First Fifty Years, 1933–1983* (Tucson, AZ: Green Fields Country Day School, 1983), 5.
68. Ibid., 12.
69. Ibid., 12, 7.
70. Ibid., 12, 16, 20.
71. "Minna Vrang Orme," *Arizona Women's Hall of Fame*, AHS, 19891, 17–19.
72. Orme School 1951–1952 yearbook, private collection of Jeb John Rosebrook, Scottsdale, AZ.

73. Orme School 1948–1949 yearbook, private collection of Jeb John Rosebrook, Scottsdale, AZ.

74. *Rattler*, 1931, Judson School, vol. 2, 8, private collection of Gloria Judson, Phoenix, AZ.

75. Laura Judson to George Judson, personal letters written June through Sept. 1948, private collection of Gloria Judson, Phoenix, AZ.

76. W. Hudson Kensel, *Dude Ranching in Yellowstone Country: Larry Larom and Valley Ranch, 1915–1969* (Norman, OK: Arthur H. Clark Company, 2010), 7–58.

77. Ferris interview; Sylvia Byrnes, *Jokake Inn: One of the Earliest Desert Resorts* (n.p., n.d.). Sylvia Byrnes, who was Barbara Ferris's mother, clearly stated that both Barbara and George started the school.

78. John Donaldson, Howard Bremond, David C. Wilhelm, and Alexander (Sandy) Woods, interview by author, Tucson, 2006.

CONCLUSION

1. Alfred E. Stearns, *The Challenge of Youth* (Boston, MA: W. A. Wilde, 1923), 6.

2. Ibid., 32–34, 92–95, 106.

3. C. Ralph Tupper, *A Survey of the Arizona Public School System: A Study of the Elementary and Secondary Public Schools of the State* (Arizona State Board of Education, January 1, 1925), 53.

4. Tupper, *Survey of the Arizona Public School System*, 5.

5. Richard De Ritter, "'This Changeableness in Character': Exploring Masculinity and Nationhood on James Boswell's Grand Tour," *Scottish Literary Review* 2 (Spring/Summer 2010): 24–29, 36.

6. Michele Cohen, "The Grand Tour. Language, National Identity and Masculinity," *Changing English* 8 (2001): 132.

7. Abigail A. Van Slyck, "The Spatial Practices of Privilege," *Journal of the Society of Architectural Historians* 70, no. 2 (June 2011): 230.

8. Porter Sargent, *The Continuing Battle for the Control of the Mind of Youth* (Boston, MA: Porter Sargent, 1945), 21–22.

9. Letter in the private collection of Gloria Judson written to Patty D. Judson, who was the sister-in-law of Gloria and Barney Judson. This letter originated from The Greenbrier and Cottages, White Sulphur Springs, West Virginia, where Patty's family lived. In this letter the writer relayed a conversation he/she had with Mrs. James Conley from Charleston, WV.

10. Porter Sargent, *Education in Wartime* (Boston, MA: Porter Sargent, 1942), 36–37.

11. *Gopher World*, 1942, Judson School, private collection of Gloria Judson, Phoenix, AZ.

12. Orme School 1948–1949 yearbook, Orme School Archives, Mayer, AZ.

13. Sybil Ellinwood, "East Meets West in the Field of Education," *JAH* 15, no. 3 (Autumn 1974): 293.

14. Porter Sargent, *Education in Wartime*, reprinted from the 26th edition of *A Handbook of Private Schools* (Boston, MA: Porter Sargent, 1942), 29.

15. Arthur G. Powell, *Lessons from Privilege: The American Preparatory School Tradition* (Cambridge, MA: Harvard University Press, 1996), 68.

16. Suzanne Tumblin Gary, *Green Fields Country Day School: The First Fifty Years, 1933–1983* (Tucson, AZ: Green Fields Country Day School, 1983), 21.

17. Mark Pry, *The Town on the Hassayampa: A History of Wickenburg, AZ* (Wickenburg, AZ: Desert Caballeros Western Museum, 1997), 122.

18. Ibid., 127.

19. Martin Nussbaum, "Sociological Symbolisms of the 'Adult Western,'" *Social Forces* 39 (Oct. 1960): 26, quoted in Michael Kimmel, *Manhood in America: A Cultural History* (New York: Free Press, 1996), 252.

20. Powell, *Lessons from Privilege*, 103.

21. Ibid.

22. "Two Ranch Schools for Boys Will Consolidate February 26," unidentified newspaper clipping, n.d., private collection of Gloria Judson, Phoenix, AZ.

23. "Dismissal of School Director is Learned," *Arizona Daily Star*, Apr. 16, 1953, Tucson Schools, Arizona Desert School, AHS.

24. "Desert School, Morgan Sued," unidentified newspaper clipping, May 23, 1953, and "Desert School Closes Doors," Sept. 23, 1953, both in Tucson Schools, Arizona Desert, AHS.

25. Powell, *Lessons from Privilege*, 89.

26. Ibid., 90.

27. Susan Adams Samuelson, "The Orme School on the Quarter Circle V Bar Ranch," *JAH* 25, no. 4 (Winter 1984): 420.

28. Powell, *Lessons from Privilege*, 144.

29. Bonnie Henry, "Prepping in Desert: School Was Born Because of WWI Vet's Cough," May 3, 1989, Tucson Schools, AHS.

30. Gary, *Green Fields Country Day School*, 24.

31. Janet Wooddancer, "Green Fields Acclaimed Among Nation's Best Schools," unidentified newspaper article, Mar. 13, 1986, Tucson Schools, Green Fields, AHS.

32. Verde Valley School brochure, 1948, Arizona Collection (AC), Arizona State University Libraries (ASUL), Tempe.

33. Franklin Patterson, "Citizens and Scholars for a Free World: The Verde Valley School's Contribution to American Secondary Education, 1948–1958," *Verde Valley School Newsletter*, no. 28, AC, ASUL.

34. Ibid.

35. Ibid., 12.

36. Patterson, "Citizens and Scholars for a Free World."

37. Hamilton Warren, "The School in Action," AC, ASUL, 2.

38. Verde Valley School brochure, Oct. 1953, 11.

39. Gary, *Green Fields Country Day School*, 10, 24.

40. Verde Valley job announcement, 1959, Verde Valley Ephemera File, AC, ASUL; Patterson "Citizens and Scholars for a Free World."

41. Edward H. Peplow Jr., "Verde Valley School," *Arizona Highways*, June 1966, 38.

42. The Fenster School brochure, n.d. (received by the Scottsdale Public Library in 1969), Southwest Vertical File, SPL.

43. "3R'S: Reading, 'riting, red rocks," *Arizona Republic*, Jan. 9, 2000, newspaper clipping, Private Schools, Southwest Vertical File, Scottsdale Public Library (SPL); "'Far Away Places' Send Students to Fenster Ranch," Tucson, Aug. 1964, unidentified newspaper clipping, Fenster School archive; *Cactus*, Judson School yearbook, 1955, SPL; and *Cactus*, Judson School yearbook, 1967, Arizona State Library, Archives and Public Records, Phoenix.

44. Fenster School brochure, c. 1998, Fenster School, Tucson, AZ.

45. *The Orme School Bulletin*, Winter 2002.

BIBLIOGRAPHY

ARCHIVES AND MANUSCRIPTS

Alberts, Robert C. MS 0037 Series II, Box 3, Folder 3. Thomas and Katherine Detre Library and Archives, Senator John Heinz History Center, Pittsburgh, PA.

Anderson, C. L. G., MD. "Arizona as a Health Resort." Paper read at the second meeting of the Washington County Medical Society. Hagerstown, MD, Apr. 9, 1890. Arizona Collection, Arizona State University Libraries, Tempe.

Arizona Desert School Ephemera File. Arizona Historical Society, Tucson.

Arizona Sunshine School Ephemera File. Arizona Historical Society, Tucson.

Brandes School Ephemera File. Arizona Historical Society, Tucson.

Burden, Sophie Collection. Desert Caballeros Western Museum, Wickenburg, AZ.

Cactus, Judson School yearbook, 1967. Arizona State Archives, Phoenix.

Collection of H. J. Heinz Company. Thomas and Katherine Detre Library and Archives, Senator John Heinz History Center, Pittsburgh, PA.

Fenster School Ephemera File. Arizona Historical Society, Tucson.

Foxboro Ranch Ephemera File. Arizona Collection, Arizona State University Libraries, Tempe.

Fresnal Ranch School Ephemera File. Arizona Historical Society, Tucson.

Goldsberry, Louise Dunham. "The Open-Air School and Out-Door Education." 1921. Library of Congress, Prints and Photographs.

Green Fields Ephemera File. Arizona Historical Society, Tucson.

"Guest Ranches Along Southern Pacific Lines." Southern Pacific, 1934, 1938, and 1951. University of Arizona Special Collections, Tucson.

Hacienda del Sol School Ephemera File. Arizona Historical Society, Tucson.

Jokake Inn. Arizona Vertical File, Phoenix Public Library, Phoenix.

Jokake School: A Desert School for Girls. Jokake, AZ, n.d. Private collection of Barbara Ferris, Paradise Valley, AZ.

Jokake Yearbook. 1937, 1939, and 1940. Arizona Collection, Arizona State University Libraries, Tempe.

Judson, George. Arizona Biography File, Phoenix Public Library, Phoenix.

Judson, Mrs. George A. Arizona Biography File, Phoenix Public Library, Phoenix.

Judson School for Boys brochure. Arizona Collection, Arizona State University Libraries, Tempe.

Judson School for Boys brochures. Private Collection of David C. Lincoln, Phoenix, AZ.

Lincoln, David C. Arizona Biography File, Phoenix Public Library, Phoenix.

The Ocotillo. Judson School for Boys yearbook. 1938. Private Collection of David C. Lincoln, Phoenix, AZ.

Organization and Services of the Secondary Education Board. Milton, MA, 1928. Library of Congress.

Orme School. Arizona Historical Foundation, Hayden Library, Arizona State University, Tempe.

The Orme School Annual Report, 1982–1983. Arizona Department of Library, Archives, & Public Records, Phoenix.

Orme School Ephemera File, Arizona Collection. Arizona State University Libraries, Tempe.

Palo Verde Ranch School Arizona Collection. Arizona State University Libraries, Tempe.

Palo Verde Ranch School brochure. Mesa Southwest Museum, Mesa, AZ.

Private Schools—Arizona. Southwest Vertical File. Scottsdale Public Library, AZ.

Private Schools of Tucson, Arizona. Arizona Collection, Arizona State University Libraries, Tempe.

Quarter-Circle V-Bar Ranch Summer Camp brochure. N.d. Arizona Collection, Arizona State University Libraries, Tempe.

"A Ranch School for Younger Boys." Brochure, Tucson, AZ, 1932. Private collection of David C. Wilhelm.

The Round-up. Vol. 1. First Classmen of the Valley Ranch School, Valley, WY, 1925. American Heritage Center, University of Wyoming, Laramie.

Russell Ranch School Ephemera File. Arizona Historical Society, Tucson.

"Souer Plans Ranch School in Mountains." *Benson News*, Feb. 1927. University of Arizona Special Collections, Tucson.

Southern Arizona School for Boys. Arizona Collection, Arizona State University Libraries, Tempe.

Southern Arizona School for Boys Ephemera File. Arizona Historical Society, Tucson.

Southwestern Academy: Beaver Creek Ranch 1924. Brochure. Arizona Historical Foundation, Hayden Library, Arizona State University, Tempe.

Thomas School Ephemera File. Arizona Historical Society, Tucson.

The Valley Ranch Co. 1915. Brochure. American Heritage Center, Laramie, WY.

The Valley Ranches, Valley, WY, 1940. Booklet. American Heritage Center, University of Wyoming, Laramie.

The Valley Ranch: Horseback Trip in the Rockies for Young Men 1929. Brochure. Valley Ranch. American Heritage Center, University of Wyoming, Laramie.

The Valley Ranch's Horseback Trip in the Rockies for Boys, Yellowstone National Park Wyoming Big Game Country, July–Aug. 1922. American Heritage Center, University of Wyoming, Laramie.

Verde Valley School Ephemera File. Arizona Collection, Arizona State University Libraries, Tempe.

Wick, David. Arizona Biography File. Phoenix Public Library, Phoenix.

Wick, Henry III. Arizona Biography File. Phoenix Public Library, Phoenix.

Works Progress Administration, Arizona Writers Project Manuscript. History and Archives Division, Arizona Department of Library, Archives, & Public Records, Phoenix.

GOVERNMENT DOCUMENTS

Burke, Avis Tarrant. "The Open-Air School Idea." *Bulletin of the Extension Division, Indiana University*, Mar. 1922, vol. vii, no. 7, Bloomington, Indiana.

Kingsley, Sherman C., and F. B. Dresslar. "Open-Air Schools." United States Bureau of Education Bulletin, no. 23. Department of the Interior, Washington, D.C.: Government Printing Office, 1917.

Myers, William Starr. "Country Schools for City Boys." United States Bureau of Education Bulletin, no. 9. Department of the Interior, Washington, D.C.: Government Printing Office, 1912.

Tupper, C. Ralph. *A Survey of the Arizona Public School System: A Study of the Elementary and Secondary Public Schools of the State.* Arizona State Board of Education, January 1, 1925.

Warren, B. S. *Open Air Schools for the Prevention and Cure of Tuberculosis Among Children.* Treasury Department, United States Public Health Service. Public Health Bulletin, no. 58. Washington, D.C.: Government Printing Office, Oct. 1912.

ORAL HISTORY INTERVIEWS

Dalzell, Fred. Interview by author, Phoenix, AZ, Mar., 2004. Tape recording.

Donaldson, John, Howard Bremond, David C. Wilhelm, and Alexander (Sandy) Woods. Interview by author, Tucson, AZ, 2006. Tape recording.

Ferris, Barbara. Interview by author, Paradise Valley, AZ, Dec. 29, 2002. Tape recording.

Judson, Gloria. Interview by author, Phoenix, AZ, Feb. 2002. Tape recording.

Kilmarx, Robert. Interview by author, Barrington, RI, Sept. 2003. Tape recording.

Lincoln, David. Interview by author, Phoenix, AZ, Aug. 2000 and Feb. 2002.

McAndrews, Anita. Interview by author, Newport, RI, July 9, 2003. Tape recording.

Orme, Charles. Interview by author, Mayer, AZ, Feb. 2002.

Parke, Ormonde. Interview by author, Phoenix, AZ, Feb. 16, 2002.

Porter, Jean Dunn. Interview by author, Tucson, AZ, Feb. 17, 2002. Tape recording.
Porter, Robert. Interview by author, Tucson, AZ, Feb. 2002. Tape recording.
Rosebrook, Jeb John. Interview by author, Scottsdale, AZ, Feb. 2002. Tape recording.
Wick, David. Interview by author, Scottsdale, AZ, Dec. 2002. Tape recording.
Wilhelm, David. Interview by author, Denver, CO, May 31, 2011. Digital recording.

DIRECTORIES

A Handbook of Private Schools for American Boys and Girls. Boston, MA: Porter
    Sargent, 1920–1950.
Private Independent Schools. Wallingford, CT: Bunting and Lyon, Inc., 1993.

PERSONAL JOURNALS

Cummings, Philip H. *A Poet in the Sagebrush: The Day-to-Day Journal of a Young
    Teacher at the Valley Ranch School for Boys, Valley, Wyoming, September 1932–
    1933.* Edited by Patricia A. Billingsley.

ARTICLES

Adler, Stan. "They Tell Me I Was an Easterner." *Arizona Highways,* Sept. 1947, 4–7.
Amundson, Michael A. "The British at Big Horn: The Founding of an Elite Wyoming
    Community." *Journal of the West* 40, no. 1 (2001): 49–55.
———. "'These Men Play Real Polo': An Elite Sport in the 'Cowboy State,' 1890–1930."
    Montana The Magazine of Western History 59, no. 1, Spring 2009, 3–22.
"Arizona Attracts Many Notables." *Arizona Highways,* Jan. 1945, 9–14.
"Arizona Ranch Schools." *Arizona Highways* 15, no. 9, Sept. 1939, 2, 19.
Atwood, Albert W. "The Rich Man's Son." *Saturday Evening Post,* Nov. 10, 1928.
Baur, John E. "The Sporting Life in Early Los Angeles." *Californians* 6, no. 4 (1988):
    26–37.
Bingmann, Melissa. "Prep School Cowboys: Arizona Ranch Schools and Images of the
    Mythic West." *Journal of Arizona History* 43, no. 3 (2002): 205–36.
Blair, Emily Newell. "Why I Sent My Children Away to School." *Harper's Monthly
    Magazine,* Mar. 1926, 428–36.
"Capital City Sojourn: The Pierre Journal of Philip H. Cummings." Edited by Patricia A.
    Billingsley. *South Dakota History* 39, no. 2 (Summer 2009): 7–8.
Cobb, Irvin S. "The Generation that Comes Next." *Saturday Evening Post,* Sept. 17,
    1921.
Cohen, Michele. "The Grand Tour. Language, National Identity and Masculinity."
    Changing English 8, no. 2 (2001): 129–41.
Compton, Mel, and Roseann Compton. "Junior Rodeo." *Arizona Highways,* Feb. 1960,
    8–10.

Cook, James E. "And You Thought Split Sessions Were Bad." *Arizona*, Nov. 7, 1971, 6–11.

"Directory." *Arizona Highways*, Sept. 1947, 30–44.

De Ritter, Richard. "'This Changeableness in Character': Exploring Masculinity and Nationhood on James Boswell's Grand Tour." *Scottish Literary Review* 2, no. 2 (Spring/Summer 2010): 23-40.

Ellinwood, Sybil. "East Meets West in the Field of Education." *Journal of Arizona History* 15, no. 3 (Autumn 1974): 269–96.

Everitt, Don. "Excavations at the Sabino Canyon Ruins, 1937–1950." *Old Pueblo Archaeology* (Dec. 1996).

Ferguson, H. N. "They Go To School on a Ranch." *Desert Magazine*, May 1962, 14–15.

Fox, Kel M. "Of Dudes and Cows: The Foxboro Story." *Journal of Arizona History* 32, no. 4 (Winter 1991): 413–42.

Goodchild, Lester F. "G. Stanley Hall and an American Social Darwinist Pedagogy: His Progressive Educational Ideas on Gender and Race." *History of Education Quarterly* 52, no. 1 (Feb. 2012): 62–98.

Grant, Julia. "A 'Real Boy' and Not a Sissy: Gender, Childhood, and Masculinity, 1890–1940." *Journal of Social History* 37, no. 4 (Summer 2004): 829–51.

Gusmorino, Paul A. III. "Main Causes of the Great Depression." *Gusmorino World*, May 13, 1996. http://www.gusmorino. com/pag3/greatdepression/index.html. Accessed Aug. 29, 2008.

Harris, Kevin L. "Horses, Polo, and the Cavalry Define the Life of this Great American." *Password* 43, no. 3 (1998): 125–35.

Hough, Emerson. "Owners of America VIII: The Swifts." *Cosmopolitan Magazine*, Mar. 1902, 399–407.

Hudman, Lloyd E. "Tourism and the American West." *Journal of the West* 33, no. 3 (1994): 67–76.

Kennedy, Winifred. "Southwestern Academy: Where Education Is More Than Absorbing Facts and Acquiring Knowledge." *Arizona Highways*, Feb. 1972, 4–7.

Kimmelman, Alex Jay. "Luring the Tourist To Tucson: Civic Promotion During the 1920s." *Journal of Arizona History* 28, no. 2 (1987): 135–54.

McAlpine, Jocelyn. "Rodeo . . . University Style." *Arizona Highways*, Feb. 1960, 11–15.

"Miss Chapin's, Miss Walker's, Foxcroft, Farmington." *Fortune*, Aug. 1931, 38–44, 84, 86.

Morton-Keithley, Linda. "Those Were the Days: Polo in the Boise Valley." *Idaho Yesterdays* 38, no. 3 (1994): 10–15.

Myrick, Donald. "Recollections of an Arizona Ranch School in 1911." *Journal of Arizona History* 12, no. 1 (1971): 52–63.

Niehuis, Charles. "Hunting in Arizona." *Arizona Highways*, Oct. 1944, 2–5.

Overend, William. "Intricacies of Private Education: The Brothers Wick." *Arizona Days and Ways Magazine*, Mar. 14, 1965, 11–14.

Parker, Charles Franklin, and Kitty Jo Parker Nelson. "Arizona's Independent College Preparatory Schools." *Arizona Highways*, June 1961, 8–15, 28–30.

Peplow, Ed. "Verde Valley School." *Arizona Highways*, Aug. 1954, 4–9.

Peplow, Edward H. Jr. "Verde Valley School." *Arizona Highways*, June 1966, 38–39.

Premo, Bianca. "Recreating Identity: Recreation on the Arizona-Sonora Border, 1880–1930." *Studies in Latin American Popular Culture* 16 (1997): 31–52.

"Private Schools of Southern Arizona." *Magazine Tucson*, June 1948, 40–41, 48.

Reed, Allen C. "Cow Country Campus." *Arizona Highways*, Apr. 1952, 18–27.

Rosenwald, Julius. "The Burden of Wealth." *The Saturday Evening Post*, Jan. 5, 1929.

Rothman, Hal K. "Selling the Meaning of Place: Entrepreneurship, Tourism, and Community Transformation in the Twentieth-Century American West." *Pacific Historical Review* 65, no. 4 (1996): 525–57.

Rymph, Catherine E. "From 'Economic Want' to 'Family Pathology': Foster Family Care, the New Deal, and the Emergence of a Public Child Welfare System." *Journal of Policy History* 24, no. 1 (2012): 8–25.

Samuelson, Susan Adams. "The Orme School on the Quarter Circle V Bar Ranch." *Journal of Arizona History* 25, no. 4 (Winter 1984): 399–422.

Saveth, Edward N. "Education of an Elite." *History of Education Quarterly* 28, no. 3 (Autumn 1988): 367–86.

"Schooling." *Time*, Feb. 8, 1926, 20.

Sokol, Marienka. "From Wasteland to Oasis: Promotional Images of Arizona, 1870–1912." *Journal of Arizona History* 34, no. 4 (1993): 357–90.

Stearns, Alfred E. "A Square Deal for To-morrow's Citizens." *Outlook*, May 16, 1923.

Stein, Ewald A. "Guest Ranching Out Wickenburg Way." *Arizona Highways*, Nov. 1945, 10.

Tibbetts, John C. "'Arizona Jim': The Westerns of Douglas Fairbanks, Sr." *Journal of Popular Film and Television* 39, no. 2 (2011): 41–49.

Van Slyck, Abigail A. "The Spatial Practices of Privilege." *Journal of the Society of Architectural Historians* 70, no. 2 (June 2011): 210–39.

Varga, Vincent. "Gentlemen Ranchers—High-Class Cowboys." *Journal of the West* 23, no. 4 (1984): 48–56.

Wilson, M. L. "How New Deal Agencies are Affecting Family Life," *Journal of Home Economics* (May 1935): 274–80.

BOOKS

Adams, Robert C. *The Good Provider, H. J. Heinz and His 57 Varieties*. Boston, MA: Houghton Mifflin, 1973.

Apple, Rima. *Perfect Motherhood: Science and Childrearing in America*. New Brunswick, NJ: Rutgers University Press, 2006.

Arizona Health Resorts. Atchison, Topeka, and Santa Fe Railway Company Passenger Department. Chicago, IL: Henry O. Shepard Co. Printers, November 1902.

Athearn, Robert G. *The Mythic West in Twentieth-Century America*. Lawrence: University Press of Kansas, 1986.

Badham, Robert J. *Preparatory School Manual for Boys and Parents: A Handbook for the Use of Parents and the Guidance of School Boys.* Philadelphia, PA: Robert J. Badham, 1932.

Basso, Matthew, Laura McCall, and Dee Garceau, eds. *Across the Great Divide: Cultures of Manhood in the American West.* New York and London: Routledge, 2001.

Batinski, Michael C. *Pastkeepers in a Small Place: Five Centuries in Deerfield, Massachusetts.* Amherst: University of Massachusetts Press, 2004.

Baxter, Kent. *The Modern Age: Turn-of-the-Century American Culture and the Invention of Adolescence.* Tuscaloosa: University of Alabama Press, 2008.

Bederman, Gail. *Manliness and Civilization: A Cultural History of Gender and Race in the United States, 1880–1917.* Chicago, IL: University of Chicago Press, 1995.

Borne, Lawrence. *Dude Ranching: A Complete History.* Albuquerque: University of New Mexico Press, 1983.

Byrnes, Sylvia. *Jokake Inn: One of the Earliest Desert Resorts.* N.p., n.d.

Chapman, William. *Roots of Character Education: An Exploration of The American Heritage From the Decade of the 1920s.* Schenectady, NY: Character Research Press, 1977.

Chester, Ronald. *Inheritance, Wealth, and Society.* Bloomington: Indiana University Press, 1982.

Church, Fermor S., and Peggy Pond Church. *When Los Alamos was a Ranch School.* Los Alamos, NM: Los Alamos Historical Society, 1998.

Cole, Robert Danforth. *Private Secondary Education for Boys in the United States.* Philadelphia, PA: Westbrook, 1928.

Columbia University, Teachers College. *Studies in the Nature of Character, by the Character Education Inquiry, Teachers College, Columbia University in Coöperation with the Institute of Social and Religious Research.* Vol. 1, *Studies in Deceit.* New York: Macmillan, 1928.

Cook, Brian. *Frank Boyden of Deerfield, The Vision and Politics of an Educational Idealist.* Lanham, MD: Madison Books, 1994.

Cookson, Peter W., and Caroline Hodges Persell. *Preparing for Power: America's Elite Boarding Schools.* New York: Basic Books, 1985.

Cremin, Lawrence. *The Transformation of the School: Progressivism in American Education, 1876–1957.* New York: Vintage, 1964.

Cutler, Irving. *The Jews of Chicago: From Shtetl to Suburb.* Urbana and Chicago: University of Illinois Press, 1996.

Deloria, Philip J. *Playing Indian.* New Haven, CT: Yale University Press, 1998.

Dennis, Jeffrey P. *We Boys Together: Teenagers in Love Before Girl-Craziness.* Nashville, TN: Vanderbilt University Press, 2007.

Dewey, John. *Democracy and Education: An Introduction to the Philosophy of Education.* New York: Macmillan, 1916.

Dewey, John, and Evelyn Dewey. *Schools of To-morrow.* New York: E. P. Dutton, 1915.

Dumenil. Lynn. *The Modern Temper: American Culture and Society in the 1920s.* New York: Hill and Wang, 1995.

Engleman, J. O. *Moral Education in School and Home.* Chicago, IL; New York; and Boston, MA: Benj. H. Sanborn, 1920.

Filene, Peter G. *Him/Her/Self: Gender Identities in Modern America.* 3rd edition. Baltimore, MD: Johns Hopkins University Press, 1998.

Fraser, Steve, and Gary Gerstle, eds. *Ruling America: A History of Wealth and Power in a Democracy.* Cambridge, MA: Harvard University Press, 2005.

Garraty, John A. *Henry Cabot Lodge: A Biography.* New York: Alfred A. Knopf, 1953.

Gary, Suzanne Tumblin. *Green Fields Country Day School: The First Fifty Years, 1933–1983.* Tucson, AZ: Green Fields Country Day School, 1983.

Glassberg, David. *American Historical Pageantry: The Uses of Tradition in the Early Twentieth Century.* Chapel Hill: University of North Carolina Press, 1990.

Hawes, Joseph M. *Children Between the Wars: American Childhood 1920–1940.* New York: Twayne Publishers, an Imprint of Simon & Schuster Macmillan, 1997.

Hine, Robert V., and John Mack Faragher. *The American West: A New Interpretive History.* New Haven, CT: Yale University Press, 2000.

Hoganson, Kristin L. *Fighting for American Manhood: How Gender Politics Provoked the Spanish-American and Philippine-American Wars.* New Haven, CT: Yale University Press, 1998.

Holden, Horace. *Young Boys and Boarding School.* Boston, MA: Gorham Press, 1913.

Horowitz, Daniel. *The Morality of Spending: Attitudes toward the Consumer Society in America, 1875–1940.* Baltimore, MD: Johns Hopkins University Press, 1985.

Hulbert, Ann. *Raising America: Experts, Parents, and a Century of Advice About Children.* New York: Alfred A. Knopf, 2003.

Hyde, Anne F. *An American Vision: Far Western Landscape and National Culture, 1820–1920.* New York: New York University Press, 1990.

Internationalize Your School: A Handbook. Boston, MA: National Association of Independent Schools, 1977.

Isenberg, Nancy. *Fallen Founder: The Life of Aaron Burr.* New York: Viking, 2007.

Jaher, Frederic Cople. *The Urban Establishment: Upper Strata in Boston, New York, Charleston, Chicago, and Los Angeles.* Urbana: University of Illinois Press, 1982.

Johnson, G. Wesley, Jr., ed. *Phoenix in the Twentieth Century: Essays in Community History.* Norman: University of Oklahoma Press, 1993.

Jones, Billy M. *Health-Seekers in the Southwest, 1817–1900.* Norman: University of Oklahoma Press, 1967.

Kammen, Michael. *Mystic Chords of Memory: The Transformation of Tradition in American Culture.* New York: Knopf, 1991.

Kasson, John F. *Houdini, Tarzan, and the Perfect Man: The White Male Body and The Challenge of Modernity in America.* New York: Hill and Wang, 2001.

Kasson, Joy S. *Buffalo Bill's Wild West: Celebrity, Memory, and Popular History.* New York: Hill And Wang, 2000.

Kensel, W. Hudson. *Dude Ranching in Yellowstone Country: Larry Larom and Valley Ranch, 1915–1969*. Norman, OK: Arthur H. Clark Company, 2010.

Kimmel, Michael. *Manhood in America: A Cultural History*. New York: Free Press, 1996.

Kravetz, Robert E., MD, and Alex Jay Kimmelman. *Healthseekers in Arizona*. Academy of Medical Sciences of Maricopa Medical Society, 1998.

Lears, T. J. Jackson. *No Place of Grace: Antimodernism and the Transformation of American Culture 1880–1920*. New York: Pantheon, 1981.

Levy, David M., MD. *Maternal Overprotection*. New York: W. W. Norton, 1966.

Limerick, Patricia Nelson. *Something in the Soil: Legacies and Reckonings in the New West*. New York and London: W. W. Norton, 2000.

Macleod, David I. *Building Character in the American Boy: The Boy Scouts, YMCA, and Their Forerunners*. Madison: University of Wisconsin Press, 1983.

Makepeace, LeRoy McKim. *Sherman Thacher and His School*. New Haven, CT: Yale University Press, 1941.

May, Elaine Tyler. *Great Expectations: Marriage and Divorce in Post-Victorian America*. Chicago, IL: University of Chicago Press, 1980.

May, Larry. *The Big Tomorrow: Hollywood and the Politics of the American Way*. Chicago, IL: University of Chicago Press, 2000.

———. *Screening Out the Past: The Birth of Mass Culture and the Motion Picture Industry*. Chicago, IL: University of Chicago Press, 1980.

McClellan, B. Edward. *Moral Education in America: Schools and the Shaping of Character from Colonial Times to the Present*. New York and London: Teachers College, Columbia University, 1999.

McLachlan, James. *American Boarding Schools: A Historical Study*. New York: Charles Scribner's Sons, 1970.

Milner, Clyde A., ed. *A New Significance: Re-envisioning the History of the American West*. New York: Oxford University Press, 1996.

Mintz, Steven. *Huck's Raft: A History of American Childhood*. Cambridge, MA: Belknap Press of Harvard University Press, 2004.

Moley, Raymond. *The American Century of John C. Lincoln*. New York: Hawthorne Books, 1965.

Morris, Edmund. *The Rise of Theodore Roosevelt*. New York: Modern Library, 1979.

Morris, Sylvia Jukes. *Edith Kermit Roosevelt: Portrait of a First Lady*. New York: Modern Library, 1980.

Nash, Gerald D. *The American West in the Twentieth Century: A Short History of An Urban Oasis*. Englewood Cliffs, NJ: Prentice-Hall, 1973.

Nash, Roderick. *The Nervous Generation: American Thought: 1917–1930*. Chicago, IL: Elephant Paperbacks, 1990.

Osgerby, Bill. *Playboys in Paradise: Masculinity, Youth and Leisure-Style in Modern America*. Oxford and New York: Berg, 2001.

Paris, Leslie. *Children's Nature: The Rise of the American Summer Camp*. New York: New York University Press, 2008.

Pearce, Charles S. *Los Alamos Before the Bomb and Other Stories*. New York: Vantage Press, 1987.

Plant, Rebecca Jo. *Mom: The Transformation of Motherhood in Modern America*. Chicago, IL: University of Chicago Press, 2010.

Pomeroy, Earl. *In Search of the Golden West: The Tourist in Western America*. New York: A. Knopf, 1957.

Post, Emily. *By Motor to the Golden Gate*. Edited by Jane Lancaster. Jefferson, NC: McFarland, 2004.

Powell, Arthur G. *Lessons from Privilege: The American Prep School Tradition*. Cambridge, MA: Harvard University Press, 1996.

Price, George B. *Gaining Health in the West (Colorado, New Mexico, Arizona)*. New York: B. W. Huebsch, 1907.

Pry, Mark. *The Town on the Hassayampa: A History of Wickenburg, AZ*. Wickenburg, AZ: Desert Caballeros Western Museum, 1997.

Rothman, Hal K. *Devil's Bargains: Tourism in the Twentieth-Century American West*. Lawrence: University Press of Kansas, 1998.

Sargent, Porter. *The Continuing Battle for the Control of the Mind of Youth*. Boston, MA: Porter Sargent, 1945.

———. *Education in Wartime*. Boston, MA: Porter Sargent, 1942.

———. *What Makes Lives*. Boston, MA: Porter Sargent, 1940.

Shaffer, Marguerite S. *See America First: Tourism and National Identity, 1880–1940*. Washington, D.C.: Smithsonian Institution Press, 2001.

Simon, Scott. *The Invention of the Western Film: A Cultural History of the Genre's First Half-Century*. Cambridge, UK: Cambridge University Press, 2003.

Slatta, Richard. *Cowboys of the Americas*. New Haven, CT: Yale University Press, 1990.

Smith, Henry Nash. *Virgin Land: The American West as Symbol and Myth*. New York: Random House, 1950.

Smith, Susan Harris, and Melanie Dawson, eds. *The American 1890s: A Cultural Reader*. Durham, NC: Duke University Press, 2000.

Stearns, Alfred E. *The Challenge of Youth*. Boston, MA: W. A. Wilde, 1923.

Stearns, Alfred E., Samuel S. Drury, Endicott Peabody, R. Heber Howe Jr., W. L. W. Field, and William G. Thayer. *The Education of the Modern Boy*. Boston, MA: Small, Maynard, 1925.

Stearns, Peter N. *Anxious Parents: A History of Modern Childrearing in America*. New York: New York University Press, 2003.

Teague, David W. *The Southwest in American Literature and Art: The Rise of a Desert Aesthetic*. Tucson: University of Arizona Press, 1997.

Thurer, Shari L. *The Myths of Motherhood: How Culture Reinvents the Good Mother*. Boston, MA: Houghton Mifflin, 1994.

Tompkins, Jane. *West of Everything: The Inner Life of Westerns*. New York: Oxford University Press, 1992.

Troth, Dennis Clayton, ed. *Selected Readings in Character Education.* Boston, MA: Beacon, 1930.

Turner, Frederick Jackson. *The Frontier in American History.* New York: Henry Holt, 1950.

West, Elliott. *Growing Up with the Country: Childhood on the Far Western Frontier.* Albuquerque: University of New Mexico Press, 1989.

White, G. Edward. *The Eastern Establishment and the Western Experience.* New Haven, CT, and London: Yale University Press, 1968.

Wilhelm, David. *Cowboy Ace: The Life Adventures of David Wilhelm, An Autobiography.* Parker, CO: Thornton, 2010.

Wirth, John D., and Linda Harvey Aldrich. *Los Alamos: The Ranch School Years, 1917–1943.* Albuquerque: University of New Mexico Press, 2003.

Wrobel, David M. *Promised Lands: Promotion, Memory, and the Creation of the American West.* Lawrence: University Press of Kansas, 2002.

Yeomans, Edward. *Views of Childhood and Education Through Two Centuries.* Boston, MA: National Association of Independent Schools, 1976.

VISUAL MEDIA

The Adventurous Soul. Directed by Gene Carroll. Hi-Mark Productions, Superlative Pictures, 1927.

A Fight to the Finish. Directed by Reaves Eason. Columbia Pictures Corporation, 1925.

Girl Crazy. Directed by Norman Taurog and Busby Berkeley. Metro Goldwyn Mayer, 1943.

THESES AND DISSERTATIONS

Coderre, Harry. "Disciplinary Problems in the Western Ranch School." Master's thesis, Massachusetts State College, Amherst, 1942.

Zeman, Scott. "Traveling the Southwest Creation, Imagination, and Invention." PhD diss., Arizona State University, Tempe, 1998.

WEBSITES

http://www.lanl.gov/worldview/welcome/history.html.

INDEX

Page numbers in italic text indicate illustrations.

classical studies: Greek and Latin, 47–48
clothing, 81–82
Coderre, Harry, 53, 151, 156
Cody, Buffalo Bill, 67
Cole, Robert Danforth, xx, 1, 26, 52, 54, 108, 137, 142, 157
College Board Exam, xii, xviii, 41, 47–50, 58, 100, 176
Connell, Albert J., 97, 133
consumerism, xii–xiii, xiv, 7, 20, 23–24
cowboys, 23, 65–69, 75, 81, 88, 93, 95–98, 100, 107, 113, 118, 120, 128–36, 140, 157, 171
Cummings, Philip, 1, 47, 52, 53, 60, 68, 85, 102, 123, 129, 131–32; salary at Valley Ranch School, 8

death, desertion, and divorce, 137–39, 142–44, 164, 167
Deerfield Academy, 51–52, 61–62
De Grazia, Ted, 41
Dewey, John, 39, 46, 59, 62
Donaldson, John, 74, *103*, 180
dude ranching, xv–xvii, 31, 66, 68, 70–74, 94, 96–98, 101, 156, 173

El Coronado Ranch School, 84
Evans, H. David, xii, x, 54–55, 96, 98, 100, 116, 119
Evans School, xi, xiii, xvi, 24, 27, 47, 51, 53–55, 69–70, 80, 85, 100–102, 119–21, 125, 171; farm and ranch, 96; location, 98; tuition, 1
Everitt, Don, 83

Fairgrieve, Mabel Baker, 34, 159
Fairgrieve, Russell, 34, 70, 129–30, 133, 159, 173
Fenster School, 84, 92, 176, 179–80
Field, Joseph Blake, 56, 162
Fight to the Finish, A (1925), 17–18
Flexner, Abraham, 40

Fowler, A. S., xii
Foxboro Ranch School, xvi, 34, 81, 95
Fresnal Ranch School, xvi, 22–23, 41, 47, 51, 95, 118, 153, 156, 158
Fuller, Philo C., 33

Girl Crazy (1943), 19
Goldsberry, Louise Dunham, 46, 76, 124, 127
Green Fields Preparatory, 41, 44, 50–51, 54–55, 73, 91, 126, 159–61, 174–76, 178, 180; alfalfa farm, 95, 160
guns, 126–28
Gyberg, Frank, 95, 99

Hacienda del Sol, xvii, xix, 27–29, 41, 52, 83, 98, 101, 172
Hall, G. Stanley, 111–12, 117, 124
Hammarstrom, Grace, 55, 161
Heinz, Henry John (Jack), II, xi–xiii, xxiii, 21, 25, 51, 74, 99, 105, 122
Heinz, Howard, 5, 51, 129
H. J. Heinz Company, xiii, xx, 5
Hopi Indians, 84, 92, 175, 178
horses, 2, 8, 20, 23, 25, 88, 93, 96, 98–105, 122, 171; boys' companionship with, 135; breaking, 129; disappearance from ranch schools, 176; riding, 41, 45, 65, 73, 79, *80*, 83–84, 88, 97, 99, 100–101, 116, 121–22, 125, 128, 130, 171; Verde Valley School, 177
hunting, 72, 120, 123–28
Hutchinson, James S., 55, 132

Indian Ruins, 82–85
inherited wealth, xv–xvii, 2–15

Jokake School for Girls, xvii, 28, 31–33, 74, 98, 101, 158, 163–64, 172
Judson, George, 32, 54, 56, 59, 108, 127, 133, 143, 162, 174
Judson, Laura, 59, 143, 162
Judson School, xvi, 28–33, 41, 44–45, 51,